SPENT CARTRIDGES
OF REVOLUTION

SPENT CARTRIDGES OF REVOLUTION

An Anthropological History of Namiquipa, Chihuahua

DANIEL NUGENT

THE UNIVERSITY OF CHICAGO PRESS • CHICAGO AND LONDON

DANIEL NUGENT is Assistant Professor of
Anthropology at the University of Arizona.

The University of Chicago Press, Chicago 60637
The University of Chicago Press, Ltd., London
© 1993 by The University of Chicago
All rights reserved. Published 1993
Printed in the United States of America

02 01 00 99 98 97 96 95 94 93   1 2 3 4 5

ISBN: 0-226-60741-0 (cloth)
        0-226-60742-9 (paper)

Library of Congress Cataloging-in-Publication Data

Nugent, Daniel.
    Spent cartridges of revolution : an anthropological history of Namiquipa,
Chihuahua / Daniel Nugent.
        p.   cm.
    Includes bibliographical references and index.
    1. Namiquipa (Mexico)—History.   2. Peasantry—Mexico—Namiquipa—
History.   3. Land reform—Mexico—Namiquipa—History.   4. Ethnohistory—
Mexico—Namiquipa.   5. Mexico—History—Revolution, 1910–1920.   I. Title.
F1391.N15N8   1993
972'.16—dc20   93-15997
                                                                        CIP

CONTENTS

v

PREFACE

Starting in 1958 and continuing through the 1980s a remarkable and valuable series of studies of the Mexican revolution called *Hechos reales de la Revolución* appeared in print. Authored by Alberto Calzadíaz Barrera, *Hechos reales* is in large part based on incredibly rich oral histories from veterans of the 1910–20 revolution, many of them from the town of Namiquipa, located in the Guerrero District of western Chihuahua, recognized by many as "the cradle of the Mexican Revolution." Born in Namiquipa shortly after the turn of the century, as a child Don Alberto had personally known Pancho Villa, Candelario Cervantes, Juan B. Muñoz, and other persons of whom he writes in his books.

In the late 1960s *El rugir del cañon,* a remembrance of the opening period of the revolution by Teodosio Duarte Morales, also from Namiquipa and a veteran of the 1910 uprising, was published. Shortly thereafter another book by Duarte Morales appeared, *Villa y Pershing: Memorias de la Revolución (20 de noviembre de 1910 a 1913).* The latter title is curious, since the text itself deals with events that happened in Namiquipa long after 1913. But Duarte Morales has a clear and definite sense of *when* the revolution was; and also of *what* it was. Describing the people of Namiquipa during the Mexican revolution he writes, "We were hardworking people; and overnight we made up what it was to be revolutionaries."

Duarte Morales's books convey, above all, a sense of loss. In 1913 he and some *compañeros* were tricked into capture by *huertista* adversaries, disarmed, stripped naked, and jailed. Records of his participation in the 1910 uprising were destroyed. He concludes the description of this low point in his life with the following remarks: "Now it is impossible to recover any evidence that would testify to our valor, or to secure recognition of us as the real initiators of the armed struggle. We are left in the end like spent cartridges with no support whatsoever. The few of us that are still around live in poverty, and the only thing we have left are our memories" (Duarte Morales 1968:23).

The present book is not a study of Namiquipa during the revolution. That story has been told—much better than I could—by writers and protagonists such as Calzadíaz Barrera and Duarte Morales. One task I did set for myself, though, was to recover some of the evidence allowing us to recognize and appreciate the valor and value of the people of Namiquipa. I attempt to situate the circumstances under which some Mexican peasants fought and died for the construction of a new basis for social life, winding up as spent cartridges on the battlefield of a violent social struggle that was won, in the final analysis, by other groups of people.

One central claim of this book is that it is possible to combine anthropological and historical research and writing in an integrated investigation and analysis by just getting on with the work rather than speculating endlessly about the possibility or impossibility of integrating the disciplines of anthropology and history. My interest in anthropology owes a great deal to my parents, who took their children to the Navajo reservation and Japan during summer vacations in the 1950s and 1960s. The closest we ever got to Disneyland was a visit to William Randolph Hearst's castle at San Simeon, so perhaps it is fitting that the research on which the present book is based was carried out in a community, Namiquipa, that bordered the hacienda of San José de Babicora, one of Hearst's largest estates in Mexico.

My efforts were brought to fruition through more than a decade of collaboration in research with Ana Alonso and with the help of the people of Namiquipa, Chihuahua. The force and vision that informs their accounts of history, their understanding of the state, and their lives—made evident during our residence in their community—were a constant challenge and inspiration.

Between June 1983 and October 1985, Ana and I lived for twenty months in Namiquipa. From March to May 1985 we worked in archives and consulted other investigators in Mexico City. Engaged in similar activities, we spent another two months in Chihuahua City (the state capital) and Guerrero City (the district capital). We returned to Namiquipa during the summers of 1986 and 1989. My fieldwork in Namiquipa and travel to archives in Mexico and the United States were supported by grants from the Doherty Fellowship Committee Program in Latin American Studies, and the Center for Latin American Studies, University of Chicago. We spent the academic year 1986–87 as visiting research fellows at the Center for U.S.-Mexican Studies, University of California, San Diego, and still harbor fond memories of the center's director, Wayne Cornelius. The Fellowship for Recent Recipients of the Ph.D. from the American Council of Learned Societies in 1989 allowed me to set aside teaching for one semester and concentrate on writing.

The entire community of Namiquipa made our research and residence there pleasant and productive. What follows is only an abbreviated list of the many people who helped us during the research. Daniel Salazar Quintana, interim municipal president in June 1983, expedited our entrance into life in the pueblo in his typically thoughtful and humorous manner. We lived in the houses of the Morales Carrasco family from June to August 1983 and the Ruiz Rodríguez family from August to September. From October 1983 to December 1984 we lived with our good friends José María (Chalía) Cano and Elba Salinas de Cano; their children, José Luis and Mónica; and their dogs, Atilla and Palomo. From December 1984 until October 1985 we looked after the house of Carlos Vásquez and Licha, friends of ours who had moved out of Namiquipa.

Don Luis Bustillos befriended us when we first arrived in the valley, as did Dr. Florencio Aguilera of El Terrero, who introduced us to a number of older informants in the *municipio* and shared with us his considerable knowledge and interesting analysis of Namiquipan history. Dra. Prisciliana Reyes and her husband, Jacobo Antillon, provided hospitality, and medicines through their pharmacy. The entire staff of the Presidencia Municipal was always helpful, particularly during the regime of Rafael Ruiz Barrera from mid-October 1983 onward, as were the officers of the *ejido*. El Pato donated space for an office next to his paint and liquor store. Teresa Carrasco de Maldonado and Oscar Maldonado frequently forced items from their hardware store upon us. Chulario (Jesús Morales) taught me about farming and helped repair my pickup truck on countless occasions. Samaniego told me about running an orchard. La Gorrilla and his brother took me hunting. Jacobo told me about fighting cocks. El Mono Chirisco (now, tragically, deceased) taught me about laying adobe, pouring concrete, plastering walls, and getting plastered oneself. Jesús Morales, Oscar Maldonado, Heriberto, Manuel, and Rubén Muñoz Franco of Armera, Pancho Muñoz, and Alvaro Carrasco were great drinking buddies most Sundays. The musicians with whom I played (Chalía, Carlos, Salomón, and Chelino of the group Fase Cinco, and Professor Luis Rascón, Chuma Muñoz, *los cuates* of La Guajalota, and El Shato) were great fun whether we were playing *corridos, cumbias,* or country western songs. Professor Colmonero motivated the high school students to help us finish organizing the municipal archive in the spring of 1985. Salomón and I built shelves for the municipal archive.

In Cruces, Carlos Ruiz Terrazas and Amalia Camarena de Ruiz frequently put up with our visits. Don Carlos also took us to El Tascate to meet the descendants of Cruz Chávez of Tomochi. Ana Cervantes (daughter of Candelario) also entertained us during several visits to Cruces. Medardo Heras of Casas Coloradas introduced us to many informants living outside of Namiquipa.

In Chihuahua City we received help and direction from Lic. Sergio Campos, Professor Apolinar Frías, Everardo at the Notarial Archive in the Government Palace, Jaime Pérez Mendoza, José Rascón Iguado, Jesús Vargas Valdez and the rest of the staff at the Centro de Investigación y Documentación del Estado de Chihuahua (CIDECH), and most significantly the Salazar Cano family, with whom we stayed during our visits to the capital. But it was above all Dr. Rubén Osorio and his wife, Guadalupe, who provided advice, guidance, and assistance in Chihuahua City and throughout the state. Rubén Osorio is a medical doctor, but also a translator and author of prize-winning books on the revolution in Chihuahua as well as one of the hardest-working popular historians in the world. He shared with us his extensive knowledge of the revolution in Chihuahua and the original results of his own investigations, and generously and openly directed us toward obscure archival collections and other sources of knowledge about Chihuahuan history.

In Guerrero City, Presidente Municipal Victor Peregrino—during whose tenure more than three hundred boxes of historical documents were consolidated, indexed, housed in the town hall, and made accessible to researchers in the early 1980s—provided hospitality and assistance. Padre Gabriel, an Augustinian priest, put us up in his house, showed us the church archives, and took us on a visit to Tomochi. Lic. Héctor González y Gonzáles, a lawyer in Guerrero City, permitted us to use his photocopy machine to reproduce thousands of documents from the Guerrero archive.

In Mexico City we received help from Javier Garciadiego Danton at the Universidad Nacional Autónoma de México (UNAM) Hemeroteca y Biblioteca; Eugenia Meyer, director of the Instituto de Investigaciones; Dr. José María Luis Mora; Armando Ruiz at the Archivo General de la Nación; and Robert Holden, whose research in the Archivo de Terrenos Nacionales preceded Ana's. (Thanks to Alejandra Moreno Toscano for writing the letter that secured admission to that collection.) Friedrich Katz helped us gain admission to the Ministry of Foreign Relations archive, the National Library, and the Porfirio Díaz Collection. Alberto Calzadíaz Barrera received us in his apartment in 1983, and Héctor Aguilar Camin, then editing the newspaper *La Jornada,* and Jane-Dale Lloyd at the Universidad Iberoamericana took time from their busy schedules to discuss the history of popular movements in northern Mexico with us. Adolfo Gilly met with us in Mexico City in 1985 and then and over the years since has discussed our research, read our papers, and compared notes on recent developments in the north. During the few moments when we were not working, we enjoyed the company of Ulises Beltran and his family.

In Washington, D.C., George Chalou, director in charge of the Military Reference Branch of the United States National Archives, sorted boxes himself to help locate misplaced documents from the Pershing Punitive Expedition containing information on Namiquipans.

César Caballero, head, Special Collections Department, University of Texas–El Paso Library, was very helpful.

In Tucson, Arizona, the late Thomas Naylor and the staff of the Documentary Relations of the Southwest files (Arizona State Museum, University of Arizona) allowed us unrestricted access to their holdings, as did the University of Arizona Library. Susan Deeds shared *datos* on Namiquipa from the Archivo de las Indias in Sevilla, Spain. My parents, Charlie and Peggy Nugent, put up with the many visits that occurred when we slipped out of Mexico to renew our visas between 1983 and 1985.

To all the individuals and organizations mentioned above, and particularly to Ana, a warm thanks. The research would not have been possible without their generous assistance.

Different from carrying out the research, writing this book involved chaining myself to the keyboard in the years since living in Namiquipa and drawing on other experiences from farther afield. The possibility of writing a historical anthropology was first encouraged by Milton Singer and Terry Turner when I was a student in the Department of Civilizational Studies at the University of Chicago from 1972 to 1976. That possibility was further nurtured (even if at times negatively) while I was a graduate student in the Department of Anthropology from 1978 to 1988. My sister Sara gave me the idea that allowed me to stay in graduate school, where I was supported as a National Science Foundation graduate fellow. John Comaroff, Friedrich Katz, R. T. Smith, and Terry Turner supervised my thesis in a consistently stimulating, critical, and supportive manner. As should be evident in what follows, each in their own way has shaped my thinking on a vast range of topics and I appreciate very much the opportunity to have worked with them.

While writing this book I also learned a great deal through discussions with friends and colleagues in San Diego, Riverside, Austin, and Tucson, especially Marjorie Becker, Ira Buchler, John Calagione, Guillermo de la Peña, Gil Joseph, Hermann Rebel, Bryan Roberts, Noel Samaroo, Michael Woost, and Leon Zamosc. Collaborative work and writing with John and Gil since the late 1980s has been immensely stimulating and valuable, and John's influence in particular is evident throughout the text (at least to me). My brother Stephen has helped in more ways than he knows over many years as a skeptical critic and source of brutal insights and inspiration. Rodolfo Stavenhagen offered words of encouragement as I was finishing my thesis and starting the book.

The *equipo* working on the history of Chihuahua at the Universidad Autónoma de Ciudad Juárez—particularly Chantal Cramaussel, Carlos González Herrera, and Rubén Lau Rojo—is setting new standards for understanding the region from a multidisciplinary perspective, and meeting with them in Austin in 1988 and in Juárez in 1989 stimulated me to reconsider a number of the issues I address in this book. I also benefit tremendously from working with the editors of the *Journal of Historical Sociology:* Philip Corrigan, Derek Sayer, Jane Schneider, and Gavin Williams. Philip's prolific correspondence especially, and the discussions when he, Derek, Jane, Gavin, and I are able to meet are invariably eye-opening. Ana Alonso, Michael Kearney, Alan Knight, Bill Merrill, and Bill Roseberry read the entire manuscript at various stages of its preparation, offering devastating criticisms alongside fruitful suggestions and strong encouragement. I also owe a lot to the trenchant readings offered by Gilbert Joseph and an anonymous external reviewer for the University of Chicago Press. T. David Brent, my editor at the Press, has been especially sensitive in undertaking the forbidding task of helping me transform an unwieldy manuscript into a readable book.

Mr. OSquared aided me with his computer expertise in July 1992, and Tom Ireland later corrected the manuscript. Susan Long and Barbara Montgomery drafted the maps. I also received assistance from the University of Arizona Provost's Author Support Fund.

Most upsetting are memories of the help and friendship of Namiquipans who passed away even as the research was going on. Cruz Tena, one of the town's most lucid and interesting elders, died in the winter of 1984. Aurelia Muñoz was a hardworking and imaginative person who would have been a great anthropologist—or, as she wished, a private investigator. Mikey Maldonado died suddenly and unexpectedly in the winter of 1986, depriving Namiquipa of one of its more committed, engaged, and well-informed local historians.

Cruz Chávez Gutiérrez, grandson of the Cruz Chávez of Tomochi, was born in the *municipio* of Namiquipa in 1916. His father and uncle fought and died during the revolution. In an interview in 1986—the year Halley's comet returned—he was asked whether people had fought for land during the revolution. His response was that they fought for land, freedom, and justice, and still enjoyed neither of the latter two. "Put it that we have land, but that was a fight. And justice? And freedom? When will those arrive? Can you tell me?" Here's hoping the next generation of Namiquipans can answer those questions positively in their own lifetime.

ABBREVIATIONS

Note: A description of the archives and primary sources that appear in this list may be found in the bibliography.

AEN	Archivo Ejidal de Namiquipa
AF	Archivo Franciscano
AGCCA	Archivo General del Cuerpo Consultativo Agrario
AGN	Archivo General de la Nación
AGN.Cyp	Archivo General de la Nación, Ramo Carceles y Presidios
AGNCh	Archivo General de Notarias del Estado de Chihuahua
AGN.PI	Archivo General de la Nación, Ramo Provincias Internas
AGN.PR	Archivo General de la Nación, Ramo Periodo Revolucionario
AGN.Ptes	Archivo General de la Nación, Ramo Presidentes
AGN.V	Archivo General de la Nación, Ramo Virreynato
AGRA	Archivo General de Reforma Agraria
AHSRE	Archivo Histórico de la Secretaria de Relaciones Exteriores
AJBT	Archivo Jacinto B. Treviño
AJN	Archivo del Juzgado de Namiquipa
AMC	Archivo Municipal de Cruces
AMCG	Archivo Municipal de Ciudad Guerrero
AMN	Archivo Municipal de Namiquipa
AP	Archivo de la Palabra
APHS	Arizona Pioneer Historical Society
APN	Archivo Parroquial de Namiquipa
ATN	Archivo de Terrenos Nacionales
Bando	The Bando of Teodoro de Croix, issued on November 15, 1778, establishing the pueblos or *villas* of Janos, Casas Grandes, Galeana, Cruces and Namiquipa

BANRURAL	Banco Nacional de Crédito Rural (National Rural Credit Bank)
BETA	Brigada de Educación Tecnológica Agropecuaria #331, a technical assistance group assigned to Namiquipa in 1983 by the Ministry of Education.
BL	Bancroft Library
BL.AST	Bancroft Library, Archive of Silvestre Terrazas
BN	Biblioteca Nacional
BN.AF	Biblioteca Nacional, Archivo Franciscano
BN.AFM	Biblioteca Nacional, Archivo Francisco I. Madero
BN.Ms.	Biblioteca Nacional, Manuscritos
c.	*Caja* (box)
Cd.	*Ciudad* (city)
CE	Comisariado Ejidal (Ejidal Administration)
Chih.	Chihuahua City (in correspondence); the state of Chihuahua
CIDECH	Centro de Investigación y Documentación del Estado de Chihuahua
CLA	Comisión Local Agraria (Local Agrarian Commission). Subordinate to the CNA (see below), CLAs operated on a regional level (often encompassing multiple states) and directed their recommendations to governors of the states.
CNA	Comisión Nacional Agraria (National Agrarian Commission); bureaucratic apparatus of the agrarian reform in Mexico during the 1920s that directed its recommendations to the president of the Republic
CNA.Actas	*Actas* (minutes) from meetings of the CNA
CNA.RP	*Resoluciones presidenciales*, presidential resolutions, granting land to villages on the recommendation of the deliberations of the CNA
CNC	Confederación Nacional de Campesinos (National Confederation of Peasants); a state-controlled peasant league, closely linked to the PRI (see below)
CONASUPO	Compañía Nacional de Subsistencias Populares. A state agency that purchases basic grains (maize and beans) cultivated by peasant producers at controlled prices, it also maintains grain warehouses in the countryside.
CPA	Comité Particular Administrativo (local administrative committee of an *ejido*).
CPD	Colección Porfirio Díaz
CRO	Colección de Dr. Rubén Osorio
DPP	Dictamen del Perito Paleografo (the conclusions or judgment of the expert paleographer); assessment of the legitimacy and au-

	thenticity of documents presented to the CLA or CNA by members of communities petitioning the state for an *ejido*
DRSW	Documentary Relations of the Southwest
e.	*expediente* (file)
Edo.	*Estado* (state)
fo.	folio(s), page
Gob°·	*Gobierno* (government)
INS	Immigration and Naturalization Service
JM	*Jefe municipal* (municipal boss or chief); title assumed by municipal presidents during the late Porfiriato in Chihuahua
JPG	*Jefe político,* Distrito Guerrero (political boss or chief of the Guerrero District). *Jefes políticos* were appointed by the governor or in some cases by President Díaz himself as the guardians of order and progress during the Porfiriato. Districts encompassed multiple *municipios* (see below).
JPyCM	*Jefe político y comandante militar* (political chief and military commander); title assumed by *jefes políticos* during the revolution in Chihuahua
LCC	Luna County Courthouse
MEBCh	*Manual de Estadísticas Básicas del Estado de Chihuahua*
Mpio.	*Municipio* (municipality); a territory and unit of governance, comparable to a county in the United States
Nam.	Namiquipa (in correspondence)
PAN	Partido Acción Nacional (National Action Party)
PEMEX	Petróleos Mexicanos (Mexican Petroleum)
PHO	Proyecto de Historia Oral; research project of the Instituto de Investigaciones Dr. José María Luis Mora, directed by Eugenia Meyer
PLM	Partido Liberal Mexicano (Mexican Liberal Party); the most radical challenge to the Díaz dictatorship in the first decade of the twentieth century. The PLM was actually anarcho-syndicalist in orientation rather than "liberal." Its followers were also known as *magonistas* (after Ricardo and Enrique Flores Magón, who founded the party).
PM	*Presidente municipal* (municipal president)
PRI	Partido Revolucionario Institucional; the ruling political party in Mexico since the revolution
Prot.	Protocolos
PST	Partido Socialista de los Trabajadores (Socialist Workers Party)
PSUM	Partido Socialista Unificado de México (Unified Socialist Party of Mexico)

RG	Record Group
RPP.CdG	Registro Público de la Propiedad, Ciudad Guerrero; property register for the Guerrero District, Chihuahua
RPPCh	Registro Público de la Propiedad, Estado de Chihuahua; state property register
SAM	Sistema Alimentario Mexicano (Mexican Food System); a short-lived state program of the early 1980s to increase agricultural production of basic grains such as maize and beans
SARH	Secretaría de Agricultura y Recursos Hidráulicos (Ministry of Agriculture and Water Resources)
SCP	Sociedad Civil Particular (Private Civil Society); the popular organization established by Namiquipans in 1906 to defend the community's land
Sec^a.	*Secretaría* (government ministry)
SEP	Secretaría de Educación Público (Ministry of Education)
SGM	*Sitio de ganado mayor.* A unit of land equivalent to a square that is one league to a side (approximately 1,755 hectares), this measure was used during the colonial period.
SRA	Secretaría de Reforma Agraria (Ministry of Agrarian Reform); successor to the CNA
USMHI	United States Military History Institute
USNA.MRB	United States National Archives, Military Reference Branch
UTEP	University of Texas-El Paso
WNRA	Washington National Records Administration

SPENT CARTRIDGES OF REVOLUTION

1
Cartuchos Quemados: Ethnography and Social Analysis

APPROACHING THE FIELD

Is it any longer possible to "imagine yourself suddenly set down surrounded by all your gear, alone on a tropical beach close to a native village, while the launch or dinghy which has brought you sails away out of sight" (Malinowski 1922:4)? I like to think my imagination is fairly fertile, but the images flashing through my brain in June of 1983 upon first arriving in Namiquipa, Chihuahua—and those that I can summon forth from my memory nine years later—are a far cry from the ones Malinowski and subsequent generations of ethnographers have evoked.

Our pickup truck started leaking oil shortly after we'd gotten past Ojinaga a week earlier, but I was able to find a brass fitting in Chihuahua City—something it would never have occurred to me to look for even in Chicago for a sixteen-year-old vehicle. It not only stopped the leak but also rendered the oil gauge functional. "Set down" we weren't. Ana and I have driven to the end of the paved road, and presuming the truck kept running, we could leave anytime we wished. It was not far to the United States border; seven hours to Agua Prieta, Sonora, six to Palomas, Chihuahua, and a beautiful drive either way.

This is not a distant tropical beach with native villages. In fact, the region, of pine- and oak-covered mountains and high, semidesertic plains, was almost familiar. My family has lived in southern Arizona since 1970, and much of my own indolent youth involved time in pine forests and mountain ranges similar to the ones around Namiquipa. Ana remarked more than once about the degree to which living in Namiquipa reminded her of the *aldea* (village) in Asturias where she had stayed before coming back to the New World in the 1960s.

Malinowski must have struck a strange figure in the eyes of Trobriand islanders and may have bemoaned the fact that the only other "whitemen" he could anticipate encountering were the usual assortment of missionaries, traders, colonial officials, and explorers, each less sensitive

1

than the next to living among "the natives." We, on the other hand, were not intending to study "natives" in the first place, and the people we met in Namiquipa did not appear profoundly different from us, nor we from them. I, for example, had worn high-heeled boots, denim pants, and cowboy shirts—Sunday "dress up" clothes for Namiquipan men—for a decade before setting foot in Chihuahua.

We were, though, like Malinowski, surrounded by our gear. The back of the pickup truck was fully loaded. We also brought an assortment of cultural and scholarly baggage. In my own case that involved a strong desire not to be in the United States during 1984, along with an interest in living and working in what I understood to be a "revolutionary" town.

The present study began as an attempt to understand what happens to a revolutionary town after a revolution. The town in question was Namiquipa; the revolution, the one that occurred in Mexico at the beginning of the twentieth century. According to many accounts of the Mexican revolution, its key achievements were related to the distribution of land to the peasantry, the enactment of progressive social legislation, and the encouragement of popular participation in the political life of the nation (Simpson 1937; Tannenbaum 1930; Whetten 1948; Knight 1986; Hamilton 1982; Leal [1975] 1985; Córdova 1973; Aguilar Camin et al. 1979). The people of Namiquipa fought throughout the period of armed struggle in Chihuahua from 1910 to 1920, and the town recovered control of its lands by 1926. Six decades later one might expect that conflicts over land or emerging as contingent results of transformed production relations would be, if not totally resolved, at least muted, and not the first items of a popular agenda.

Nevertheless, struggles for land and political conflict were widely manifest in Namiquipa in the 1980s. During our fieldwork, when we told people we were interested in studying "the Mexican revolution," they would often ask, "Which one?" In the opinion of many, the events we witnessed during the 1980s constituted the elements of another "revolution" in Namiquipa, more profound in many ways than the events of 1910–20. After watching the state police (*judiciales*) club, tear-gas, and shoot at a crowd gathered for an opposition political rally in the plaza in front of her house, one elderly women remarked that she had never witnessed such a degree of mobilization and brutality even though she had lived in the same house through the years of the revolution.[1] (For another description of the events this woman was talking about, see the first section of Alonso 1988a.)

Key published texts including information about Namiquipa (Almada 1964; Calzadíaz Barrera 1979; Katz 1981; Olea Arias 1961; Duarte

Morales 1968) dealt with the decades immediately before and during the Mexican revolution of 1910–20, but little had been written about what had happened to the town since then. Did Namiquipans regain control of land and local politics as a positive outcome of the revolution, as the official view of the state claims? Or were they merely the *cartuchos quemados*, the burnt or spent cartridges of a struggle in which the victory went to other social classes, as a peasant revolutionary from Namiquipa eloquently asserts (Duarte Morales 1968:23)? Can such questions even be answered in terms of a time frame restricted to the twentieth century?

To the question, "What happened to this revolutionary town after the revolution?" one possible answer—more or less consonant with official history in the 1980s—would run something like this: The economic, political, and ideological bases of prerevolutionary conflict have eroded. In the decades since the revolution the people of Namiquipa recovered their land, very fast. Community-state conflicts were softened by the integration of the community into a national political party and the subsumption of community livelihood into the life of a new nation, which was the explicit political project of the revolutionary state (Córdova 1973; Womack 1986).[2] Finally, as the result of a combination of advances made by other sectors of the rural population of western Chihuahua and a relative deterioration for the Namiquipans, Namiquipa is now less distinct from other rural towns than in the past; its colonial glory days (it had been settled as a presidio in 1778) no longer bear much weight. According to this interpretation, the Paz Porfiriana—the regime of "order and progress" instituted in Mexico while President Porfirio Díaz ruled between 1876 and 1911—has been supplanted by the Paz Revolucionária in the decades since 1920.

This book answers the question differently, giving voice to an interpretation according to which peasants from Namiquipa and elsewhere were the *cartuchos quemados* of national revolutionary struggles in Mexico in the decades following the revolution of 1910. It indicates the ways they were "burnt" or "spent" by the revolution and the postrevolutionary state in the course of examining forms through which the relationship of Namiquipa to the state developed as a historical process prior to and following the violent decade of social revolution. By adopting a time frame that extends back to the eighteenth century, the analysis permits us to understand why a community that was earlier established as a military settlement colony should today occupy a structural position vis-à-vis the state curiously similar to that of the indigenous peoples the settlers were originally commissioned to suppress.

The ethnographic and historical research for this book was conducted

through the 1980s during the height of the political, economic, and social crisis in Mexico. Early on in fieldwork it became evident that despite
six decades of agrarian reform, political integration, and cultural-
ideological homogenization through a revolutionary-nationalist "imagining" of community (Anderson 1983), daily life in the pueblo was
plagued by conflicts similar to those that occurred on the eve of the
revolution of 1910. Land invasions and agrarian struggle, various indi-
cations that particularist rather than universalist ideological battles were
still very much alive in the pueblo, and fights over political succession
appeared endemic.

Such circumstances might convince the naive ethnographer that
French social theorists and structuralists are correct when they insist,
"Plus ça change, plus c'est la même chose" (the line is from de Tocque-
ville, but this sort of position is advanced by Lévi-Strauss 1963:320–38;
1966; or Sahlins 1976, 1981). However, such a manifestly ahistorical
formulation is inadequate because it sweeps the issue of change under
an essentialist rug. Agrarian, political, and ideological conflicts in contemporary Namiquipa are outcomes of the way land, labor, politics, and
consciousness have been transformed since the revolution; and those
transformations were in turn shaped by prior processes of ecological,
economic, and political formation and deformation, the contents and
organizations of which were provided not by "the Mexican Revolution"
but by the history of the community, the people who created it, and the
internal and external relationships through which the community had
been reproduced.

An appreciation of the need to develop an alternative periodization
of the history of Namiquipa—one that challenges the centrality of the
1910 revolution in Mexico—emerges from reflections on the settlement
of the region. Descriptions of the North of Mexico generally, and of the
state of Chihuahua in particular, have noted the historical, social, and
political peculiarities of certain towns in the mountains of Chihuahua.[3]
Studies of the revolution in Chihuahua, as well as accounts written by
participants, identified the singularly important role played by the inhabitants of these sierra towns throughout the revolution.[4]

One feature of the pueblos that were sites of agrarian and political
conflict before the revolution, of mobilization by their inhabitants during the revolution, and of successful restitution of lands in the years
immediately following the revolution is that many had been established
as military settlement colonies during the eighteenth and early nineteenth centuries (Katz 1976b:64–65). The colonies, as Friedrich Katz
calls them, were given land by the colonial state in return for fighting
the Apaches, and the inhabitants constituted a unique social group on
the northern frontier.

The inhabitants of the colonies were privileged in many respects compared to the free villagers of central and southern Mexico. Unlike the villagers, they were not wards of the crown during the colonial period but enjoyed rights generally reserved for Spaniards and their descendants, the criollos. They owned their land individually and were allowed to sell it, or buy additional land. They usually owned more land and more cattle than the free peasants of Mexico's other areas. Their communities were entitled to greater internal autonomy, and the military colonists had not only the right but the duty to bear arms (Katz 1981:8).

Three general points or lines of research emerged from Katz's work on peasant mobilization in Chihuahua (see Katz 1976a, 1976b, 1980, 1981, 1988a, 1988b). First is his hypothesis regarding the significance of the origin of these towns as military settlement colonies in shaping the possibilities for popular mobilization in subsequent decades (cf. Gilly 1986, Aguilar Camin et al. 1979, Holden n.d.). Ethnographic, popular historical, and archival evidence supports that hypothesis.[5] Second, Katz's archival discoveries, combined with the findings of other anthropologists and historians—petitions for control of land, judicial briefs filed against landlords invading pueblo lands, reports of electoral conflicts, complaints about caciques (local political bosses), tax revolts, contemporary land tenure arrangements and their popular historical exegesis—indicate Chihuahuan peasants developed a historical consciousness of their role in the pacification of northern Mexico and the relationship of that project to the maintenance and reproduction of their communities.[6] Third, the sometimes mutually supportive relationships between the state and the communities before the revolution and the pueblos' important military role in forging the possibilities for the revolutionary state aside, little was known about what occurred in these towns since the 1920s.

The present volume corroborates the first of these points and explores the latter two through an examination of the history of one of the former colonies, Namiquipa. From the 1770s, when the town was resettled as a presidio, through the 1910s and beyond, the people of Namiquipa forged a distinct and militant ideology, distinct both from that of the great majority of laboring masses in Mexico and that of the "modernizing" elites who controlled the region and the country by the 1890s and who still rule in the 1990s (Katz 1981:9ff.; Knight 1986, 1; Alonso 1988b). Until the Porfiriato, Namiquipa had enjoyed a relatively privileged, autonomous development (Katz 1976b, 1981). But throughout Mexico the Porfiriato was a period of headlong capitalist development, the effects of this economic transformation—of the countryside as much as of urban areas—registering even in relatively isolated rural communities (Carr 1973; Katz 1986; Lloyd 1983). Labor and work (abstract social labor, and the action of individual workers) were transformed, assuming new characteristics in relation to the reorganization of the production process in the countryside (Lloyd 1987).

In part as a reaction to this process of social and economic reorganization, Namiquipa was the site of agrarian and political conflicts in the decades preceding 1910 (Wasserman 1980). It was a consummately revolutionary town in Mexico from 1910 to 1920,[7] the site for and its inhabitants the protagonists of some of the more celebrated events of that violent decade. Like the *zapatistas* of southern Mexico (see Gilly [1971] 1983, 1986; Warman 1978, 1980, 1988b; Womack 1969), Namiquipans realized in their own political practice—however ambiguously—the popular demands for *tierra y libertad*. They wrested control of the administration of pueblo lands from outsiders, successfully pushed back invasions by landlords, and restored local autonomy in government, an "end to boss rule" (Womack 1969). Further, before the end of the 1920s, and anticipating by a decade the implementation on a national scale of a massive agrarian reform in Mexico under President Lázaro Cárdenas (1934–40), Namiquipans recovered undisputed control of their lands.

In August 1926 the *ejido* of Namiquipa was established when the revolutionary state acknowledged that almost 100,000 hectares of land, a third of which would eventually prove suitable for cultivation, belonged to this town and its inhabitants, then numbering only a few thousand. One might have anticipated that this community would enjoy a strong, and positive, relationship with the postrevolutionary state in the decades to follow. And while a few Namiquipans did cultivate their connections to the emergent power structures in Mexico—one Francisco V. Antillon was even interim governor of Chihuahua in the 1930s—many more cultivated instead their agricultural fields and their memories, memories rooted in experiences and constructed through practices that were no less at odds with the Mexican state in the 1980s than in the 1900s. But the postrevolutionary state of recent decades is not identical to the state in the decades before and during the revolution. And so, too, recent challenges to the power of the state, popular questionings of the character of Namiquipa's relationship to the state, have assumed new and different forms.

WRITING HISTORY THROUGH THE ETHNOGRAPHIC PRESENT

The chapters that follow examine modalities of community-state relations in Namiquipa by indicating the different ways land and labor have been the foci of political struggles within the community from 1778 to the present. Such a grand sweep is possible owing to the temporal depth, richness, and variety of archival sources that provide information about Namiquipa. The representation of that information in the present analysis should not, however, be construed as a transparent reflection of "the data." For what is interwoven throughout the narration are analyses of contemporary popular ideologies of history and land, of labor and politics.

More pertinent than simply the quantity of the data was the opportunity to develop an interpretation of documentary sources through discussions with Namiquipans while living with them through yet another epoch of struggle, during which the relationship of the community to the state was once again redefined and recast. During the fieldwork it became clear that popular historical exegesis deployed time frames and periodizations that challenged official history (Nugent 1985:78, 82). This long time frame is required to keep the interpretation from being overly weighted by the celebrated events of the revolutionary decade and, by implication, overdetermined by an official version of history, until very recently promulgated by the state, which privileges "The Revolution" (Joseph and Nugent 1994). Time frames such as this also challenge the conventional ways anthropologists write about the peoples they study, even as they provide a critical basis for enriching the ethnographies we produce (see Stern 1987).

Conventional ethnographies, say those written during the heyday of structural-functional anthropology, typically dealt with nonliterate populations inhabiting peripheral regions of what came to be called the Third World. Often as not, the ethnography would start with a short chapter providing a "historical background" to the chapters that followed. Those would offer a synchronic analysis "from the ground up" (geography, economy, marriage and kinship, politics, religion, myth) of the people, community, or culture being studied. The synchronic analysis was presented in that "violation of the normal use of tenses" long distinctive to anthropological writing, "the ethnographic present" (Service [1958] 1971:xv).

This book inverts that conventional order of presentation. It starts with a description of Namiquipa during the 1980s from the ground up and proceeds to a diachronic analysis of community-state relations from the late eighteenth through the late twentieth centuries. The ethnographic present is not being used only at the outset as a provisional descriptive device, however. Rather, I want to demonstrate how any reliance on such a notion, even one as committedly tongue-in-cheek as my own, requires a critique of the concept that can direct anthropological writing away from the sterility of abstract, centrist, and presentist description and towards a form of historical explanation. Such a critique makes possible an analysis of community-state relations in terms of state formation and the formation of community, the relationship between peasant and capitalist economies, the multiple significations of agrarian reform in Mexico, and how some subjects of the Mexican state regard themselves.

The mid-1980s in Namiquipa—the ethnographic present—can be represented from a variety of perspectives. Thirty years hence, or next week, one could develop a different way of representing that period in this locale in relation to other events—biographical, political, ecological—and produce an incommensurable yet equally coherent and valid description of the same community and the same events. While this problem is notorious in Mexican anthropology, especially since Redfield's and Lewis's studies of Tepoztlán (Redfield 1930; Lewis 1951), neither is it one uniquely afflicting ethnographers. Agents and agencies of the state have a lot invested in representations of the conditions enjoyed by subjects of the state. So too do the state's subjects manipulate, even as they are manipulated by, representations, whether their own or those imposed from outside their communities (see Orlove 1991). Namiquipans, for example, produce contrasting and mutually irreconcilable accounts of the mid-1980s, the different effects of truth registering (validly) in relation to distinguishable and sometimes contradictory experiences, interests, and terms of reference (see Alonso 1988a). Any rush to assert the obvious point that the ethnographic present is profoundly partial and incomplete, however, runs the risk of ignoring the related point that it can at the same time serve as a useful construct for imparting some information and be quite meaningful as an account. Of more immediate importance, though, is that by its very partiality and incompleteness an account constructed in the ethnographic present may indicate important areas of further investigation. It is toward the end of developing the latter point in particular that the following experiments with the ethnographic present are offered.

THE STATE OF CHIHUAHUA

Chihuahua is the largest state in the Republic of Mexico, comprising some 245,612 square kilometers, bordering Coahuila to the southeast, Durango to the south, Sinaloa and Sonora to the west, New Mexico to the north, and Texas to the northeast (*Compendio Estadístico* n.d.). Much of Chihuahua is semidesertic plains interrupted by lines of hills running north and south. The Sierra Madre Occidental dominates the western third of Chihuahua.

The Río Bravo (Grande) runs along the border with Texas. Much of the interior of Chihuahua is drained by the Río Conchos and its tributaries, which join the Río Bravo near Ojinaga (Presidio, Texas). For much of its length after leaving the sierra, the Río Conchos runs through desert, though its middle stretches now constitute an irrigation zone developed largely since the 1920s (Aboites 1988). The Papigochic and Urique rivers cut through the sierra to the west, running to the Pacific Ocean. Several rivers of western Chihuahua—Casas Grandes, Santa María, and Carmen or Santa Clara, never reach the ocean. During particularly rainy years they form in shallow lake beds in northwest Chihuahua, but usually they just peter out in the desert (map 1).

According to a view shared by forest industry cartographers and Marxist sociologists,[8] there are three agricultural regions in Chihuahua: the sierra, the valleys on the margins of the sierra and the desert, and the irrigation districts. Somewhat less rigorous, and occasionally even poetic, descriptions that advance the same threefold categorization of land and people-land relationships in Chihuahua are found in Lister and Lister 1966 and Jordan [1956] 1981.

In the sierra, impoverished peasants, many of them *indígenas* (mostly Tarahumara or Rarámuri), cultivate maize on small, level patches of land. The irrigation districts are controlled by private, commercial farmers. Namiquipa is located on the marginal lands which in the past (and in parts until very recently) comprised parts of enormous cattle ranches controlled by Chihuahuan or North American families such as the Terrazas, the Zuloagas, and the Hearsts, or companies such as the Palomas Land and Cattle Company. While the land is primarily suitable for cattle grazing, parts of this region have been cultivated for centuries, and today it constitutes a zone of rainfall or seasonal (*temporal*) agriculture, though there is some irrigation on the immediate margins of the rivers.[9]

Alexander von Humboldt's characterization of *norteños*—egalitarian, more "Spanish" than "Indian" (or even "Mestizo") in their orientation and self-identity, but too engaged in the hard work of transforming the frontier to be overly preoccupied about ethnic distinctions within their communities—is in many ways as accurate today as when he penned his observations a century and a half ago.[10]

A slightly less dated characterization of Chihuahuans than von Humboldt's, written by Enrique Creel in 1928, reveals as much about Creel's ideology as it does about the people of Chihuahua.[11] Creel presented two lectures on Chihuahua, the first a history, the second a discussion of geography and natural resources; he talks about people in the second of the two lectures (Creel 1928). In the midst of a discussion of the disagreeableness of the Chihuahuan climate he suddenly remarks, "The inhabitants, principally those of the countryside, are more developed and more strong than those of the South of Mexico. . . . There are towns in the Guerrero District where a growing number of the inhabitants can

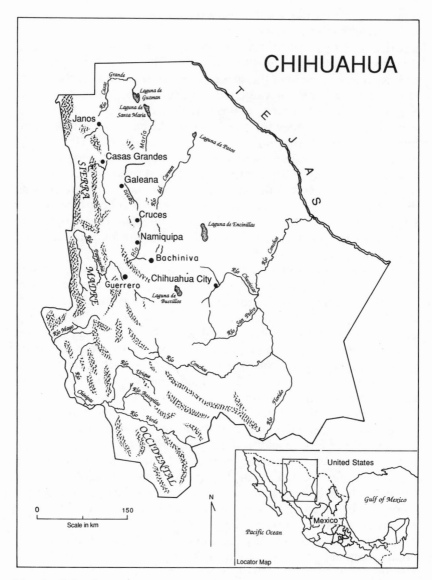

Map 1. Chihuahua.

place ten shots from a rifle in exactly the same spot" (Creel 1928:45).

Can such people be characterized in more precise sociological terms? Appendini's study (1983) of the agricultural sector in Chihuahua focused on the differentiation between groups of agricultural workers in terms of distinct socioeconomic class characteristics defined by people's relationship to means of production and the kind of exploitation to which they are subjected (or to which they subject others). Using these criteria, Appendini was able to identify capitalist entrepreneurs, shopkeepers and artisans, peasants, semiproletarians/semipeasants, and proletarians inhabiting contemporary Chihuahua. By far the largest group were the farmers ostensibly engaged in "peasant" production (oriented to household reproduction), whose labor is organized as a kind of petty-commodity production by the character of their relationship to an encompassing capitalist political-economic structure. Both their labor power and the products of their labor enter into capitalist markets and circuits of exchange and distribution. One thing analyses such as these indicate is that the differentiation of social classes in terms of ideology may not be axiomatically derived from structural class position.[12] Rather, individuals may assume any or several of these identities over time *or* simultaneously, as many Namiquipans do.

Finally, the region has been profoundly affected by its contiguity with the U.S. border. Foreign, but particularly North American, capital investment has been made at a local level for more than a century. This includes not only investment in railroads, smelters, enormous sawmills, and the like, but also in small mines and commercial establishments, ranches, repair shops, and orchards.[13] Similarly, North Americans themselves have physically penetrated the region during the same period. But transborder penetration is not a unidirectional movement; Mexican inhabitants of this region have worked in the United States for more than a century.[14] Today most adult males from Namiquipa have worked for longer or shorter periods of time in the United States either legally (e.g., as *braceros* until 1965; by securing U.S. residence papers) or illegally. They have not only brought back dollars, machinery, tools, and pickup trucks to their communities but have also experienced subjection to "alien" or "non-Mexican" forms of work discipline and the organization of time (Alonso 1992a). Out of these historical experiences in their own country and abroad the Chihuahuans have developed a distinctive perception not only of "the Other Side" but also of the Mexican state and national development (Nugent 1992).

THE PUEBLO OF NAMIQUIPA

The pueblo of Namiquipa is located on the eastern margin of the Sierra Madre Occidental, about two hundred miles south of the inter-

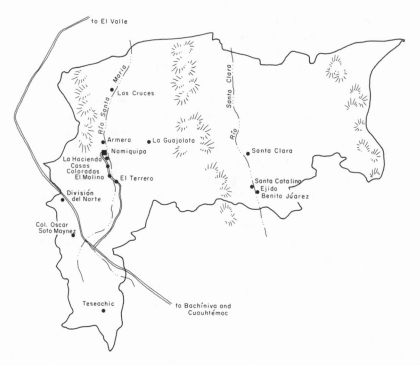

Map 2. The *municipio* of Namiquipa.

national border at latitude 29°15' and longitude 107°25' (*Compendio Estadístico* 1958; SPP map 1981). Namiquipa is the *cabecera* or county seat of a rural municipality 4,212.58 square kilometers in extent. The *municipio* (also called Namiquipa) is shaped like a rectangle—the longer part running east to west—with a "handle" extending perpendicular to the main rectangle south along the *municipio*'s western edge (map 2).

Two rivers, running south to north and separated by a parallel range of hills, pass through the *municipio*. Río Santa Clara to the east passes through the pueblos and *ejidos* of Benito Juárez, Santa Catalina de Villela, Santa Clara, and Emiliano Zapata and thence north through the former haciendas Carmen and San Lorenzo before disappearing into the desert. The Río Santa María starts in Bachiniva to the south, drains the plains above Namiquipa—the zone of most concentrated habitation—and then runs through Cruces and proceeds north, watering the *municipios* of San Buenaventura and Galeana before petering out in Ascensión. West of the Río Santa María is a line of mountains beyond which, towards the south, is a river valley which eventually empties into the Sea of Cortez (the Río Papigochi). Towards the north, where the mountains abut much nearer to the western bank of the Río Santa

María, is a high plain (Babicora Alta), beyond which the terrain is pure sierra.

What significance, if any, there is to the name "Namiquipa" was never determined. Namiquipa or some variant such as "Mamiquipa," "Amiquipa," or "Anamiquipa" was used in colonial documents to refer to the site from as early as the 1660s. It is probably a word from the language of the indigenous peoples of the area, the Conchos, who lived in a *ranchería* at the site when a Franciscan mission was established there in 1663 (Gerhard 1982). It is not a Tarahumara place name, though a few Tarahumara families were living in Namiquipa as early as the 1760s. Some informants insisted Namiquipa was an Apache word. While philologically impossible, the suggestion is interesting from the standpoint of demonstrating the reciprocal imbrication of identity and social memory in the meanings attached to place names; for Namiquipa is located in a region where eighteenth- and nineteenth-century settlers fought the Apaches for control. Informants suggested a variety of meanings, for example that Namiquipa signified "place of the flagstones." The more flattering, widely subscribed to, and in a way the most accurate notion is that it means *"valle bonito"* (beautiful valley).

"Namiquipa" can refer to the *municipio* as well as the pueblo. However, the pueblo of Namiquipa itself specifies multiple territorial and social entities. Between the 1770s and the 1910s, the majority of the inhabitants of the present-day *municipio* were concentrated along the Río Santa María in or near the pueblos of Cruces and Namiquipa. Namiquipans were eventually able to adopt a typical riverine settlement pattern, with habitations spread along the banks of the river and the arroyos which feed the river. Consequently, by the 1920s, areas which were regarded as "neighborhoods" (barrios) of the pueblo of Namiquipa were located along a ten-mile stretch up and down the river, extending from what is now El Terrero to Armera. The arroyos feeding into the Río Santa María marked the boundaries between barrios (see map 3).

Some locations which were in the past barrios of Namiquipa are regarded by present-day inhabitants as pueblos in their own right. Indeed, two former barrios, El Molino, and El Terrero have larger populations than the barrio La Plaza, or Namiquipa proper, the political and administrative center of the modern *municipio*, the site of colonial-period settlement, and the location of a church dating from the eighteenth century. "Namiquipa," then, can refer to the *municipio*, the ten-mile stretch of the Río Santa María along which the barrios of the central community or locale are located, and one barrio in particular, La Plaza.

According to preliminary results of the 1980 census, in that year 32,566 inhabitants in the *municipio* of Namiquipa were living in 6,337 houses (an average of slightly more than five persons per household) in

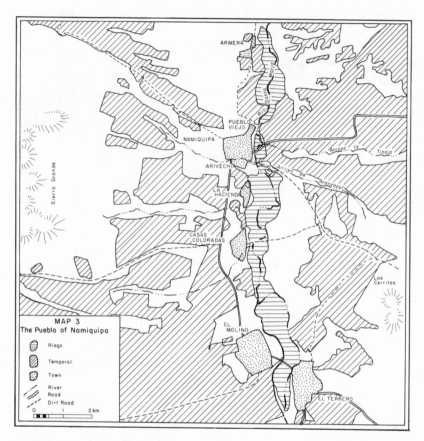

Map 3. The pueblo of Namiquipa.

approximately forty villages and towns (Monografías Municipales 1982:
63–68). Official use of the same figures estimated a population approaching 40,000 in the *municipio* by 1985 (draft of Professor Gándara's
informe for Monografías Municipales that year), but that is an exaggera-
tion which fails to take account of several factors. First, the increasing
tendency for young people in particular to work outside the *municipio*
hides the fact that some Namiquipans are only infrequently resident in
the *municipio*. Many young people go to the United States, and while in
the past it was primarily single men or husbands without their families
who went north, in the last ten years increasing numbers of women
have left the pueblo as well. A second factor is the dramatic depopula-
tion of one of the *municipio*'s larger pueblos from 1983 onward as the
result of a shooting war which developed out of a conflict over lands.
During the mid-1980s, several thousand people left what had been a

vigorous pueblo of almost 5,000 people. A third factor is the economic crisis throughout Latin America in the 1980s. As the real value of the official minimum wage and crop prices in Mexico collapsed through the 1980s, many rural peoples looked north, and those in the Chihuahuan countryside were particularly well positioned to migrate—if only temporarily— to the United States. I estimate the population of the *municipio* in 1983 at 35,000 and suspect it declined modestly over the next three years, a decline attributable to permanent and temporary outmigration from the region as the effects of the economic crisis in Mexico were felt in rural Chihuahua during the 1980s.

Of these 35,000 people, most live along the Río Santa María in Santa Ana (Colonia Oscar Soto Maynez), El Terrero, El Molino, Namiquipa, and Las Cruces. Namiquipa proper (including Pueblo Viejo and Arivechi, but not La Hacienda or Casas Coloradas) has about 2,200 inhabitants. The clearest and most exact statement one can make about the Namiquipans' ethnic background is that they are not Indians. Cruces and Namiquipa were the sites of military settlement colonies by the end of the eighteenth century. A significant proportion—though by no means all—of the early settlers were Spaniards and *criollos* (descendants of Spaniards born in the New World). Many Namiquipans have the hair color, blue or green eyes, and tall, lanky figures more characteristic of their Spanish and Basque antecedants than of their Indian and mulatto antecedants. *Güero/a* (blond or fair one) and *gringo/a* are frequent nicknames and terms of reference used by Namiquipan men and women to address one another.[15]

In Namiquipa the valley of the Río Santa María is approximately 6,000 feet in altitude (1,850 m). The pueblo is situated on bluffs on the western bank of the river from which one can view a large plain cut by several arroyos and ringed with hills stretching out to the east across the river. The Sierra de Babicora, or Sierra Grande, towers over the pueblo from the west. There are small pieces of irrigated land on either side of the river, planted with wheat in the past but now devoted almost exclusively to apple orchards. Much of the plains have been cleared and fenced for planting corn and beans; cattle graze freely on the periphery of the plains and in the sierra. The dirt is vaguely red tending to vaguely white, or clayey tending to sandy. (The 1983 BETA study includes a technical description of qualities of the soil. See "A Note on Archival Sources" in the Bibliography.) The foothills are unevenly covered in scrub oak, and there are stands of pine trees higher in the sierra.

The climate is temperate, with a mean average temperature of 60° Fahrenheit. It gets as hot as 100° in August, and as cold as 15° in January. There are frosts from October until April. It snows in the winter. Winds come pouring out of the sierra in the months after winter, and then the countryside slowly heats up until "the rainy season," which did not begin until late June during the period of fieldwork (1983–86), and usually not in earnest until well into July. Whether "the rainy season" any longer exists in western Chihuahua is a matter for debate. Older Namiquipans complained that the summer rains came later and later with the passing of the decades, an observation corroborated by meteorological records for the *municipio* of Namiquipa from the late nineteenth century to the present found in the Archivo Municipal de Namiquipa (AMN). During the five summers we passed in Namiquipa, the proverbial rainy season figured less as a fact of nature and more like the figure from Beckett's play for whom the characters only wait. I once went with a farmer to examine his field with him and see if it was ready to plant with beans. I asked, "When does the rainy season begin?" and he, poking around with his fingers in the dust, replied, "This *is* the rainy season."

The pueblo of Namiquipa is at the end of a paved road, a 28-km spur departing from the Cuauhtémoc-San Buenaventura highway a mile south of Santa Ana. The spur was paved in the early 1970s. Like almost all the other towns and villages in the *municipio*, Namiquipa has electricity. Unlike most of the smaller and more distant locales, it has "potable" water, that is, untreated ground water pumped into a holding tank and drained into plastic pipes through which it is delivered to individual households.

Most houses in the town are constructed of adobe, though concrete block and *adobón*,[17] neither of which insulate as well, are used in some recent constructions. Older roofs are made of wooden beams and boards covered with dirt. Newer houses and recently repaired roofs use sheets of corrugated metal (*lamina*), but the value of a thick dirt roof for insulation is universally acknowledged.[18] Window and door frames are wooden, but they are frequently repaired using reinforced concrete. The inside walls of the houses are usually plastered, at least roughly, but in the houses of poorer families they sometimes are not. Exterior walls are often left uncovered except for the side exposed to the street, which is plastered with a mix of cement and sand (*mezcla*) and sometimes painted or whitewashed. Almost all of the houses in Namiquipa have concrete floors, and some have wooden floors. Dirt floors were found in only 4 of the 325 occupied houses in the town in 1983 (BETA).

Houses front right onto the street. Behind them are enclosed patios or lots, where householders keep chickens, turkeys, pigs, milk cows, horses, tractors, farming implements, and trucks. Most houses in Namiquipa today have more than one room, one of those serving as a kitchen, another a space in which visitors may be received, which frequently serves as a bedroom as well.

The issue of "quien manda en la casa" (who rules inside the house) is an interesting one. The insides, especially the kitchen, the area of transformation of food, is a preeminently female domain; the male domain is the street. For example, when women go calling, they ask to be admitted, then stride right into the kitchen or living area. When men go calling they do not leave the street so readily, often not even getting out of their trucks, but honking from outside. They remain outside on the street, where the man of the house comes to receive them, and the men usually stay outside unless the visitor is a close kinsman or *compadre*, or their visit is the occasion of some formal or informal gathering or festivity.

Most of the people who live in these mostly adobe houses are members of families in which men work on the land as agriculturalists and keepers of cattle. Different sources suggest that of the "economically active population," anywhere between 70 and 85 percent of the working people, are agriculturalists.[19] The higher figure is more meaningful because many households and individuals that appear in the censuses as "merchants," "artisans," "government functionaries," and so on are also involved, to varying degrees and in various capacities, in working the land. One pertinent argument in this regard is that the relevant unit in determining people's relationship to the local economy is not the individual "worker" but the household, and a higher proportion of households than of individuals in the "economically active population" is involved in agriculture and ranching than census figures may indicate. Additionally, and perhaps more important from the standpoint of the community as a whole (rather than the individual worker, or the household), is a shared sense of collective identity among Namiquipans as belonging to a fundamentally agropastoral community. Finally, there are problems with the very term "economically active population." It provides a basis for *not* counting domestic or reproductive or household labor and is absurd when applied to the action of people whose lives revolve around the transformation of nature by plowing dirt, sowing seeds, waiting for rain, or rounding up cattle from the sierra twice a year, according to rhythms which dictate that, by the very nature of these activities, they are decidedly *inactive* for much of the year.

In other words, the census definition hides (or celebrates) the fact that agriculturalists in Namiquipa are "unemployed" for half the year. Additionally, even individuals whose actual involvement in the agricultural production process is tangential insist they are farmers—for example, "landlords" who in some way derive part of their income from rent or a share of the crop, even someone who rents out a small parcel from year to year because they haven't the tools to work it. In defiance of sociological and official categories, people formulate self-identities through their relationship to the land as members of a community even if that does not correspond to the way they are identified according to the regularizing descriptions and identifications of the state.[20]

That an overwhelming proportion of the inhabitants of Namiquipa not only identify themselves as such, but *can* be, farmers and ranchers underscores the more astonishing fact (astonishing vis-á-vis rural Mexico as a whole) that they actually have land to work on. Despite the tendency to out-migration of the past decade, and despite the ninefold increase in population of the *municipio* over the last sixty years (the population of Namiquipa proper has actually scarcely doubled during the same period), the circumstance that many Namiquipans today have land to work and are working it underlines the importance of the land, and control of the land, in everyday life in the pueblo.

The censuses classify all of these people as "rural,"[21] which is valid since the inhabitants of Namiquipa live in pueblos and ranchos (towns, villages, and hamlets), and most are existentially involved in agriculture or in the production and transformation of the region's now "traditional" products: corn, beans, cattle, apples, and human labor-power. Namiquipans are not simply located in geographical space but have a relation to that space mediated by the historical experience of the people who settled the pueblo and their descendants, by the activities of the present-day inhabitants on the land, and by organizations of power linking the pueblo to the state.

A key feature of Namiquipa determining the relationship of people to the land and of the pueblo to the state is that the town is the center of an enormous *ejido* or corporate landholding more than 100,000 hectares in extent. Later chapters detail the history of that extension of land, exploring the meaning of the pueblo's currently holding the land in this form. The *ejido* was established in 1926 immediately after the period of revolutionary violence in Chihuahua, yet its size, the timing of its establishment, and its location make Namiquipa anomalous compared to the rest of rural Mexico.[22] Before examining some of the issues this paradox raises and how, theoretically, to get a handle on them, conditions in the pueblo of Namiquipa will be contextualized in terms of struggles between people during the period of my fieldwork.

The Big Picture

Winds out of the Nevada Test Site were blowing around the world the first time Ana and I stepped out of our pickup truck in the plaza of Namiquipa in June of 1983. By the time we departed in October of 1985 those winds were still blowing, but so too were the winds of Bhopal. Added to those when we returned in the summer of 1986 were the winds of Chernobyl. Billions of people throughout the world survived

1984; many did not. Indira Gandhi, for example, was assassinated: I first learned of that when a Namiquipan friend told me of the murder of a woman candidate for the presidency of England named Ferrara. In the United States, Ronald Reagan was reelected, the island of Grenada was "rescued," and much of Central America was being "rescued" ever more vigorously. "Civilian governments" assumed power in Brazil, Uruguay, and Argentina, and civilian resistance to the Chilean junta was more widely reported. The rulers of some western European states were clamoring for cruise missles while Macluhanites extoled nuclear weapons as "the ultimate information medium" (*New York Times*, Feb. 12, 1984). As Mengele's body was identified (once again), Kurt Waldheim was preparing to stand for election in Austria.

The Republic of Mexico faced new threats from abroad to its sovereignty, one novelty of which was that they were openly recognized, discussed, and criticized throughout the society (see, e.g., Loret de Mola 1986). As the U.S. Congress struggled to formulate a labor law disguised as an immigration reform bill to deal with the "tsunami" of illegal migration from the south,[23] the U.S. Immigration and Naturalization Service (INS) increased its violent attacks on Mexicans in the United States and Mexico. At the same time, Mexico had its own "wetback problem" on its southern border. Tens of thousands of Guatemalan refugees, mostly indigenous peoples, were illegally crossing into Mexico in a desperate attempt to escape the Guatemalan state's policies of genocide and ethnocide directed against its own citizens. Economic policies encouraged by the World Bank and the International Monetary Fund were implemented by Mexican government officials. Internally, some efforts were made to revitalize a moribund "private sector" involvement in manufacturing and services, but the primary outcomes were registered in the linked processes of capital flight and a spiraling external debt (see Branford and Kucinski [1987] 1988). The Sistema Alimentario Mexicano (SAM) was dismantled almost before official announcements of its success could be proclaimed, and long before scholarly analyses of its possibilities for success or failure appeared in print.[24] Within Mexico, annual rates of inflation surpassed 100 percent; government corruption of a previously only imagined extent was revealed; electoral violence moved out of isolated communities, where caciques could no longer control the situation, onto the state-wide level, where a different order of caciques was no longer competent to control the situation; and then there were the earthquakes in September 1985. The government of Miguel de la Madrid Hurtado (1982–88) was truly, as suggested in the title of a recent book by Héctor Guillén Romo, "the regime of zero growth."

Alongside these international and national issues Chihuahuans confronted an additional series of local crises. These were terrible years for farmers of *temporal* (rain-irrigated) fields; what little precipitation there was sometimes came in the form of crop-damaging hail. Credit for farmers was available only at usurious rates.[25] Teams of animals were used to work fields which in the previous decade had been worked with tractors. Production of basic grains was routinely 50 percent of the harvest anticipated by agricultural engineers at the start of the growing seasons. A Chihuahuan steel plant belatedly discovered that the steel rods used for reinforced concrete in the construction of thousands of houses were irradiated to such an extent that they posed a health threat to the residents of those dwellings.

During the 1983 municipal elections the PRI (Partido Revoluciònario Institucional, the Institutional Revolutionary Party, which has ruled throughout Mexico in one form or another since the 1920s) lost control of every major urban area in the state of Chihuahua, and its supposedly unchallenged appeal and authority in the countryside was questioned to a much greater extent than has figured in most post-1983 analyses (cf. Cornelius 1986; Amaparan Gonzáles et al. 1987; Lau Rojo 1989). The PRI permitted the PAN (Partido Acción Nacional, the National Action Party, a right-wing opposition party with old links to the provincial bourgeoisie and the Catholic church, which nevertheless secured massive and genuine popular support, especially in the North, in the 1980s) to assume office in all the major cities of Chihuahua in 1983. However, the PRI also lost elections in rural municipalities in northwestern Chihuahua, including Madera and Nuevo Casas Grandes (to the PAN), Cuauhtémoc and Namiquipa (to the PST [Partido Socialista de los Trabajadores, the Socialist Workers Party, a reformist "loyal opposition" slightly to the left of the PRI]), and Ignacio Zaragosa (to the PSUM [Partido Socialista Unificado de México, the Unified Socialist Party of Mexico, a coalition of left parties and political organizations to which the Mexican Communist Party had brought the most members]). In only two of the bitterly contested elections in the countryside where the PRI lost—Ignacio Zaragosa and Cuauhtémoc—were opposition party candidates for municipal president permitted to assume office.

Triple-digit rates of inflation were linked to a continuing deterioration of the peso against the dollar. In late 1984 three enormous irrigated marijuana plantations were discovered in the state of Chihuahua, covering hundreds of hectares and at the time employing more than ten thousand migrant agricultural workers. The U.S.-Mexico border was effectively closed by the United States on several occasions during 1985 in actions related to the disappearance and murder of Enrique Camarena Salazar. Increased vigilance—supposedly to thwart the possibility of "terrorist" attacks on U.S. border stations—took the form of harassment of Mexicans and others, with and without papers, crossing the border.

Camarena Salazar was an armed U.S. Drug Enforcement Administration agent working in Mexico who was kidnapped in Guadalajara and murdered, presumably by drug dealers, in 1985. Between the time of his disappearance and the recovery of his body on a roadside in Michoacán, the U.S. Customs Service on several occasions orchestrated searches of all vehicles entering the United States, resulting in hopeless bottlenecks at the border, harassing the Mexican state and the people of Mexico and the United States (see Shannon 1988).[26] When Ana and I entered the United States at Columbus, New Mexico, in March 1985, INS officials trained shotguns on me while customs agents went through our truck. When I asked what all the heavy artillery was about, I was told they had received a bulletin from their regional office warning them to be on the lookout for "Mexican terrorists" who planned to attack U.S. border stations. It was unclear whether the "terrorists" were supposed to be drug dealers, angry "wetbacks," *sandinistas*, or gringo anthropologists.

In the winter of 1985–86 the inhabitants of northwest Chihuahua seized the warehouses of the Compañía Nacional de Subsistencias Populares (CONASUPO), demanding an increase in the *precios de garantía*, the prices at which the state purchased basic grains from farmers. The Chihuahuan peasants' demand was partially met, and the PRI tried to take credit for it.[27] Finally, there was an ongoing political crisis in the wake of the 1983 elections. The PRI lost key cadres in the countryside and removed Governor Oscar Ornelas from office towards the end of 1985 (his term ran for another year). Opposition coalitions appeared throughout Chihuahua in 1985–86 in the countryside and in the cities, incorporating such unlikely combinations as priests, disaffected *priístas* (members of the PRI) and communists directing organizations composed of peasants and shopkeepers, industrial workers and rentiers. University students and steelworkers, peasants and civic organizations, frequently with women in the lead, all repudiated the PRI in public gatherings, demonstrations, strikes, and massive rallies, seizing the streets of the cities and blocking highways and international bridges. It was difficult to determine exactly when the popular movements peaked between the elections for governor (in July 1986) and the new PRI governor's assumption of office in October. By the summer of 1986 the popular mobilization in Chihuahua arguably was "a revolution not against this or that, legitimate, constitutional, republican or Imperialist form of state power. It was a revolution against the *State* itself, of this supernaturalist abortion of society, a resumption by the people for the people of its own social life" (Marx and Engels [1871] 1971: 150).[28]

The issue of how electoral struggle in Chihuahua in 1983–86 articulated with the nationwide uprising of 1988 during presidential elections is too complex to consider in any detail here (but see Lau Rojo 1989). In any event, that would draw us away from developing an appreciation of how to represent the ethnographic present in the pueblo of Namiquipa itself, a topic to which we now turn.

THE LITTLE PICTURE

The preceding account of world, Mexican, and Chihuahuan "history" in the mid-1980s mentioned events that people in Namiquipa were aware of to varying degrees and which people talked about. While there is no disputing that "the ethnographer" authored that account, I "made it up" only after recalling how the events described were discussed in the course of day-to-day conversation during the 1980s. International events *did* have a significant impact both on people's material life and on the way they viewed the world and their own possibilities within it in the *municipio* and the pueblo. For example, two Namiquipan physicians noted the recent increasing incidence of cancer deaths in the *municipio*. This was related by other residents to the poisoning of the atmosphere through nuclear tests and the widespread use of pesticides manufactured by transnational chemical companies such as Union Carbide. While many Namiquipans expressed affection for the people of the United States, North American military adventurism was perceived as a "message" to the people of Latin America, Mexicans included. While the U.S. immigration "reform" bill was perceived as a generalized (if legally formulated) attack on Mexicans, the increasingly outrageous and violent behavior of *la migra* (agents of the INS) along the border was experienced directly by Namiquipans leaving from and returning to their country. To this must be added the routine, and no less violent and outrageous, insults to which Mexicans are subjected by Mexican customs and immigration officials.

The crises in the ecology, economy, and politics of Chihuahua also have direct consequences for Namiquipans. Scarce rainfall means that agriculturalists watch their invested labor-power dry up and wither away in the fields. With inflation approaching or surpassing 100 percent annually, farmers' opportunities are limited. What credit exists is available only at usurious interest rates, to which are added the exactions of corrupt bank officials. Also, by the time grains are delivered to the warehouses they are almost completely devoid of monetary value, lending to the whole agricultural production process in the region a surreal and futile cast (see Nugent 1987; Amparan González et al. 1987). One index of Namiquipan involvement in the state-wide political upheavals from 1983 to 1986 is the fact that during the 1985 elections for Congress in the fifth electoral district of Chihuahua, all four of the opposition-party candidates were from the *municipio* of Namiquipa.[29] Finally, comments and analyses by Namiquipans about the drug traffic; PEMEX (Petróleos Mexicanos); the "moral renovation" campaign with which President Miguel de la Madrid began his tenure in office; and political leadership in the community, the nation, and the world all suggest they understand there is a crisis of legitimacy in Mexico even though experts have agreed to conspire with the state in furthering the baseless contention that there is none. During a discussion of local and state-level politics in 1984, for example (one that I will return to later), an *ejidatário* from the *municipio* of Namiquipa wryly commented, "Pues, que ya no hay valientes" ("Thing is, there are no brave and honorable men anymore.") Another man from El Terrero—in his sixties, very well read, but going blind—once explained to us that most of Mexico's problems had to be understood in terms of foreign domination. He insisted that all of Mexico's presidents since the revolution of 1910 had really been Spaniards, for example, and the fact that the then-current president's name was Miguel *de la Madrid* lent strength to his argument.

In addition to external factors shaping events in Namiquipa, however, there were local or internal factors defining several local crises. These included an agrarian war in the *municipio*, political violence related both to elections and the routine exercise of the powers of governance, and continuing criticism and questioning by Namiquipans about how they were expected to survive in an apparently disintegrating world.

During the spring of 1983 a "war" broke out in one of the largest pueblos of the *municipio*. The municipal president, his family, and friends, all landowners or prosperous ranchers, engaged in a two-day shoot-out against a group of "land invaders." The fighting occurred within a large *ejido*. In *ejidos*, land is held communally, farmers are assigned individual lots to cultivate, and each member of the community is supposed to have equal access to pasture lands and other commons. The municipal president's family (whom I will call the Ricos) controlled much of the irrigated land in the *ejido*, and asserted rights in property to vacant land on which their cattle grazed and from which cattle belonging to other members of the community were excluded. The so-called land invaders were known as Los Malvinos and had earlier demanded a redistribution or reassignment of irrigated lands. Failing that, they decided to seize and cultivate vacant lands of the Ricos. The land Los Malvinos "invaded," that is, seized control of, fenced off, and prepared for planting, was former grazing land near the pueblo which the Ricos claimed was their "private property."

During the first few months of living in Namiquipa we were told that the war of 1983 was a new and unprecedentedly violent interruption of

the normally peaceful state of affairs in the *municipio* and that Los Malvinos were recent immigrants to the region who only wanted land so
they could sell it. Upon meeting the Malvinos—who a year later had
effective control of the "invaded" land but had to arm themselves and
guard their fields at night—we quickly determined that many belonged
to families that had lived in the pueblo for a century and the conflict
with the Ricos was decades old. Land was so unequally distributed
within this *ejido* that twenty years earlier, families whose members now
belonged to the Malvinos group or faction had petitioned the state for a
land *dotación* (grant) because they were landless—in spite of belonging
to a community that had been granted almost 60,000 hectares of land
thirty-five years earlier (AGCCA e.23:434, 8-ii-1960). During the gun-
fighting in the spring of 1983, several Malvinos were killed, the limbs of
others shattered and later amputated. If the "land invaders" were initially defeated, so too was the municipal president, removed from office
in May 1983 in an effort by the state to pacify the situation.

The land invasion and fighting did not take place in the pueblo of
Namiquipa, but some individuals from the town participated by lending
firearms to the Ricos, the landowner faction. (The fact that Los Malvinos
were underarmed was an often-invoked explanation for their initial defeat.) Furthermore, although President Rico was widely reviled in the
pueblo of Namiquipa, many people there identified their interests as
landholders with those of the faction supporting the municipal president and were unsympathetic to the struggle of the "land invaders."

When President Rico was removed from office, a school teacher and
functionary of the Sindicato Nacional de Trabajadores Educativos (SNTE,
the state-controlled national teachers union) who had married a woman
from Namiquipa was appointed by the governor of the state as interim
municipal president. He presided for six months over a *municipio* which
appeared to be coming apart at the seams. Beside the "war" during May
1983, several political homicides occurred in Ejido Benito Juárez over
the summer. The struggle of the Malvinos became implicated in the fight
for the election of a new municipal president in July and his assumption
of office in October 1983.

Enjoying the support of Los Malvinos and thousands of other Namiquipans, the PST candidate received the most votes during the July election. But as even *priístas* acknowledged, the elections were "stolen" by
the PRI. Throughout the summer there were more political homicides,
mass rallies, and opposition and official mobilizations. State and federal
police occupied key plazas in the *municipio*. This process culminated
in a PST rally in Namiquipa on October 9, 1983, the day before the
recently "elected" *priísta* was supposed to assume office. The rally ended
abruptly when an effort by some PSTistas to enter the Presidencia Mu-

nicipal (the town hall) and physically as well as symbolically "seat" their candidate in the municipal president's office chair was met with gunfire. *Judiciales* (state police), assisted by two dozen armed adherents of the newly "elected" *priísta*, proceeded to club, shoot, and tear gas the crowd until the plaza was cleared. Two people were shot dead that afternoon in the plaza, and another died several months later as the result of the beating he received that day.

The *priísta* who was installed as municipal president on October 10 was removed from office ten days later. The governor, in part at the suggestion of the Chihuahuan leadership of the PST, appointed a different *priísta* to serve out the three-year term. This man led the *municipio* somewhat inconsistently, warding off attempts by the municipal council (still linked to the individual whom the appointed municipal president supplanted on October 20, 1983) to have him removed by mobilizing the populace and his allies in various branches of the state government. Challenges to his authority by popular organizations were met by buying off the opposition or again calling in favors from state and party officials to effect repression. The *judiciales* were removed from the plaza of Namiquipa by the spring of 1984, and their absence restored a patina of normalcy and peace to the pueblo. But the state's efforts to pacify the situation and mediate conflicts between political factions within the *municipio* continued unabated, just as factions formed, disappeared, reformed, but above all continued to fight each other over the ensuing years.

Political conflicts within the pueblo and the *municipio* were sometimes linked to conflicts throughout the state of Chihuahua. Examples include the plight of Los Malvinos securing the attention and support of the PSUM, struggling to gain a foothold in the countryside; Namiquipan participation in opposition-party electoral campaigns in 1983, 1985, and 1986; and the tactics of individual *agricultores* in Namiquipa to secure an income working the land and the mobilizations of the Movimiento Democrático Campesino in 1985 and 1986.[30] But political conflicts in the *municipio* of Namiquipa served more importantly as expressions of interpueblo and intrapueblo rivalries. Among these were jurisdictional disputes between Namiquipa and El Terrero and El Molino; conflicts between inhabitants of the core communities along the Río Santa María and the "ranchos" or outlying communities; and conflicts between property owners (*pequeños propietários*) and members of collective landholding organizations (*ejidatarios*), between cattle ranchers (*ganaderos*) and farmers (*agricultores*), between fruit growers (*manzaneros*) and *agricultores*, and between merchants (*comerciantes*) and peasants (*campesinos*).

It is possible to distinguish between interpueblo and intrapueblo rivalries and conflicts by pointing out that interpueblo conflicts are linked to different ways in which identity is invested in barrio or community membership, while intrapueblo conflicts are linked to the different sorts of productive activities people engage in. But these distinctions may not be conflated. Many of the second set of differences (differences of "class") cut across the first (differences of "locale"), and there is no neat correspondence between the two such that one could say, for example, that the people of the pueblos are *pequeños propietários, ganaderos, manzaneros, comerciantes*—in short, *ricos*—while those of the ranchos are *ejidatarios, agricultores, campesinos*—*pobres*. In other words, *where* one lives (in a rancho, in a pueblo, in one pueblo in particular, in which barrio, on which street, in which lot contiguous to some other specific lot, with *whom* one shares the domestic space) may play a role in determining one's politics. But no less important for such a determination is the character of one's engagement with the processes of production and reproduction.

The different engagements of Namiquipans with the production process are underlined here because they, too, are objects of contention, negotiation, and only fleetingly resolved struggle in the 1980s. People's engagement with the production process is determined by the way land is held, how land is worked, what is produced, and the disposition of the products of labor upon the land. Within the *ejido* of Namiquipa, a complex system—or rather plurality of systems—of land tenure is in place. Although it is an *ejido*, all the best land and some of the marginal land is comprised of "illegal" "small private properties" (*pequeñas propiedades*). Over the last two decades there has been a progressively accelerating change in the use of the lands, with Namiquipans directing their energies and resources away from the officially sanctioned products (corn and beans, which are sold at set prices to state grain warehouses), towards other products (especially apples), which may be sold on private markets in Mexico and the United States. While few individuals have secured control of extensive plots of land within the *ejido* of Namiquipa (by way of contrast, such consolidations of landholdings are routine in the neighborning *colonias agricolas* [agricultural colonies, of freeholders rather than members of an *ejido*], on estates bordering the *ejido*, and for that matter *within* other ejidos in the region), the fundamentally capitalistic labor regime is a far cry from the ideal-typical formulations of what the organization of labor is supposed to look like on *ejidos*. Emigration from the pueblo by young people, especially young men, to Chihuahua City, Cuidad Juárez, or the United States and the retrogression of agricultural technology that the pueblo experienced through the 1980s was a function not only of an "economic crisis" throughout the continent, but also of the Namiquipans' efforts to determine a way they could continue to survive as agriculturalists operating as petty-commodity producers within a capitalist labor regime. For example, people work in the United States to get together *un capital* to be able to return as *agricultores*. They renounce technologically innovative or capital-intensive methods of working the land to free themselves from the bank and break the cycle of perpetual indebtedness.

This account of relations on the ground in Namiquipa in the 1980s could be summarized in terms of the agrarian war of 1983, interpueblo and intrapueblo rivalries securing a new potency and immediacy in the context of "the Crisis," and the violent political struggles waged within the pueblo and the *municipio* during this period. The "war of Los Malvinos" alone points to several of the contradictions emerging out of the crippling arrangements which must be made when *"ejidal"* and "private" properties share space within a supposedly unified land-tenure regime. It also resonates with conflicts and contradictions related to the flight of young people from the countryside to the cities or foreign lands; the uneven development of agricultural technologies; struggles between classes or class factions; and the tendency for certain elements in Namiquipa to orient production away from a state-controlled sector of basic grains and towards private markets in cash crops, in turn subjecting the communities to a different sort of exploitation and loss of value at the hands of merchants, middlemen, and speculators.

This panorama of conflict is framed by the circumstance that the "ground" on which these relationships are constituted is (to shift from metaphoric to literal use of the word "ground") considerable in extent. The *ejido* of Namiquipa includes more than 100,000 hectares of land, the *ejido* of Cruces almost 60,000. More than 60 percent (250,000 hectares) of the territory of the *municipio* of Namiquipa is in the *ejidal* sector, that is, land which has supposedly been distributed to peasant communities by the state, much of that six decades ago.[31] Nevertheless, struggles for land, struggles over how the land should be worked, and struggles to determine the power relationships according to which land is held and worked appear to be as intractable a part of daily life as they were before the revolution of 1910. The Mexican state's attempt to appropriate for itself the peasant slogan "Land and Freedom" is a failure in Namiquipa in the 1980s.

BEYOND THE ETHNOGRAPHIC PRESENT

Key sites of political struggle in Namiquipa in the 1980s include land and labor or the organization of the production process in agriculture. One possibility, and a tempting one, is to explain events and organizations in Namiquipa in the 1980s in terms of the economic crisis in

Mexico or *el caso Chihuahua* (i.e., the political crisis in the state of Chihuahua), or the nature of peasant politics and consciousness. Hence, to understand social relationships in contemporary Namiquipa the analysis would relate the critical absence of affordable credit for Namiquipan farmers to the economic crisis of the state, or the political violence in the *municipio* to political violence and mobilization throughout Chihuahua, or the complex and contradictory character of Namiquipan (or Malvinian) ideology to some generalization about "peasant consciousness." According to this line of argument, contemporary struggles in Namiquipa could be comprehended in relation to the present period in terms of what was happening in Mexico (or the world) as a whole, and through the uncritical deployment of a set of categories, concepts, and way of using them arguably appropriate for analyses of the peasantry.

Yet however valuable and interesting such a form of explanation might be, very little is to be gained by the exercise. Beyond the empirical data it might present, the analysis would also be presentist, centrist, and abstract. It would be *presentist* because it would assume the possibility of explaining historical development and socioeconomic process in terms of one particular and perhaps exceptional historical conjuncture (i.e., the "ethnographic present," itself, in any event, an invention). It would be *centrist* because the distinctive characteristics of political, economic, and ideological change in Namiquipa would be cast in terms of a supraregional, falsely national or international idiom of change. It would be *abstract* because it would presume to resolve conflicts and contradictions, and characterize distinctive engagements and processes, in terms of a set of unexamined *a priori*a. In other words, it obviates the need to deal with the problem of change even as it sidesteps the important, indeed crucial, issue of peasant ideology and culture. In the end, it would not amplify our knowledge at all, instead resulting in the reiteration of points already understood about the present and about the inexorable functioning of the capitalist world-system.

As an alternative to presentist, centrist, and abstract types of explanation, this book analyzes Namiquipa in terms of a distinctive historical process in which the community has formed in relation to the state (generally, but not always, subordinated to the latter) through struggles over land and labor or the production process. These struggles are not a novelty in Namiquipa. Neither are they cast—by the people who engage in them—in terms of a logic of development and change which can blithely be imported from the outside, whether in the form of ubiquitous "objective conditions" or in the form of elite or national or world-systemic factors and influences. *These* struggles in *this* pueblo have their own history, corresponding to a logic of development and change, and above all a mode of understanding and configuring development itself,

How do you know?

⟨which is specific to the pueblo of Namiquipa⟩and which has determined the Namiquipans' very engagement with those "objective conditions" and with "external factors." While this specificity does not preclude the possibility of making comparisons, an analysis of these struggles in this pueblo must focus not only on a series of actions by people on and in the world and relationships between groups and individuals and things, but also on the manner in which actions and relationships are organized by people both practically and conceptually.

One central problem for analysis, then, is to develop an account of the ideology of the Namiquipans. It would be inaccurate to assume the adequacy of fixed functional attributes or tendencies to describe the ideology of Namiquipans. It can only be understood in terms of the material forces and cultural forms in relation to which ideology develops, and changes, over time. A first point, then, is that popular ideology cannot be conceived as something static and is constantly reformulated by people in the course of the struggles and the quotidian activities in which they are involved. A second point, though, is that popular ideology is not autonomous. The account which follows focuses on popular ideology in Namiquipa as it has developed in relation to the power of the state in Mexico and the transformations in the character of state power over the last two centuries.

It is worthwhile asking whether *this* community (Namiquipa) and *this* state (Mexico) together provide a privileged example in addressing the general issue of community-state relations. They do, but in a paradoxical manner, the consideration of which will provide an even more nuanced sense of how Namiquipan revolutionaries were "burned" by the postrevolutionary state (Nugent 1990). The paradox of the recent history of Namiquipa and the pueblo's relations to the Mexican state is that while agrarian and production-oriented problems appear to have been resolved some decades ago in a manner favorable to the harmonious development of the community and the state together, these sites of struggles for power are still conceived and organized as arenas of conflict with the state. Since the conclusion of the period of armed struggle in Chihuahua in the twentieth century—since "The Revolution"—the pueblo of Namiquipa has recovered its lands as *ejidos*. Until recently, the state had introduced programs and implemented policies aimed at maintaining a vital segment of the country's populace in the countryside. However fragile and subject to challenge the hegemony of the capitalist state in Mexico, the ruling party in Namiquipa from the 1920s until 1992 had been the party of the Mexican state, now called the PRI. Nevertheless, land and labor remain the foci of intractable struggles for power.

Rather than explain away these conflicts—conflicts within the pueblo and the *municipio,* and between the pueblo (broadly conceived as locale and people) and the state—in essentialist terms (e.g., peasant backwardness, the inevitability of the peasantry's demise under a capitalist state, the domination inherent in the state-peasantry relationship), this book proposes a historical explanation of the current conflicts. It relies rather less on structural arguments, themselves frequently a variety of essentialism, though at times they are very persuasive in the analysis of peasant mobilizations (see Zamosc 1986), and rather more on "ideological" arguments in the course of narrating an agrarian history of Namiquipa from the 1780s through the 1980s. But definitions of key terms such as peasant society and the state, how their relationship is conceived, and where popular ideology fits in to this relationship are required at the outset.

Peasant Society or Serrano Peasantry

There exist abstract arguments for and against regarding Namiquipans as peasants. Considering those arguments will demonstrate the need for an alternative to "the peasant concept" of received anthropological wisdom to describe present-day inhabitants of Namiquipa. Such a need arises also because the variety of ways the peasant concept has been used in anthropology bear considerable loads of ideological baggage that are frequently difficult to separate out in the practice of investigation and analysis (Silverman 1979).

In many respects the people of Namiquipa are indistinguishable from millions of other Latin American countryside dwellers, making their living primarily working land they control or aspire to control and routinely discussed in the literature as "peasants." In the Mexican literature, however, the term *campesino* has been weighted with such a variety of meanings that its exact meaning is unclear; all it seems in the end to connote is politically dominated rural peoples (Gledhill 1985:33–35; see also Borah 1954). At the same time, the word "peasant" conjures up images of isolation, subordination, and backwardness, images inappropriate for describing the people of Namiquipa today.

One striking feature of the economy and society of western Chihuahua is that rural people, particularly agriculturalists, are well integrated into a regional, national, continental, and global capitalist economy and have been for the past century. This no more makes Namiquipans exceptional by comparison to other historical peasantries than does the fact that many of the details of organization of daily experience, including actions related to cultivation of land and reproduction of the domestic economy, are shaped by a market in the products of their labor rather than manifestations of some primordial peasant essence. But it does call into question the utility of the peasant concept.

In the first place, the concept máy be historically nonspecific. An example is the difficulty posed by speaking about "the European peasantry" and "the Latin American" peasantry in the same breath. Analysis of the former is freighted with the problem of the transition from feudalism to capitalism and the formation of an industrial society in a particular place and time (Hilton 1976). This has only confused the analysis of people in Latin America and the Third World generally. The identification of a set of theoretical issues and the development of a vocabulary to explain the fate of the European peasantry has been imported to a very different set of historical and cultural developments in the New World (Laclau 1978:10–52). The peoples of rural Latin America, Africa, and Asia, each with their different colonial experiences and postcolonial legacies, and today distinctive types of political domination, scarcely fit the mold of one another, never mind of the European peasantry. As William Roseberry pointed out, most peasantries are not the standard textbook case, nor of the classic European sort, "even in Europe" (Roseberry 1983:208).[32]

A second problem is the tendency to typologize in discussions of the peasantry (Shanin 1987a; Mintz 1973), resulting in the hypostatization of people and distinctive social groups in analyses. The typologies may obscure as much as they illuminate the issue of characterization, for example, so whether rural toilers are *really* "peasants" or "disguised proletarians" becomes a topic to which many words are devoted (cf. Gledhill 1985; Bartra 1974, 1975a; Roseberry 1978). Human subjects are written out of the scholarly debates, which assume the features of discourses in which categories such as peasant, proletarian, peasant/worker, and landlord are made to dance at the wave of a baton (Tristan Tzara, quoted in Alonso 1988a:34).

This in turn raises the question of how to precisely locate rural workers vis-à-vis global socioeconomic systems. Among social scientists and political activists in Mexico during the 1970s, a debate over this issue developed between *proletaristas* and *campesinistas,* who respectively argued that rural toilers in Mexico are fundamentally proletarian or peasant (see Redclift 1980 for a lucid discussion of the debate). The *proletarista* position is that it is politically defeatist, and sociologically inaccurate, to hold on to the antiquated notion of a Mexican "peasantry" (Bartra 1975b, 1982; Díaz Polanco 1982). *Campesinistas,* on the other hand, insist that the peasantry is "an integral part of today's working class. . . . [T]he peasantry not only is a class-in-itself but also forms a class-for-itself" (Lucas de Rouffinglac 1985:xvi; see also Esteva 1980). This Mexican debate and the issue of characterization mentioned in the preceding paragraph are discussed in chapter 6.

A fourth and even more extreme argument was developed by structural Marxists influenced by the work of Althusser (1970) and Hindess and Hirst (1975, 1977). The rationalist claim, made by these writers and other of their followers during the 1970s, is that there is simply no category, and hence no such thing, as peasant economy or a peasant mode of production (Ennew et al. 1977).

Yet however convincing parts or all of the preceding arguments may be, it nevertheless remains possible to view the generic features of peasant societies as elements of a type of sociocultural organization qualitatively distinct from others. Shanin's analytical definition of a "general type" of peasantry—agriculturalists dominated by outsiders working family farms in small rural communities according to specific cultural patterns—provides a compelling point of departure for theoretically informed anthropological and historical analysis (Shanin 1987a). Other classic anthropological definitions of the peasantry repudiate the notions of isolated villagers whose production is organized primarily through the household. Instead, the problem of the relationship of the peasantry to dominant social groups and organizations of power such as the state assumes centrality in the *problematique* of the definition. For example, Wolf wrote that peasants "are rural cultivators whose surpluses are transferred to a dominant group of rulers that uses the surpluses both to underwrite its own standard of living and to distribute the remainder to groups in society that do not farm but must be fed for their specific goods and services in turn" (Wolf 1966:3–4).

Namiquipans might, then, accurately be described as peasants owing to their generic similarities to other peasantries. Moreover, lumping Namiquipans with "the peasantry" may be preferable to inventing yet another type of social group or class or subclass. The sterility and finally the absurdity of picking nits over whether or not a "peasant mode of production" under capitalism is theoretically possible (Alavi 1987:188–90) is a manifestation of the increasing distance between ways of looking at really existing groups in society and what the lives of those people are about (Alavi 1982; Warman 1978, 1988a). The question should not be, "Is the peasant *concept* possible?" but rather, "*Is peasant production reproduced,* even under capitalism?" Arguably, it is.

There is little utility in entertaining either empiricist or theoreticist debates about the validity of the term "peasant" throughout this book.[33] More valuable would be a term that specifies agricultural workers' relationship to means of production, their location in relation to dominant systems of power, and their similarities to other agricultural producers around the globe, and that also provides a sense of the people comprising this social group as historical agents, locating them geographically as well as structurally. The term *serrano* provides precisely such a geographical and historical specificity to the peasant concept and is particularly apposite in discussing the people of Namiquipa as a "*serrano* peasantry."

Serrano means literally "people of the sierra"—"highlanders" or "mountaineers." Characterizing the inhabitants of many Chihuahuan communities including Namiquipa as a *serrano* peasantry amplifies our sense of them as agriculturalists located in a physically distinctive (mountainous) terrain, engaged in a political project different from that of the state and other historical peasantries, who have developed a distinctive ideology of history. This combination of ecological, geographical, political, and ideological factors distinguishes them from many other peasants in Mexico.

The historian Alan Knight used *serrano* throughout his influential two-volume history of the Mexican revolution (1986) to refer to a peripheral peasantry relatively free of landlord control and unfamiliar with the hand of political authority. The identification of the characteristic features of *serranos* owes much to Wolf's earlier discussions of peasant rebellion (Wolf 1969a, 1969b). Clearly Knight was not writing about hacienda workers or *peones*, nor about migrant agricultural workers; the closest analogy or point of comparison would be the "peculiar" (Carr 1973) free peasantry which formed in the North of Mexico in the nineteenth century (*cf.* Katz 1976b). This peasantry was peripheral both physically—in mountainous regions, on frontiers, or in internal frontiers—and in terms of degree of political-economic and sociocultural integration with the broader Mexican society (Knight 1980; Knight 1986, 1:115–27). Knight writes eloquently about what he calls *serrano* popular movements, which represented "the popular backlash of autonomous communities reacting against the incursions of central government" (Knight 1980:27; see also Knight 1986, 1:115ff., 2:339–41).

The point I emphasize is that *serrano* communities are more than just political entities enjoying a particular relationship to the state: the people inhabiting them also entertain specific relationships to the land. In Chihuahua they are farmers and ranchers cultivating fields and grazing cattle on commons which are conceived as being parts of the community as well. In other words their attachment to locale is not simply a function of physically occupying it and enjoying a degree of autonomy from outside control, but also of working upon it and transforming it. Furthermore, *serrano* peasants of Chihuahua were compelled to defend communal resources against a range of opponents (not just the power of the state) from the time their communities were established, and not only during the Mexican revolution.

Designating the people of Namiquipa as *serrano* peasants indicates what they do (i.e., the character of their engagement with the economy and their structural relation to means of production) and what their relationship to dominant power structures is (while subordinated to the state, they are largely independent of landlord control). It locates them in space and time, clarifying how their communities form parts of a regional geography and how the people behave as historical actors and as active subjects. But beside their own lands and their own communities, what do *serrano* peasants act in relation to? An important issue to address concerns the state and how the inhabitants of *serrano* communities contend with the power of the state.

THE STATE AS EXPERIENCED BY ITS SUBJECTS

A discussion of the Mexican state that is oriented in the first instance by an interest in the state's subjects cannot expect to resolve many of the controversies raging within that discursive space appositely derided as "Statolatry" (Gramsci [1929–35] 1971:268; Knight 1985b; cf. Corrigan and Sayer 1985:7).[34] But a great number can be sidestepped if it is borne in mind from the outset "that the 'same' unifying representations from the perspective of 'the State' may well be differentially understood from 'below'" (Corrigan and Sayer 1985:6). In Mexico what is "below" are a lot of pueblos. In Spanish the word *pueblo* can signify both "village" or "rural town," and "people" or "popular classes." The word assumes an appropriate resonance when it is taken to signify both simultaneously. It is precisely this multilayered meaning—referring at once to geographical locale and social totality, to physical space and political movement within it—which should be attached to the concept rendered as "community" in English.

As for "the state," a good place to begin is the familiar Engelsian/Weberian definition as an institution in society which controls a territory in which determinate property relations exist, has an apparatus for administering that territory, and enjoys the exclusive franchise on the "legitimate" use of force (cf. Hamilton 1982:4–8). According to this conception, the state is something invented in society, yet which seemingly stands apart from and above society.

Writing about the formation of the bouregois state, for example, Engels described it as

> an institution which *set the seal of general social recognition* [emphasis added] on each new method of acquiring property and thus amassing weath at continually growing speed; an institution which perpetuated, not only this growing cleavage of society into classes, but also the right of the possessing class to exploit the non-possessing, and the rule of the former over the latter.
>
> And this institution came. The *state* was invented. (Engels [1884] 1942:97)

Using somewhat more blunt and precise terms, Weber wrote that "a state is a human community that (successfully) claims the *monopoly of the legitimate use of physical force* within a given territory. . . . If the state is to exist, the dominated must obey the authority claimed by the powers that be" (Weber [1918] 1958:78). The vague specification of what exactly the state *is* (here an "institution," there a "human community")[35] aside, an important aspect of these definitions is that they characterize a relationship of power. An additional feature, more generally recognized and perhaps more nuanced in Weber—and later in Gramsci—than in Engels, is that they draw attention to how effects of power are achieved within the community (Weber's "legitimacy"; Gramsci's "active consent"; cf. Weber [1918] 1958:78; Gramsci [1929–35] 1971:244).

A stress on the relational constitution of the power of the state over "its" subjects, however, in fact undermines the very notion of the state as a thing. Philip Abrams developed this point quite forcefully with his proposal that

> we should abandon the state as a material object of study whether concrete or abstract while continuing to take the *idea* of the state extremely seriously. . . . The state is, then, in every sense of the term a triumph of concealment. It conceals the real history and relations of subjection behind an a-historical mask of legitimating illusion; . . . In sum: the state is not the reality which stands behind the mask of political practice. It is itself the mask. (Abrams [1977] 1988:75, 77, 82)

In order, then, to move away from an instrumentalist and institutional or reified notion of the state we must highlight the practical and processual dimensions of community-state relations. "The State is not a structure, . . . it is a complex of social forms organized so that it inflects all relations and ideas about relations in such a way that capitalist production [for example], and all it entails, becomes thought of as lived and natural" (Corrigan et al. 1980:10). At the same time, however, the state is not the only organized complex of social forms in society; communities and popular ideologies may figure in this regard as well. "Neither the shape of the state, nor oppositional cultures, can be properly understood outwith the context of the mutually formative (and continuing) struggle between them" (Corrigan and Sayer 1985:7). An overweening emphasis on looking *just* at "the state" obscures an understanding of alternative forms of power and identity, of movement and action which create "oppositional cultures" or *pueblos* as alternative spaces of power.

The popular identification of "the state" in Namiquipa varies considerably from any textbook definition or idle wish of a contemporary bureaucrat. Instead it is formulated by people on the basis of their current political experience *and* the complex mediations of a social memory distinct from both scholarly and ruling class or elite consensus. By developing a concept of the state in relation to a specific community with a particular history more or less consonant with this popular formulation, we might be able to inject parts at least of this popular formulation in our theoretical discourse and thereby strengthen it. A justification for considering the state in a variety of formal, temporal, and other manifestations as a confused and confusing ideal entity, at once the recrudesence of a complex series of transformations over time and the fleeting synthesis of policy formulators grappling with particular historical-political social problems, is that "the State" appears as such to the people.

POPULAR IDEOLOGY AND THE STATE

If the state "appears" to "the people" in one form or another, however, it does not do so in an unmediated fashion. One of the more important factors shaping that appearance—mediating the relation between people and state—is ideology, a form of consciousness of the world according to which configurations of meaning in social life are organized and rendered more or less coherent to social agents.

Ideology is not an autonomous or readily abstractable "level" or "domain" of "meaning," "values," or "structure," as is characteristic of the concept of culture employed by some anthropologists (see the excellent discussion in R. T. Smith 1984). Rather it is constrained by, expressed through, and linked with the material it organizes and the historical context in which the configurations of meaning (which often have to do with power) it renders coherent are *recognizable* to social actors.

> The link between structures and history . . . is people, who are the bearers of structures, live through time, and perpetuate themselves and their labor-power through their children. In doing these things over a discernible period (and periodization is a major problem in the writing of history) they reproduce a particular pattern of association for the purposes of meeting material needs which implies cognition of material reality and the preservation of a certain distribution of power within and among structures. (Post 1978:467)

The condition according to which the organization by people of material objects and social relationships may be formulated differently (re-cognized) over time means that this concept of ideology articulates a fundamentally historical phenomenon, revealing growing contradictions in social relations. Further, it is not only an official or dominant ideology that is entailed, but also popular ideologies, the contours of

which are revealed in the course of historical action and may be transformed as a result of that historical action.

Inquiry into popular ideology has a special pertinence for the study
of the Mexican peasantry, which, however violently it was defeated during the revolution of 1910, still remains to be understood "ideologically." A distinguished Mexican anthropologist pointed out more than
a decade ago,

> This insistence on ideology may seem a little out of place today
> when many are speaking of the death of ideologies and of the
> anachronistic nature of political parties. . . . [Nevertheless,] ide-
> ology takes on greater importance in agrarian countries [such as
> Mexico] in which the socioeconomic characteristics of industrial-
> ism have not yet crystallized. . . . In the agrarian countries various
> modes of production coexist and industrialism, which has been
> considered the natural evolutionary model, is in profound crisis
> and seems exhausted. This opens up objective options for the fu-
> ture development of society and *these must be debated in the realm
> of ideology.*
>
> The peasant lacks a politically structured ideology, but his revo-
> lutionary acts reveal a set of persistent core ideas, which can be
> summarized in the much used slogan, "land and freedom," and
> which expresses a model of social organization: the free confed-
> eration of agrarian communities. (Warman 1978:417–18)

Now arguably Warman overstated the case for the intrinsic revolutionary potential of the peasantry. How in practical terms is it possible
to substantiate this proposition, especially in the case of Mexico, where,
however "revolutionary" it was or is, the peasantry has been succes-
sively defeated in the course of centuries of struggle (see Katz 1988b,
1988c, 1988d; Nugent 1988:1–2)? The reification of a "free confedera-
tion of agrarian communities" may be a late twentieth-century roman-
ticization of a supposed "Zapatista" ideology in another time, and in
terms of another struggle facing "the Mexican peasantry" (Knight 1988
warns of this routine error). The crucial point, then, does not have to do
with the *content* (or the imaginable content) of a "peasant utopia" as
much as the *relational* constitution or formation of a particular ideology,
the core idea of which may be summarized in the slogan, "Land and
Freedom."

This challenges Warman's contention that peasants lack "a politically
structured ideology." The demand for "Land and Freedom" is more than
just a locally relevant, inwardly directed *expression* of a particular form
of social organization providing evidence of the lack of a "politically

structured ideology." It draws into question the character of the *connection* of that form of social organization to alternative forms which enjoy a greater degree of power within the social formation as a whole. As a slogan, it articulates peasants' relationships to means of production (and productive action and the production process generally) *and* to other social groups and classes and loci of power. By posing the question, "Freedom from what?" that is, stating the slogan relationally as having to do with the peasant community and the state rather than just propositionally as having to do with the peasant community *tout court,* it is possible to proceed in the course of an inquiry into popular ideology toward an understanding of the relation between the state and its subjects.[36]

Stuart Hall, Philip Corrigan, and Derek Sayer, among others, have in recent years advanced similar formulations of the relationship between the bourgeois state and its subjects,[37] albeit referring to popular or oppositional *cultures* rather than *ideologies.* Hall insists that

> what is essential to the definition of popular culture is the relations which define "popular culture" in a continuing tension (relationship, influence and antagonism) to the dominant culture. It is a conception of culture which is polarised around this cultural dialectic. . . . What matters is *not* the intrinsic or historically fixed objects of culture, but the state of play in cultural relations. (Hall 1981:235)

Making a similar point about the "mutually formative struggle" between state and "oppositional cultures," Corrigan and Sayer remark, "Too often these have been sundered. State forms have been understood without reference to what they are formed *against.* . . . Oppositional cultures are conversely comprehended through the grid of the various selective traditions imposed as if they were all there is to say and know about 'culture'" (Corrigan and Sayer 1985:7).

This conceptualization of the relationship between state and popular ideology, then, is not a position that regards popular ideology as a category which is semantically nested within state ideology, analogous to the manner in which popular classes are subordinated by the state, and the proletariat by the bourgeoisie. Instead, what this perspective admits (or rather insists upon) is an understanding of how state and popular ideology are articulated, which is to say expressed in one another as well as connected to one another (see Foster-Carter 1978 and Post 1978 on "articulation").

The chapters that follow provide an account of the history of Namiquipa in which the narrative is organized by this "continuing tension," this "mutually formative struggle" between pueblo and state.

2
Geopolitics of the Colonial Frontier: Civilization and Barbarism, 1660s–1850s

GEOPOLITICS OF THE COLONIAL FRONTIER

Land has been a perennial object of contention between Namiquipa and the state, no less during the century and a half preceding the revolution than in subsequent decades. This account of what happened to the lands forming the "original" donation to the eighteenth-century *pobladores* (colonists or settlers, literally, "populators") of Namiquipa and which today largely comprise the *ejido* of the community is intended to provide a basis for understanding labor, politics, and ideology in Namiquipa's relationship to the state.

The area that is now Chihuahua comprised the northern half of the province of Nueva Viscaya, one of the "Internal Provinces" on the northern frontier of colonial New Spain. In contrast to the center and south of the colony, the north had only slowly and very unevenly been brought into the orbit of Spanish power. Conditions in the north were radically different from those in central Mexico: the landscape of deserts, high semidesertic plains and mountain ranges, the region sparsely populated by nomadic and semisedentary indigenous groups (Lister and Lister 1966; Jordan [1956] 1981; Spicer 1962). By the early eighteenth century, colonial settlement was concentrated near mining centers such as Santa Barbara, Parral, Santa Eulalia, and Chihuahua City (West 1949; Barnes et al. 1981; Cramaussel 1990). Missionary priests enjoyed some success in "reducing" (i.e., baptizing and congregating in villages) some of the indigenes. Jesuit priests built more than one hundred churches in the sierra of western Chihuahua, while Franciscans worked in the valleys on the eastern edge of the sierra and took over the Jesuit missions at the time of the latter's expulsion from the New World in 1767 (Sheridan and Naylor 1979; Gerhard 1982).

The greatest obstacles to colonial expansion into this region were almost all "natural," or at least conceived as such: a harsh climate, scarcity of water, great physical distances separating the region from the center and each "civilized" settlement from the next, and the indigenes. Tarahumaras revolted throughout the seventeenth century and on more than one occasion drove the white "devils" (*chabochi*) out of the most coveted of their lands, notably the region around the upper Papigochic Valley. The Spanish response to these revolts was brutal, particularly under Colonel Retana in the 1690s, whose military campaigns coincided with devastating epidemics in 1693 and 1695. By the early eighteenth century the Tarahumaras had been subjugated or driven into the sierra (see Spicer 1962; Sheridan and Naylor 1979; Jordan [1956] 1981:145–53). Colonial settlement was next threatened by Athabascan raiders driving down from still further north. Consequently, northern New Spain in the middle of the eighteenth century was a large militarized zone. But by that time Namiquipa had been a recognized Spanish settlement for almost a century.

LAND IN NAMIQUIPA BEFORE THE PRESIDIO

In the seventeenth century, Namiquipa was the site of a *ranchería* of Conchos Indians. A Franciscan mission, San Pedro de Alcantara de Namiquipa, was founded at the site in 1662 (1663 according to Solis 1936:27 and Almada 1982), and by 1668 it was a political dependency of the mining town of Cusihuiriachic (Gerhard 1982). Franciscan and Jesuit missionaries working in Chihuahua made competing claims for the privilege of "reducing" the indigenous population in a dispute that was resolved in 1675 when the Order of St. Francis got the franchise for the valley of the Río Santa María (Gerhard 1982:187–89).

It was a difficult mission for Franciscan fathers. A document from 1726 recounts the efforts of the priests Juan de San José and Felipe Palomino, who had traveled by foot from their missions to the mining city of Parral to petition their superior for a reassignment. They could no longer tolerate the minimal rewards of missionary work in Namiquipa and nearby Bachiniva. José S. López de Carbajal, the governor of Nueva Viscaya, himself ordered them to return immediately to the pueblos.[1]

Spanish and *criollo* families acquired properties in Namiquipa by the early eighteenth century. In 1708 the governor of Nueva Viscaya, Don Juan Fernández de Córdova issued a *merced* (grant) to Ignacio Gómez, at the time living in the valley of Casas Grandes, for 2 *sitios de ganado mayor* (SGM), 2 *sitios de ganado menor*, and 3 1/2 *caballerías* of land (approximately 7,000 hectares).[2] In 1725 Gómez's son Antonio registered the title to this property before a judge (the *juez privativo de composiciones*), who granted still more lands and agreed to a settlement whereby the younger Gómez assumed title to 7 SGM (12,285 hectares) all told for the sum of 315 pesos. This property subsequently came into the possession of Don Manuel González y Zamora, who sold it to Pedro González de Almoyna in 1735. Later known as the Hacienda or Rancho de Carmen, the property had magically expanded in the ensuing decade and was now said to consist of 8 SGM (14,040 hectares).

In 1733 Pascuala de la Fuente and Pedro Nevares, who lived in El Valle de San Buenaventura, registered titles to a property called Nuestra Señora de Aranzazu, near Namiquipa, consisting of 3 SGM. Pedro González de Almoyna purchased this property from de la Fuente and Nevares in 1742 for 650 pesos, making him the sole owner of 10 or 11 SGM in Namiquipa. He also owned the Hacienda de Santana del Torreón (consisting of some 20 SGM), seventy miles downriver from Namiquipa.

The fact that González de Almoyna paid 650 pesos for Aranzazu in 1742 (it had been registered for less than a tenth that amount nine years earlier) suggests these haciendas must have been reasonably productive to support such progressively grander investments. Another example is the property Santana del Torreón, which had changed hands for only 1,000 pesos twenty years earlier, yet was seven times as large as Aranzazu. While land values were increasing during this period, though, there is little data concerning who actually lived and worked in Namiquipa.[3]

The region was hard hit by Apache attacks that occurred with ever greater frequency in the second half of the eighteenth century. The Archivo Franciscano includes an account by Father Pedro Pablo Villavicencio, the priest of Namiquipa, of an encounter with Indians in 1751. Villavicencio, accompanying a party of people including thirty-four armed men, was traveling between Namiquipa and Santa Clara on January 28 of that year. Midway on their journey, they were set upon by "enemy" Indians. The Indians killed a woman from the party. "They found the dead woman completely nude, scalped as is their habit and custom, an arrow in her heart and through the part where they stuck the lance into her, which was her back, they took out her intestines and tangled them in her legs" (AF Ms.29/5771.1). The Indians were no more respectful of the priest's power. They tore up and scattered his breviary, shat upon the wafers he was taking to celebrate mass, and urinated upon his chalice and other sacred objects (AF Ms.29/5771.1).

The bishop of Durango, Pedro Tamarón, spent three years in the 1760s traveling through the Provincias Internas. His observations about the pueblos in his bishopric provide a sense of conditions in the region at that time. Tamarón noted that the mission at Cruces, near Namiquipa, had almost been wiped out by the Apaches. He laments that this region, which earlier boasted productive haciendas shipping grains to Chihuahua City (established in 1708), could no longer do so. The Apaches, he said, "enter and leave when they care to, steal whatever they want, and also kill people. The Apaches have reduced San Buenaventura . . . to a deplorable condition and would have wiped it out altogether were it not for 30 soldiers" sent there from the presidio of Guajoquilla (Tamarón, BN, Ms.1765:60). Tamarón's description of Namiquipa includes the following:

> Namiquipa is the *cabecera* of a Franciscan mission, having thirteen families with forty-two Indians . . . in the district of this pueblo, and in sites served by the priest live nine non-Indian families[4] consisting of seventy individuals. In September of 1763 the enemy Indians [Apaches] killed the *fiscal,* a local official. The Franciscan priest Father Ignacio Fernández witnessed this murder, and despite the fact nothing was done to him personally, he died of fright the following day. (Tamarón, BN, MS.1765:61)

It is unclear exactly when Don Pedro González de Almoyna abandoned his properties in Namiquipa, though probably he did so around 1760, the year he abandoned Santana del Torreón.[5] He donated titles to his properties of Carmen, Aranzazu, and Torreón—some 33 SGM in Namiquipa and San Buenaventura—to the Crown precisely for the purpose of creating new towns which would be protected by presidios (AGCCA 24/434 [I], DPP, p. 12). According to Gerhard, the Franciscan mission at Namiquipa was abandoned by the end of 1763 (Gerhard 1982:187).

Father Ignacio Jiménez, the priest of San Andres, conducted a census of the *visitas*[6] of his church in March of 1778. Included in the "Census of the Families in the Pueblo of Sainapuchi, Visita de San Andres" is a list for "the pueblo of Namiquipa, attached to Sainapuchi," (AF Ms.16/328.1, pp. 1–5). In the list appear names of twenty-eight individuals in eleven families. These are all indigenes, bearing last names, if any, such as de la Cruz and Domingo. The first entry is "Don Lazaro, *Gobernador,*" the title routinely bestowed upon "native" "chiefs" in northern New Spain by missionary priests and colonial officials (Bennett and Zingg 1935). The oldest individual, a man of ninety, was named Pedro Llepomera, clearly indicating that he was a Tarahumara who moved to Namiquipa from the neighboring Papigochic Valley. (Yepomera is the name of a Tarahumara pueblo west of Namiquipa.) One forty-five-year-old man is named Antonio Concho, a brutal irony since his identifying badge—a family name that follows, in the Spanish fashion, a personal name—is the name of the group of people who, at that point in time, appear to have been completely exterminated or absorbed into frontier Hispanic society, the Conchos Indians (Barnes et al. 1981:129; Spicer 1962).

A curious feature of this census is that only five children (aged 1, 8, 8, 10, and 11) appear. This suggests several possibilities, including that the Namiquipans in March of 1778 had some reason for hiding their children from the priests, that great strides have more recently been made at reducing infant mortality, or that many children had been "stolen" by the Apaches.[7]

During the eighteenth century, the valley of the Río Santa María had been the object of somewhat desultory missionary activity by Franciscan fathers. Control of the lands around Namiquipa was assumed by *criollo* settlers from other pueblos of the region who established productive haciendas. Land values increased through the first half of the eighteenth century. The greatest obstacle to continued settlement of the region was the Apaches, who began to "terrorize" the region in 1748 (Escudero 1839). The González de Almoyna haciendas were abandoned in the 1760s, as was the Franciscan mission. By 1778 Namiquipa was home to eleven wretched families, none of them *gente de razón* ("people of reason"), its haciendas abandoned, its future in doubt.

TEODORO DE CROIX AND COLONIAL AGRARIAN IDEOLOGY

Namiquipa was not the only pueblo facing such a predicament. By the 1770s the entire province of Nueva Viscaya was swept by Apache attacks, many of its pueblos and haciendas abandoned by settlers to the "barbarians" as the region entered a period of "permanent warfare" (Lister and Lister 1979:77; see also Escudero 1834; Jordan [1956] 1981:179ff.; Griffen 1988:37ff.). Spanish colonists faced a formidable enemy, as indicated in the by and large respectful and admiring—almost sympathetic—words of Teniente Coronel Antonio Cordero, who had been a presidial soldier from his youth, fought the Apaches for decades, and spoke their language. Writing in 1796, Cordero insisted, "The Apache is proud of nothing, except being brave, this attitude reaching such a degree, that he despises the man of whom no bold deed is known" (in Matson and Schroeder 1957:341).

Control of the territory became an important determinant of the definition of power relations on the frontier for both the Apaches and the Hispanic settlers of the region. These issues captured the attention of the architects of Spanish colonial policy in the region, resulting in the encouragement of what can only (in the context) be called "white settler colonies" (cf. Emmanuel 1972).

> The northernmost territories of New Spain required more compelling authority from local administrators because of the distance from viceregal control in Mexico City. The Spanish crown was keenly aware of the lack of administrative control in the northern

provinces which resulted partially from failure to pacify native groups and partially from pressures exerted by other European powers encroaching on the poorly defined perimeters of New Spain (Barnes et al. 1981:62).

After two decades during which Apache attacks and raiding accelerated (Escudero 1839), the Provincias Internas were reorganized in 1776 and removed from viceregal control. Authority over them was invested in a governor and *commandante general* reporting directly to the Crown. The individual put in charge of the Provincias Internas in 1776 was Teodoro de Croix, "Caballero de Croix del Orden Teutonico, Brigadier de los Reales Ejercitos, Segundo Teniente de la Compañía Flamenca de Reales Guardias de Corps, Gobernador y Comandante General de las Provincias Internas de Nueva España."

To de Croix fell the task of staffing strategically placed military settlements—presidios—designed to defend Spanish settlers against marauding Indians and other colonial powers as well. A series of presidios stretching from the Gulf Coast to the Pacific Coast was already in place by the middle of the eighteenth century (Moorhead 1975). Under Hugo O'Conner in the early 1770s efforts had been made to reinforce this east-west line, making it impregnable to Apache and foreign attack. Troops were assigned to the presidios and arrangements made to supply them from central Mexico.[8] In addition, a number of "flying companies" (*compañías volantes*) were formed to patrol more extensive stretches of this porous frontier (see Moorhead 1975:98–99).

Teodoro de Croix began his tenure as governor by touring the territory. He observed that the east-west line of presidios was routinely penetrated by Apaches, especially along the eastern flank of the Sierra Madre Occidental. Civilian settlers were ill-prepared to deal with the Apaches themselves, and there were far too few soldiers to defend the Spanish communities. De Croix saw a value in further colonizing the region with civilian as well as military settlers. The former could bring a "civilized" style of life to the region and develop the frontier with farms, ranches, and industries, the products of which could provision the mining settlements, thereby reducing the region's dependence on imports from the center. With these objectives in mind, in 1778 de Croix ordered the establishment of five towns, with the designation *villa*, in a north-south line along the eastern flank of the mountains. Several of these (Janos and San Buenaventura, now called Galeana) were situated at or near already existing presidios, others (Casas Grandes, Cruces and Namiquipa) at the sites of pueblos or abandoned missions (see Griffen 1988). It was as an element in this strategic project of the colonial state that the pueblo of Namiquipa's relationship to the state originated, and it was through this program of colonization that settlers to Namiquipa received lands.

On November 15, 1778, de Croix dictated an order for the "creation and firm establishment of towns in the most important sites on the frontier" to the end of minimizing hostilities in the region, to provide work and property for people who had neither, and to "expand commerce, encourage agriculture, and bring knowledge of industry" to this region.[9] The five pueblos were staffed with soldiers, "under whose protection the happy settlers might make use of the fertility and beauty of the lands assigned to the new pueblos, the abundance of waters, the promise of mineral wealth . . . and the fruits of their labor and Industry" (Bando).[10] The Second Flying Company was assigned to Namiquipa.

Each pueblo was given 64 SGM of land ("cuatro leguas por viento," four leagues to a wind [in each direction] from the center in a square), for *ejidos,* common use, and agricultural plots which the settlers would be obligated to develop. Regardless of their "class, caste, or quality," people were encouraged to move to the new towns. Each family that arrived would be given a salary of two *reales* a day for one year to help them survive until the first harvest was in. Initially a common field was cultivated to provide seed and grains for new settlers and serve the entire community collectively in the event of some catastrophe. As families settled in the towns, there would be an "equal distribution of house lots, agricultural plots, and water" among the inhabitants, to which each would be given title (Bando).

To secure title to land and other rights of membership in the community, settlers had to remain in the new pueblos for ten years, during which period they would be exempt from taxes. Properties could not be broken up, and "the first settlers will be preferred over outsiders in whatever contract or rental agreement is made in regard to these rights" (to land, tax exemptions, etc.). After ten years, settlers could do what they wished with their properties, but authority over them would be invested first in the captains of the presidios or leaders of the royal troops resident in the community

> until such a time as the inhabitants are brought together and, the functions of governance secured, may proceed to elect alcaldes and other municipal employees annually . . . with the clear understanding that the primary obligation of the Spanish settlers was to have small arms and horses, of the Indians to have *carajes,* arms, bows, arrows, and lances, to defend themselves from, and to direct themselves against, the enemies. (Bando)

The Bando indicates how much land was given to the settlers of Namiquipa, where it was, who was to control it, what was to be done with it and by whom. It also included information and stipulations not directly pertinent to the land question in the strict sense. Namiquipa was formed with its 64 square leagues of land as a *militarized* town, as a presidio.[11] Colonists were to remain in the community and arm themselves for its defenses. Heads of families assumed possession of house lots, agricultural plots, and other rights of membership in the community (cf. quotations from Bando in AGCCA 24:432 [721.1], DPP, and AGNCh Prot. Namiquipa, libro 1, 26-v-1906), and rights to land, among other things, were given to individuals regardless of their class or caste. The land of the pueblo was an indivisible, collectively owned unit. But joining the community entailed a set of obligations, most important of which were that the settlers work the land and defend it by fighting the Apaches. In other words, land was given to settlers as part of an exchange with the colonial state.

By 1785, 145 soldiers, many with families, were living in Namiquipa.[12] By the 1790s there were probably an equal number of civilian settlers and families in the town as well (APN, AGN.PI). The proportion of civilian settlers increased as decommissioned soldiers stayed on in the pueblo, working the land and fighting the Apaches. There were still more than 150 soldiers assigned to the Second Flying Company as late as 1820, but many of those, particularly in the 1810s, were actually posted outside Namiquipa.[13] In 1787, Jacobo Ugarte y Loyola, then governor and *commandante general* of Nueva Viscaya, had authored an analysis of the Apache problem and suggested offering rations of corn and tobacco in exchange for peace.[14] In the 1790s truces were achieved with some Apache bands which settled near the presidios (see Griffen 1988:72ff.), and for several decades the need for well-equipped soldiers was no longer so pressing. Provided the Indians stayed at peace and settled near presidios, they received their rations of food, tobacco, and clothing.[15] One Chaar-Ul-Li, with wife and child, assumed residence in Namiquipa in 1791. A band led by Ojos Colorados settled there as well after earlier making overtures to settle in Janos and San Buenaventura, and others were maintained at other presidios.[16] Within the towns the distinction between soldiers and civilians became meaningless, since both groups shared "soldierly" and "civilian" duties simultaneously, fighting when necessary and engaged in agriculture the remainder of the year. In addition, ethnic distinctions between the settlers were of progressively diminishing importance.[17]

Settlers of Namiquipa, whether soldiers or civilians, Spaniards, *criollos, mestizos, mulatos,* or even *indios mansos* ("tame Indians"), enjoyed equal rights to the land of the community. The apparent occupational (soldier/farmer) and ethnic (Spanish/Indian/etc.) diversity of the settlers is mentioned to underline the fact that the significant differences between these ideologically constructed categories were fairly rapidly eliminated or destroyed on the frontier. The community formed in such a way that superficially primordial or natural differences between individuals and groups disappeared and were absorbed through the no less ideological—but also political, economic, and military—constitution of a new category of person, which became in the colonial period and the nineteenth century "soldier/farmers" or "an armed peasantry." As will be demonstrated, this armed peasantry was reproduced through the nineteenth century and the Mexican revolution, and its continued reproduction into the twentieth century played an important role in shaping the relations of the community to the state.[18]

But that is to anticipate the argument which follows. For now it is enough to note that during the colonial period, individual household heads in Namiquipa assumed possession of *solares* (house lots) and *tierras para sembrar* (agricultural fields), the men of the community owners in common of the remaining lands within the boundaries of the pueblo. Those boundaries were considerable in extent, describing a square 33 kilometers (21 miles) to a side. There was an abundance of land for distribution among new settlers, who put under the plow the lands along the margins of the Río Santa María and of several arroyos which fed the river, particularly from the east. Houses were initially built near the central plaza, but as the decades wore on (particularly while the Apaches were at peace), neighborhoods were created up and down the river (more up than down because more irrigable land is above the plaza than below.)[19]

There is no evidence of conflict over lands among the *originarios* (original settlers), as they called themselves. But conflicts with "outsiders" (*foráneos*) began even before the end of the colonial period. In 1807 María Martina Salazar, the daughter-in-law of Pedro González de Almoyna, brandishing Don Pedro's titles to Santana del Torreón (in Galeana) and Carmen and Aranzazu (in Namiquipa), and admitting her father-in-law had donated (the magically expanded total of) 36 SGM of land for the purpose of establishing presidios at Namiquipa and San Buenaventura, insisted nevertheless that 3 SGM constituted the "Hacienda de Aranzazu" in Namiquipa legally belonged to her aged and impoverished husband, Juan Antonio Gil de Almoyna. Furthermore, she charged, these lands had been invaded and illegally usurped by one Francisco Vásquez, a retired *alférez* (second lieutenant) of the presidial company at Namiquipa.[20] The commander of the Second Flying Company characterized Salazar's petition as "ridiculous,"[21] and to make a long story short, her petition that property be returned to her family was rejected. But the longer story is more interesting for what it reveals about how Namiquipans conceived of the land of the pueblo and how they regarded outsiders in the colonial period.

Francisco Vásquez's response provides a profoundly different view of what the lands of the pueblo consist in and how people determine and understand their relationship to the land than the view manifest in the Salazar petition of November 14, 1807.[22] According to Vásquez, María Salazar's argument is cynically legalistic, based as it is on a piece of paper. Hers is a quantitative (rather than qualitative), amoral view which values the land as real estate rather than as instrument of production for the owner. First, Vásquez points out that the very description of Aranzazu offered by Salazar was inaccurate:

> Aranzazu was never a hacienda nor even fruitful agricultural land [*tierra de pan llevar*], but a few eroded, arid plains, as all Namiquipans could certify; the hacienda to which Almoyna[23] refers, and where his parents and ancestors lived, is the hacienda *del medio*[24] where the fields and even the houses of the Almoyna still stand, but which are currently in the possession of the inhabitants of this military post. (Namiquipa)

Second, while Vásquez admits that the lands he occupies and works were once part of Aranzazu, he demonstrated with what right he occupied them, prepared fields for planting, and built houses on them. He retired from his military position in 1785, filed a request with the presidio's captain, Juan Antonio Arce, for the lands, and ten years later had his rights to and possession of that land confirmed by Captain Alberto Maynes, "for which reason I call these lands and houses mine."

Third, Vásquez refers to the Bando ("which may be found in the archive of this [presidial] Company") of Teodoro de Croix guaranteeing "four leagues to a wind of land for the crops and cattle of the people who wish to settle the military post." "Since my fields may be hit by a shotgun fired from the wall of the presidio," he goes on, "it appears as though they are within that four-league perimeter, and that I, like my neighbors, am in possession of the lands." Finally, he expresses the view that the land should go to those who work it, and that he himself has, by his labor, transformed an arid plain into a productive field.

On July 4, 1808, Salazar renewed the petition to Governor Salcedo, suggesting the titles to 36 SGM still in the possession of her husband might at least merit the donation of a small parcel of the best lands in Namiquipa to maintain herself and her husband in their old age.[25] On July 8, 1808, Governor Salcedo directed another query to the captain of the Second Flying Company regarding whether any such lands existed in Namiquipa. The captain denied that any such lands were to be found in Namiquipa and suggested offering the Almoynas a few *suertes* (10-hectare lots) near the pueblo of Cruces (August 8, 1808). With the support of the presidial captain, Namiquipans resisted the Almoyna petition out of hand and further set the terms for who did or did not settle in the pueblo after 1778, with all the rights of an *originario*.

Francisco Vásquez and other settlers of Namiquipa emerged from this conflict with the upper hand, the Almoyna descendants frustrated in their attempts to resecure ownership of Aranzazu or any other properties in Namiquipa or Galeana/San Buenaventura.[26] In fact the fate of the Almoyna properties in Namiquipa and Galeana had been on the agenda in 1778, at which time de Croix proposed to settle any conflict in advance by offering to return to the Almoynas a sixth part of their abandoned properties in Galeana, *provided they immediately occupied and worked upon the land* (de Croix, letter to Nicolas Gil, captain of presidial company at San Buenaventura, Nov. 15, 1778. AEN, DPP). In other words, de Croix's policy in regard to the land assigned to the "five new pueblos" was one of "land (and other rights) to the tiller (and the warrior)." This policy was faithfully and rigorously adhered to by the *originarios and their descendants* (cf. material from nineteenth century in AMN, AMCG, AGCCA, passim).

The Vásquez letter indicates elements of an agrarian ideology that also figure in nineteenth- and twentieth-century land conflicts, and indeed in the apprehension of contemporary Namiquipans. The notion that land and other rights and obligations should go to the tiller *and* the warrior highlights the fact that land has always been something which has to be fought for and defended in Namiquipa. Namiquipans' rights to the 64 SGM of land were conferred by the Bando of 1778. Individuals who secured those rights for themselves were scrupulous in their attention to fulfill legal obligations regarding those rights. But going beyond these narrowly legalistic definitions of rights, Namiquipan power over the land was predicated on an immediate knowledge of and physical intimacy with the land and labor upon it, the work of transforming it, engaging it, and defending it.

The rights of the settlers of Namiquipa to the lands of the pueblo were strongly supported by the colonial state. Conflicts over land were between Namiquipans and outsiders, whether landlords—or presumptive landlords—or Apaches. Through the early decades of the nineteenth century there appears to have been little ethnic or class differentiation within the community predicated on putatively distinct "origins" or varying degrees of control of land, animals, and labor enjoyed by different members of the community. Differential access to objects and instruments of labor, above all to land, was severely limited by the circumstance that among the approximately three hundred families that

settled Namiquipa at the end of the colonial period and the early decades of the nineteenth century there was a more or less equal distribution of land, as prescribed by the Bando of 1778 (evidence on this
point in SCP, May 1906, *acta* in AGNCh, RPP.CdG). Furthermore, it was
the lands of the *pueblo as a whole* which were defended by the settlers.

From 1778 through 1821 Namiquipan settlers were simultaneously
privileged subjects of the colonial state and its agents. Invested with
undisputed control of the land and local political autonomy, and em-
powered to subdue the *"indios bárbaros,"* the people were able to work
the land when not defending it from the Apaches (see Terrazas 1905;
Terrazas Sánchez 1973; Escudero 1839; Solis 1936:81; Griffen 1988).
However, once the colonial state was destroyed as an outcome of the
Wars of Independence (1810–21) and the Namiquipans no longer enjoyed the state's protection of those rights, they were not immediately
dispossessed of the land by either landlords or capitalists. Instead the
entire region was once again swept up in a struggle against "barbarians"
as the Apache Wars of the nineteenth century rendered further expansion into or development of the region impossible. Once again pueblos
and haciendas of the region were depopulated, and the settlers again
spent as much of their time defending their land and cattle from the
Apaches as they did working on and benefiting from "the fertility and
beauty of the lands assigned" them. But in contrast to other pueblos in
the region, until the late nineteenth century, Namiquipans retained a
control of their land that, while contested by other social groups, including the Apaches, was not decisively usurped.

APACHE WARS AND DISPOSSESSION OF LANDS

The Second Flying Company was maintained at Namiquipa until 1821
(AGN.PI, AGN.CyP, *listas de revista* that late). Namiquipan soldiers were
involved in the Wars of Independence to the extent that some of them
participated in campaigns against the insurgency, which did not in any
event secure much of a foothold in the region near Namiquipa. It should
be recalled that after the rout of his troops in early 1811, Miguel Hidalgo
moved what remained of his armed insurgent followers to the North,
where he was promptly captured, led in chains from Monclova, Coahuila, to Chihuahua City, and there tried and later put before a firing
squad. In the 1820s the Provincias Internas ceased to exist as an administrative unit; Namiquipa was now in the department (later state) of
Chihuahua. While the national state made desultory efforts to maintain
a few key presidios after 1821, Namiquipa was not among the sites receiving such support.[27] The resurgence of Apache attacks in Chihuahua
after independence resulted in the energies and initiatives of the state

being directed against the "barbarian" menace. Similarly, landlords, property owners, and settlers of the region were compelled to take up arms and campaign against the Apaches.

Apache raiding from the 1830s into the 1880s posed a threat to the physical existence of Chihuahuan communities, whether "Spanish" or "Indian." In a pamphlet published in 1839, José Agustín de Escudero, a native Chihuahuan, lamented the disuse into which the presidio system had fallen.

> Chihuahua has been the Department [state] most victimized by the general condition of disorder. In addition to being eaten alive by incredible domestic problems, . . . [Chihuahua] has always been open to attack; and now more than ever before this has assumed a decidedly malignant character, poison to the most essential organs of social life; we are speaking of the cruel war which for centuries . . . the barbarian indians have waged against the northern frontier. . . . Chihuahua enjoyed 40 years of fairly solid peace [1793–1832] . . . but recently the presidios have been suppressed; and that has been the signal for the barbarians to advance over their natural dam. (Escudero 1839).

Despite the dissolution of the system of presidios on the northern frontier (cf. Escudero 1839; Holden n.d.), Namiquipans were still able to claim some of the privileges earlier accorded the original settlers. For example, tax exemptions were routinely extended to the Namiquipans, figuring as reciprocal favors granted them by the state for their role in Apache campaigns. But little money circulated in the pueblos in any event. Owing to continual attacks, agricultural production and the maintenance of animal herds were seriously hampered, and Namiquipans were barely producing enough to support themselves, never mind the state.

There exists little evidence of agrarian conflict in Namiquipa until the 1860s, when for the first time rents were supposed to be charged to *vecinos* (literally, "neighbors," inhabitants or members of a community) for use of pueblo lands. But local authorities proved incapable of raising the proposed taxes. Similarly, in the same decade when landlords attempted to assume control of parts of the pueblo lands and state officials tried to survey the pueblo lands for the first time since 1778, these efforts from without to reshape social life within the pueblo were stalled in their tracks. These developments are best understood by comparison to agrarian conflicts in neighboring pueblos, which underline the exceptional circumstances within Namiquipa.

Namiquipans' lands were much greater in extent than the lands of other pueblos in the region (with the exception of Janos, Casas Grandes,

Galeana, and Cruces), most of which had one square league or less each. Yet although other pueblos had much less to give up, their lands were stolen by ranchers, farmers, *hacendados,* capitalists, and *gente de razón* in general. *Indígena* communities were the most frequent victims of attack. After the war of 1846–48, for example, at the conclusion of which the United States assumed control of half the Mexican territory in the New World, some former residents of New Mexico relocated to Chihuahua. *Despojos de tierras* (dispossessions of land) of *indígenas* in the Sierra Tarahumara committed by New Mexicans and other recent settlers to Chihuahua followed soon thereafter in the 1850s.[28]

Another development affecting peasants in western Chihuahua was the implementation of the Ley de Desamortizaciones (or the Ley Lerdo), passed in 1856 (Mendieta y Nuñez 1981:119–31). This law was designed to break up the enormous landholdings of corporations, particularly the church, and divide the land into small lots which would be available for purchase by a "new class" of yeoman farmers. But in addition to church properties, the collectively held lands of Indian villages were also subject to division and sale. This problem was much more generalized in the center and south of the country (Mendieta y Nuñez 1981:130–31) but did have its effects in Chihuahua. Since communal and corporate holdings were prohibited under the Ley Lerdo, it was easy for a "person of reason" to convince villagers to sign away their rights to land. Also, some villages were forcibly dispossessed. Tarahumara villages were parceled and the lots sold, often to outsiders, since the indigenous inhabitants had neither capital to invest nor familiarity with a legal system that required them to secure with money a piece of paper giving them legal rights to land they already possessed and worked.[29]

Sometimes whole valleys or mountain ranges were affected by the Ley Lerdo in the Guerrero District of Chihuahua. In the early 1870s, Tomás Dozal y Hermosillo, member of an influential family in Cuidad Guerrero, denounced (i.e., identified and claimed rights to) former properties of the Jesuits in the sierra and in the Papigochic Valley.[30] The Jesuits had been expelled from the country in 1767, and the properties he was among the first to denounce included multiple villages within their borders. In a similar manner, Luis Terrazas, while governor of Chihuahua in the early 1860s, supervised the sale of church lands in the state, acquiring some properties for himself, but also turning others over to deputies in his congress (Katz 1986:6–7).

Finally, Apache attacks resulted in the abandonment of many pueblos and villages. A very Mexican view of the Apaches appears in Manuel Orozco y Berra's *Geografía de las lenguas y carta etnográfica de México,* published in 1864.

> The Apaches, . . . in devastating and continuous war with our establishments; without ever having been led to Christianity; with no hope of destroying them either by means of arms or preaching because the presidios and the missionaries have disappeared together; the Apaches, we repeat, are for Mexico nothing but a constant and disastrous peril; a nation which invades and wipes out territory; savages in their primitive form; such as ought not to be found here more than three centuries after the discovery of America. (Orozco y Berra in Matson and Schroeder 1957:335)

For Chihuahuans the impact of Apache raiding was immediate: they lost their land, their means of livelihood, and often their very lives. The former presidio at Cruces (under the authority of Namiquipa after 1821, and today a section of the *municipio* of Namiquipa) was abandoned twice during the 1800s (CRO, *Cuestionario geográfico*, Cruces, Luis Chávez, 20-v-1908). In the 1850s hundreds of Apache lived in the sierra of Santa Clara, east of Namiquipa.[31] By 1863, the municipal president wrote there were only 127 families still living in Namiquipa, where there had been 300 in the past, because of "los ataques de los bárbaros."[32] Namiquipans repeatedly petitioned the state government for powder and weapons to fight the Apaches, help in campaigns they initiated, recognition of campaigns they participated in, and the reestablishment of a presidio at Namiquipa (AMCG c.7, c.8 passim).

The experience of those Chihuahuans that survived the Apache Wars left a lasting impression in the popular consciousness. The colonists and their descendants were manifestly aware of their historical mission of "civilizing" the frontier. The *Proyecto de Restitución de Ejidos* for Cruces (AGCCA 24/434, 8-viii-1923), for example, includes a history "obtained from the inhabitants of this place" which remarks, "In the course of the 18th and 19th centuries and part of the 20th, there were many difficulties, primarily having to do with defending their households and their lands against Apache Indians." In 1894, a statement by the popular Municipal Council of Namiquipa affirms that

> since the year 1778 and until very recently, the descendants [of the original colonists] and those who actually possess the aforementioned land [of the pueblo] have defended it . . . against the frequent and tenacious attacks of the barbaric Indians, irrigating with their own blood, as with that of their ancestors, the land which until now they have peacefully possessed. (AMN 1-iv-1894)

Cruces was resettled in the late 1850s by a group of Namiquipans. Almost as soon as it was resettled, conflicts erupted over land and use of water from the Río Santa María. It is important to recall that these local conflicts occurred in the context of generalized political disorder in Mexico, elite struggles in the state of Chihuahua, and the invasion of the Guerrero District by large, well-armed bands of Apaches, not to mention the differences of personality and ambition between the settlers themselves. Jesús María Vásquez, instrumental in bringing people from Namiquipa to Cruces in the early 1860s, was accused by another man living in Cruces, Nicanor Ortega, of being sympathetic to the French invasion.[33] While the French encountered resistance in Chihuahua during the Intervention (1863–67), neither was the national government of Benito Juárez able to secure the uncompromised allegiance of many Chihuahuans. In fact, what was left of the Juárez government—and a Chihuahuan government faithful to him—was compelled to tax heavily the few subjects under its control. Vásquez was only one of many people in the Guerrero District who resented these exactions, which may provide some of the basis for Ortega's accusations. But Ortega's complaints halted abruptly in November 1863, when he was killed in what was reported as a fight with Apaches.[34]

Later (in 1865 and 1866) people from Cruces, Namiquipa, Yepomera, Temosachic, and other ranchos and pueblos in the Papigochic and Santa María valleys (including Jesús M[a.] Vásquez) formed a popular alliance opposed to the governments of Benito Juárez (at the national level) and Luis Terrazas (in the state of Chihuahua). It is possible that in the Papigochic Valley especially, agrarian conflicts fueled popular participation in this alliance of pueblos. Other issues, however, such as taxation, regional politics, and pueblos such as Namiquipa securing a revalidation of the military and honorific privileges they had enjoyed under the colonial state, were certainly important factors motivating this complex popular mobilization.[35]

The conflicts among elite factions in the state of Chihuahua from the 1860s onward filtered down unevenly to the remaining pueblos of the region, articulated to local struggles only to the extent that the former were refashioned in terms of ongoing conflicts between the pueblos and regional and state authorities (Almada 1955; Wasserman 1984). For example, men from Cruces participated in the killing of Manuel Ojinaga, one of Juárez's generals, during Juárez's flight from the French to El Paso (Solis 1936:109), and Namiquipans and Cruceños joined other pueblos against the Liberal state—by implication supporting the conservative, anti-*juarista* forces—in the 1860s (AMCG c.8, e.100, Guerrero, 13-iv-1865). Then again, yet other Namiquipan men had earlier participated in the battle of Arroyo del Mortero on the outskirts of Chihuahua City, fighting alongside *juarista* troops.

The behavior of pueblos in the Papigochic Valley during the Tuxtepec rebellion is another example. These pueblos wanted their own *cantón* to provide greater political autonomy at the local level, and Cantón Degollado was formed in 1876 by the *porfirista* Manuel de Herrera's concession to Santana Pérez and others (Solis 1936; AMCG c.144 passim; Almada 1980).[36] During the 1860s and 1870s, in other words, *serrano* peasants including Namiquipans were willing to align themselves with (or against) national political leaders, but their reasons for doing so and popular political action generally were invariably informed above all by local issues and demands, the coincidences of which with the programs and policies of a Juárez or a Díaz were simply that: coincidences.

A few new military colonies were established in the nineteenth century elsewhere in the North. In the Laguna region of Coahuila several pueblos were given lands by Benito Juárez after the expulsion of the French. These villagers had been entrusted with part of Juárez's archive during his flight from the French. They jealously guarded it and were awarded with lands—secured as a kind of military honor—at the time of the expulsion of the French (Barry Carr, pers. com.). The settlers of Cuchillo Parado, on the lower stretches of the Río Conchos, also received land from Benito Juárez.

The Juárez government was not so generous with the people of Namiquipa. In 1868 the municipal president was ordered to collect rents from the inhabitants for use of municipal lands (i.e., lands within the pueblo's 64 SGM to which individual title had not been assigned). The *jefe municipal* (the title given to municipal presidents at that time) was reluctant to introduce this new policy and unable to do so.[37] Four decades later, municipal authorities relate the difficulties of collecting such rents from people unaccustomed to paying them in the past (AMCG 1904). Celso González, member of an influential family from the district capital of Guerrero, attempted to acquire what he thought to be a "public" land within the borders of Namiquipa around the same time, but Namiquipans prevented González's claim from being recognized.[38] In 1869 the Zuloagas, one of the biggest landowning families in Chihuahua, tried to secure title to a property near Namiquipa, insisting that it must be "National" land and not part of Namiquipa's lands since, they argued, it was a well-known fact that presidios were no larger than $1\frac{1}{4}$ leagues to a wind.[39]

The interest of Chihuahuan families in the lands of Namiquipa motivated the state government (then in the control of Luis Terrazas) to press for a survey of the pueblo's lands in the late 1860s. The *vecinos* would have to pay for the survey. They refused to do so since they regarded the extent of the lands, the placement of the boundary markers, and who controlled properties within those boundaries—all points stipulated by the Bando of 1778—as totally unambiguous. Each time the state sent surveyors to Namiquipa, Namiquipan resistance prevented them from carrying out a survey (AMCG c.9, e.112 passim).

A new survey of the lands of Namiquipa was finally conducted in 1871, but it was a survey the Namiquipans did not pay for, and even less recognize. Neither was it carried out by the state, but instead at the behest of one Enrique Müller. In fact the survey of Namiquipa was incidental to Müller's own survey of recently acquired properties, which he was consolidating as the Hacienda de Santa Clara y Anexas. Two of the "annexes" of Santa Clara were the ranchos of Aranzazu and Carmen. Thus began the most important conflict between Namiquipans and a landlord, which continued until the 1920s. Still at war with the Apaches during the second half of the nineteenth century, Namiquipans found themselves fighting on another front as well, defending their lands and their way of life against the owners of large estates. By the end of that century they were confronting barbarism with a capitalist face.

3
Property, State, and Revolution: The New Barbarism, 1860s–1910s

NAMIQUIPA AND THE LANDLORDS

In 1855 Enrique Müller, a German-born U.S. citizen, purchased the Hacienda de Santa Clara, a property of some 12 3/4 SGM (more than 22,000 hectares) in a valley to the east of Namiquipa (AGCCA.DPP p.61). It is doubtful that he attempted to work the hacienda during the following decade since at the time hundreds of Apaches were living in the sierra between Namiquipa and Santa Clara, plundering on all sides (AMCG c.7 passim). Six years later he purchased the Hacienda de Ortega, some 9 SGM (16,000 hectares) contiguous to Santa Clara to the north, paying only 400 pesos. This low purchase price was secured because the lands were "worth no more than that, by virtue of the fact they have been completely abandoned for more than 30 years as a consequence of the frequent incursions of the Barbarians" (AGNCh, Prot., v.72, 9-ix-1861). Müller participated in business deals with Luis Terrazas (the two of them "renting" the enormous Hacienda de Encinillas before Terrazas seized it for himself), purchased mining rights in Cusihuiriachic in 1863, and set up a mining company with headquarters in San Francisco, California, to exploit them (AGNCh, Prot., v.72–73). But it was his attempt to assume control of the Santa Clara properties that generated the conflict with the Namiquipans.

In November of 1863 he purchased the old titles to Santana del Torreón, Aranzazu, and Carmen from several descendants of the González de Almoynas, including María Salazar (AGNCh. Prot., v.73). These titles were invalid and hence in their own way as worthless as the titles to Santa Clara and Ortega, unexploitable because of the Apaches. Nevertheless, Müller consolidated his Namiquipa estate in 1865, at least on paper, through a settlement (*composición*) in which the boundaries of all his properties were fixed anew, and he purchased from the federal government of Juárez any *terrenos baldíos* (unsurveyed public lands) that fell within the newly described borders (AGNCh v.74; DPP pp.61–71). In November 1865 Müller became the presumptive owner of more than

375,000 hectares of land (cf. RPP.CdG), most of it in the municipality of Namiquipa, all of it acquired with a relatively small investment, and none of which he was able to exploit at the time owing to Apache warfare. In 1871 he determined to find out what he really had by sending the surveyor Carlos Marion to Santa Clara.

According to the settlement, the western border of Santa Clara was the pueblos of Namiquipa and Cruces and the Río Santa María. Carlos Marion assumed Namiquipa's lands were no larger than 1 1/4 leagues to a wind—a square 2 1/2 leagues to a side, measuring 6 1/4 square leagues, or SGM. Consequently, the Marion measurement failed to recognize the full extent (4 leagues to a wind) of Cruceño and Namiquipan landholdings. Since some of "the Müller properties," including part of Aranzazu, fell within the smaller square, Müller conceded those lands to the Namiquipans. The conflict that ensued was over lands outside the small square the Marion measurement recognized as belonging to Namiquipa, but inside the square described by the 4 leagues to a wind of the 1778 Bando (copy of Marion survey in ATN, DPP, many letters in AMN and AMCG, 1870–1900). Namiquipans referred to the lands of the 1778 donation, exclusive of *ejidos* and individuals' lots, as the *terrenos de común repartimiento,* the commons of the pueblo. (See map 4.)

Despite the 1871 survey, Müller was unable to assume immediate control of the *terrenos de común repartimiento* of Namiquipa east of the Río Santa María in the decades following the survey. First, Namiquipans opposed and successfully resisted such a maneuver, and second, continued Apache raiding made any attempt to use the lands hazardous. That did not prevent Müller from buying still other properties in the region. In 1874 he acquired what were described as nineteen parcels of land inside the *ejidos* of Cruces on the west bank of the Río Santa María by purchasing the ranch El Tintero. With that invasion, the pueblo of Cruces was left on paper with almost none of the lands indicated in the Bando of 1778 (AGCCA 24/434 [III], e.72, p.1). Namiquipans were more steadfast in their assertion of rights to land, and more successful at challenging outside surveys. Fourteen years after the Müller/Marion survey, Namiquipans convinced representatives of another surveying company to respect their rights to the 64 SGM that comprised the community's colonial land grant (ATN 1.71 [06], e.75669; ATN 1.24 [06], e.17).

By the middle of the 1880s, the Apaches had been driven from Chihuahua and were no longer a threat to the development of the region. Müller took their removal as the signal to advance over the only remaining natural barrier (the Sierra de Santa Clara) to the *terrenos de común repartimiento* of Namiquipa. Müller ran cattle on these lands, and the cattle were just as quickly seized by Namiquipans, who complained that

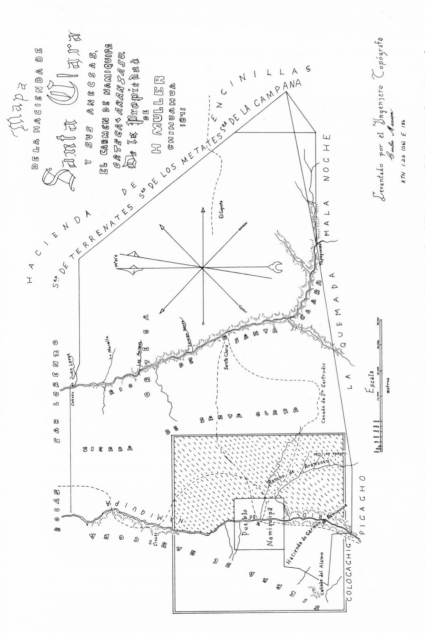

Map 4. The large double-lined square around Namiquipa, indicating the full extent of the 1778 donation of lands, was not part of the original map drawn by C. Marion. It has been added here, and so too the crosshatching indicating Namiquipan land invaded by Santa Clara.

these animals invaded their fields and compromised the interests of the inhabitants of the town, the legitimate owners of the land in question. Müller relied on influential friends and business partners in the district and state governments to validate his claims. The Namiquipans appealed to the president of the Republic, and in 1889 Porfirio Díaz issued a *dictamen* recognizing the validity and the legally binding character of the 1778 Bando, affirming that the Namiquipans collectively held legitimate title to 64 SGM of land (ATN 1.22 [06], e.182, 21-viii-1889). Müller ignored Díaz's *dictamen*, relying on influence with local political officials to circumvent its thrust.

THE FETISHISM OF COMMODITIES

The conflict between Namiquipans and the owners of Santa Clara was a fairly straightforward one concerning rights in property to contested lands and, more immediately, physical control of the land. By the 1890s, however, the pueblo was drawn into a more complex conflict precipitated by implementation of national agrarian policy that affected the very definition of land as "property." Within four years of President Díaz's 1889 decree recognizing Namiquipans as the "owners" of the *terrenos de común repartimiento*, the Government Ministry (Gobernación), while also recognizing their rights to land, ordered that it be divided up among its co-owners (ATN 1.24 [06], e.178). The state envisioned the survey and fractioning of the 112,000 hectares. Any question about the precise form this division was to take—whether it would result in about three hundred lots of about 375 hectares each or whether the land was to be divided according to the different contributions individual families had made to defending the land [1]—was a moot point since Namiquipans refused to accept a division of the *terrenos de común repartimiento*. To fully appreciate the Namiquipan's position against any division, a review of agrarian development policy during the Porfiriato is required.

The Porfiriato (1876–1911) was a period during which the national state facilitated the consolidation of land in the hands of a small rural elite. Porfirian land policy was a logical extension and rationalization of the Ley Lerdo (1856), which earlier had mandated the breakup of corporations. A direct outcome of that law encouraging the expropriation and privatization of church properties and communal villages had been that pueblos, especially of *indígenas,* lost control of their land. But much of Mexico's territory was not recognized as pueblo lands from the outset. To encourage immigration and settlement of underpopulated regions of the country, colonization laws in 1875 and 1883 authorized surveys of public lands. The 1883 law encouraged the formation of survey companies (*compañías deslindadoras*), which were allowed to keep one-third of the lands surveyed and purchase the remaining two-thirds at discount prices unless they were sold to private buyers or held onto by the state (Tannenbaum 1930:13ff.; Mendieta y Nuñez 1981:133ff.; Holden 1986). The "vacant lands" law (Ley de Terrenos Baldíos), passed in 1894, mandated the sale of public lands to individuals or private parties (see Tannenbaum 1930; Mendieta y Nuñez 1981:141–47; Whetten 1948:98–99).

Díaz exalted the privatization of land—turning agricultural fields into commodities—as an important element of national policy to modernize Mexico. Commodification of land would guarantee the orderly progress of society. Díaz argued that to "divide the *ejidos* of the pueblos among the heads of families [would have] a very beneficial outcome for that indigent class of people, for it would assure them small private properties."[2]

It is doubtful the practices of the *compañías deslindadoras* secured this "beneficial outcome." Mendieta y Nuñez, for example, wrote, "The *compañías deslindadoras* contributed to the decadence of the small private property because, while the stated intention was to survey vacant lands, the companies in fact kicked many people off their land" (1981:134). Most studies agree the work of the surveying companies in the late nineteenth century accelerated the concentration of lands in the power of rural elites at the expense of peasant villages.[3] As Friedrich Katz put it, "Mexico's economic boom (after 1884) led to the greatest catastrophe since the massive Indian mortality of the sixteenth and seventeenth centuries. Most of the villagers who had managed to retain their lands throughout the colonial period lost them in the late nineteenth and twentieth centuries to hacendados, speculators, or wealthier members of their communities" (Katz 1988d:533).

While the surveyors were obligated to respect occupied lands—and sometimes, as in the rare case of Namiquipa, they did[4]—they usually did not. In the Papigochic Valley, surveying companies, and later railroad and lumber companies (purchasers of the recently surveyed *baldíos*), invaded pueblo lands. Throughout the state of Chihuahua, Luis Terrazas and other landlords like the Müllers took advantage of the new definition of "vacant" lands, as well as the peace with the Apaches, to expand their holdings in the state. One condition of the *composición* issued in regard to Santa Clara in 1865, for example, was that Enrique Müller pay the national government 1950 pesos for the *baldíos* within the borders of Santa Clara, thereby increasing its size by more than 300,000 hectares.[5] In a similar manner, Luis Terrazas purchased San Miguel de Babicora, a ranch of some 21,067 hectares, in the 1860s, and then after the Apache Wars, in 1887, secured a *composición* from the federal government according to which the property was 318,982 hectares in extent (AGCCA 24/434 [II], p.2).

Surveys of *terrenos baldíos* in Chihuahua sometimes encountered violent resistance from residents of pueblos threatened with dispossession. A dramatic example occurred in 1895 when a North American, C. P. Morrison, was surveying lands between Guadalupe y Calvo and Baborigame in the sierra of Chihuahua. He and his party were attacked by the inhabitants of the lands being surveyed, and twenty members of Morrison's crew were killed by the "natives" (AHSRE e.15-6-29). Combined with other actions against the pueblos of Chihuahua (excessive taxation, electoral fraud, *caciquismo*, an abusive clergy, criminal charges filed against innocent peasants and muleteers), the surveys helped fuel peasant participation in a series of uprisings in the Guerrero District between 1889 and 1895, and Namiquipans were active participants in these popular mobilizations (Almada 1964:93–106; Alonso 1988b; Vargas 1989).[6]

Nevertheless, the Namiquipan lands were never surveyed by a *compañía deslindadora*.[7] Hence, while the Díaz decree of 1889 provided a tactical legal resort against the threatened invasion from Santa Clara, in the final analysis it was less a validation of municipal autonomy than part and parcel of a new definition of the land. National policy encouraged the fractioning of communal holdings: for pueblo lands to be divided, "ownership" first had to be clarified. The 1889 affirmation of the legitimacy of the Namiquipans' title to land, in other words, was merely the prelude to the 1893 order that the "property" be rationally divided.[8]

Porfirio Díaz himself was sensitive to the potentially unsettling consequences of such policies for the Mexican peasantry. In correspondence written in 1889, Díaz addressed the problem of peasants who had lost their lands to survey companies. These letters provide a striking contrast to the routine and generally accurate characterization of Díaz as a great friend of the *latifundistas* (holders of large estates).

Díaz held the opinion that adjudications of land authorized by the Spanish Crown constituted legitimate titles that should be respected by the state.[9] Díaz wrote further that in carrying our surveys of occupied land for which the occupants have no apparent legitimate title, if the peasants enjoy possession of small lots of land at the time of a survey they should be allowed to maintain possession and given title gratis or by payment of a minimal fee.[10] He complains that crooked local officials overseeing the distribution of titles to "primordial possessors" of the land caused irregularities in the distribution of land to peasants and smallholders. Conflicts and abuses had resulted from efforts made to "divide the *ejidos* of the pueblos among the heads of families."[11]

Díaz's key insight was into the subtle but far-reaching consequences his own land policy had for peasant mobilization. In August 1889 there was a "conspiracy" and intended uprising planned by people from Cruces, Yepomera, and other pueblos in the Papigochic Valley (AMCG c.20, c.21 passim; cf. Almada 1955:346, where the argument and inference is that the conspirators were actually instigated and possibly financed by Luis Terrazas—at that date no longer in the governor's office—and Carlos Zuloaga). Led by Santana Pérez and Jesús María Vásquez y Terrazas,[12] the conspiracy was suppressed before peasants took up arms against the state, and Pérez and Vásquez y Terrazas both amnestied themselves before committing any crimes. (Much of the same personnel and bases for conflict—*caciquismo*, dispossession of lands, taxes—figured in the armed uprisings that occurred in the Guerrero District in 1893 and 1894.)

Díaz saw, if no one else did, a dangerous pattern emerging, in which agrarian conflicts in Chihuahua were linked by rebellious peasants to conflicts in other parts of the country. On September 5, 1889, Díaz wrote to Albino Lertache, governor of the state of Oaxaca,

> However much we should not grant a great deal of importance to the daily rumours circulating about adjudications of land in Juchitan,[13] it is certain that in some parts [of the Republic] they have served as a stimulus to the malcontents, and in others they may serve to foment attempts against public peace/order [*tranquilidad pública*], as happened in a conspiracy which was just uncovered in Chihuahua, the members of which are now at the disposal of the local authorities. Among the plans and documents taken from them are some which make reference to an imminent uprising in Juchitan over this question of land, and *they exploit this possibility to animate and convince otherwise vacillating followers*. At the least, these *rumors give hope to those who would upset the order,* and although in the last analysis the rebels will be repressed, we were incapable of preventing this attempt which could have been so damaging at this time.[14]

Díaz's analysis clearly demonstrates his appreciation of the link between peasant dispossession and agrarian revolt (pace Holden) and his frustration at attempting to implement a new regime of property throughout Mexico. But it says little about how the Mexican state's policy of dividing communal lands affected Namiquipans or what sort of reaction that policy provoked within the pueblo.

It was in accordance with the policy of dividing pueblo lands and designating lots as private properties that the Government Ministry had ordered the division of Namiquipa's land in October 1893. The division was intended to turn the peasants into holders of small private properties (*pequeños propietarios;* cf. above quote from Díaz of September 10, 1889). Municipal authorities were to determine how the division should be effected, and Namiquipans assumed license to implement the law in their own way.

In the late nineteenth century Namiquipans distinguished between the *fundo legal,* the *ejido,* and the *terrenos de común repartimiento* of Namiquipa. *Fundo legal* referred to the center of the town, where the majority of house sites were located, while the *ejido* comprised land within a 2 1/2-league square around the pueblo. (This was the same territory which figured in the 1871 Marion measurement as *all* of the pueblo's lands.)[15] The *terrenos de común repartimiento* fell outside what was called the *ejido* and inside the boundaries of the 64 SGM of the 1778 donation. Namiquipans insisted that all *originario's* of the community owned the *terrenos de común repartimiento* collectively and refused to divide them up, preserving them instead as commons. The *ejido* was already "divided" to the extent that there was recognition of cultivable plots which Namiquipans possessed and worked. Individual use, for example cultivation, of the *terrenos de común repartimiento* by *originarios* was permitted provided they did not fence off land within the *terrenos de común repartimiento* or claim individual parcels as property.

In short, there was no new division of land in Namiquipa in the 1890s even though that was precisely what the Government Ministry decree called for. Instead there was a revalidation of an existing state of affairs, a formalization of Namiquipan's interpretation of the Bando of 1778 in terms imputed locally to correspond to the new guidelines. Namiquipans took the decrees of 1889 and 1893 as the basis for a formulation of the rights of the descendants of the original colonists. Those rights, to a house lot, possession of an agricultural plot, and use of common lands for grazing cattle or exploiting timber resources, were restricted to families of the original colonists and were contingent upon the *vecino* laboring upon the land and participating in collective projects (e.g., of defense and maintenance of irrigation works).

This popular definition of rights (*derechos*) to land in terms of possession rather than property had important implications restricting the possibility of turning agricultural land and labor power into commodities. Since the concept of *posesión* of agricultural land was dependent upon an individual working it, and not just exercising control over it, this popular formulation challenged the validity of an abstract separation of land and labor power. Further, the circulation of land as a commodity within the broader regional economy was made difficult if not impossible, since the stipulation that possessors of rights to land be accepted as members of the community required a vetting of individual claims to rights that was not structured by the hidden hand of market relations nor, for that matter, by agencies of the state. Rather, Namiquipans held popular juntas (meetings of the pueblo) to determine admission or non-admission of new members of the community. Finally, at a more prosaic level, Namiquipans' resolute insistence on maintaining the commons as an indivisible unit[16] for a time effectively removed the possibility of parts of that considerable expanse of land circulating as commodities.

Posesión involves a peasant holding a plot of land and working it. Assignment, or more commonly *recognition,* of *posesión* was made by local authorities who were members of the community, and not by state officials. This way of holding the land was troublesome to Porfirian officials and to Díaz himself, who clearly regarded *la pequeña propiedad* (private property) as providing a more rational and just way of determining rights to land. The singular "informal" feature of *posesión* was that there was no intervention by the state, no official recording and ordering of the land. Instead, members of the community were themselves responsible for mediating disputes and validating access to land, in short, for recognizing *posesión.* It is a concept eminently well suited to the circumstances and conditions that prevailed on the northern frontier through most of the nineteenth century. And it became a problem only when modernizing, scientific-minded capitalist entrepreneurs attempted to assume control of the *posesiónes* of Namiquipans.

Luis J. Comaduran was one such entrepreneur, acquiring many properties in Namiquipa and Bachiniva in the first decade of the twentieth century. After conducting a survey of the *ejidos* of Namiquipa (preliminary to the sales of municipal lands in 1906; see below), Comaduran wrote that many members of the community refused to secure title to their lands owing to their conviction that the land was theirs to begin with. In other words, *posesión* did not require the state's blessing.[17] An individual in nineteenth-century Namiquipa may have worked a plot of land that their father had worked earlier. If that son abandoned the plot and someone else proceeded to work it a decade later for another decade, since neither had title, the second individual would continue to work the land. He would have *posesión.*[18]

Trouble began when immigrants arrived in Namiquipa in the late 1880s and 1890s, after the Apache Wars. Namiquipans' acceptance of new members into the community had in the past been conducted within the framework of popular juntas. *Naturales* (individuals born into the community) were still holding popular juntas late in the nineteenth century (in 1879, 1889, and 1900 at least, and possibly with greater frequency), which allowed *certain* individuals to purchase and assume rights in the community as *condueños* (co-owners) of the pueblo land. This gave rise to the distinction among outsiders (*foráneos*) between those with and without locally recognized and popularly sanctioned rights to land. One criterion for acceptance, beyond purchasing the right, was the agreement to cooperate in collective projects initiated within the community, such as fighting the Apaches, or the construction and maintenance of irrigation canals.[19] Another was that the new immigrants work the land themselves and not accumulate or hold the land as a speculation.

but not fictitious capital!

The records of the Registro Público de la Propiedad (RPP) for the Guerrero District for 1900 contain evidence that there was in fact a market in Namiquipan *derechos*, with individuals selling their rights to outsiders or even, as the actions of Cornelio Espinosa demonstrate, accumulating multiple *derechos* at low "insider" prices for sale en bloc to outsiders for a considerable profit.[20] This would seem to indicate that rights (including to *posesión* of agricultural fields) were indeed turned into commodities by the end of the nineteenth century. However, the full maturation of that development—the commodification of *derechos*, the transformation of possessions into properties—was interrupted since Namiquipans simultaneously and routinely repudiated the "sale" of their rights to outsiders, insisting on the continuing and inalienable character of *derechos* as a unique privilege of *originarios* (while pocketing the cash they may have secured from their sale).

One process the short-lived market in *derechos* after the 1893 decree points to is the profound ambivalence of Namiquipan response to outsiders moving to the pueblo in the aftermath of the Apache Wars. Some outsiders purchased *derechos*, while other rented land from the municipal government. But Namiquipans continued to insist on the application of their own criteria for admitting, or refusing to admit, outsiders into the community. The rights of the *naturales* or *originarios* ("native-born" members of the community or descendants of the "original settlers") were never questioned within the community. But the popular insistence on continuing to operate with a notion of *posesión* coupled with rejection of the notion of capitalist property (land being some thing to which one enjoyed title, which could be "freely" bought and sold) was challenged by the state and proved the undoing of more than one resident of the region in the decade before the revolution broke out. A group of men from Cruces who later became *villistas* complained in 1904 that cattle belonging to Pedro Loya and Julio Weckman—landlords and recent immigrants to Cruces—had destroyed their agricultural fields. The Chihuahuan Government Ministry, with authority in such matters, ruled the complaint without foundation because those individuals registering the complaint could not demonstrate title to the *labores* (fields) that had been destroyed.[21]

While all of this was going on, the owners of Santa Clara continued to advance claims on the *terrenos de común repartimiento* east of the river. In the valley south of Namiquipa, haciendas such as Cologachic, Providencia, Teseachic, and Las Chollas were established or purchased—

mostly by wealthy landowning families from Ciudad Guerrero—and later consolidated and attached to the Hacienda San José de Babicora, which occupied a high plain to the west of Namiquipa. These lands came into the possession of William Randolph Hearst. Hearst's Babicora "Ranch" (as he called it) comprised more than 300,000 hectares and invaded some 5,000 hectares of Namiquipan land from the south. And when workers from Babicora erected a fence across Namiquipan lands in 1908, an armed party of Namiquipans promptly tore it down.[22] But by then an even bigger conflict with the government of the state of Chihuahua had begun, a conflict discussed in the next section.

The policy of the Porfirian state was to turn land into a commodity. At the national level this strengthened *latifundismo* throughout Mexico (Stavenhagen 1970; Reyes et al. 1970; Whetten 1948). In Chihuahua the effect was similar, but there it coincided with the consolidation of political and economic power throughout the state by a single extended family, the Terrazas-Creels (the best discussion in English of the Terrazas is Wasserman 1984). In Namiquipa the policy forced a redefinition of the meanings of land, accentuating contradictions between local and national conceptions of the land and human action.

In deepening and extending this policy, Porfirio Díaz was aware of the palpable relationship between peasant dispossession and peasant unrest and mobilization. To deal with the latter possibility, the state could always, as it frequently did, resort to direct repression. A more interesting outcome (of this positive relationship) is the way Díaz's expressed concern for dispossessed peasants could lead to conflict between the national state and regional elites. Such was the case in Chihuahua, where the efforts of the Terrazas-Creel oligarchy to consolidate its power throughout the region had earlier led to repression (as at Tomochic in 1892 or Santo Tomás in 1893) and later to expropriation (throughout the state after 1905) of the peasantry (on Tomochic see Almada 1938; Chávez Calderón 1964; Osorio n.d.).

Through much of the nineteenth century Namiquipa survived as a pueblo largely through locally directed initiatives and forms of organization. Although in general disarray in the region as a whole, the presidial/military social organization remained important internally in Namiquipa.[23] The requirement of militant defense of the land not only affected the amount of land still in Namiquipan control at the start of the twentieth century but also informed the notions of male personhood figuring in the popular apprehension of meanings of the production process.

The wars between the Apaches and the inhabitants of Chihuahua's peasant communities (Terrazas Sánchez 1973) ended with the defeat of the Apaches in 1886. This marked a victory for landlords (primarily cattle barons) and capitalists, frequently the same cattle barons looking for alternative investment opportunities in Chihuahua. Capitalists proceeded to do to independent agrarian communities what the Apaches had failed to do: destroy the pueblos and steal the land. They also tried to accomplish something more: establish a new order of property in the region and subject the population to a new labor regime.

CONFLICT WITH THE STATE

In 1904, Luis Terrazas turned the governor's office over to Enrique Creel, his nephew and son-in-law. In his first year in office, Creel revised the state constitution to eliminate the last vestiges of local control over municipal politics and forced through a municipal tax law that substantially increased the state's share of peasant surpluses (Almada 1964:21–26, 81–83). In 1905 Governor Creel enacted the Municipal Lands Law,[24] ordering local authorities to sell off all "municipal lands," including house lots, agricultural plots, and pasture land within the *ejidos* of the pueblos to which there was no clear title, to individual purchasers. Putting land controlled by rural communities and their inhabitants in Chihuahua on the market intensified and generalized peasant discontent and delegitimated the state and federal government in the peasants' eyes (see Lloyd, 1987, 1988; Alonso 1988b, 1992b). Wealthy ranchers, *hacendados,* municipal- and regional-level officials of the state and—certainly in the case of Namiquipa—petty bourgeois immigrants purchased vacant lots, grazing land, fields, and even house lots out from under existing residents who, though descendants of colonial period settlers, could not produce "legitimate" titles to their lands.

With the support of higher-level government officials, immigrants had by 1904 assumed control of the apparatus of Namiquipan municipal administration. That provided the recently arrived *foráneos* the power required to undermine the rights to land of peasant *originarios.* One policy the recent immigrants succeeded in implementing was to charge peasants rent for small plots cultivated without titles, something prior administrations had been unable to do for almost fifty years. By 1906, approximately half of Namiquipan families were paying rent for their plots (AMN c.2, 1906). For *originarios,* a more important issue than the cost was the fact that exaction of rent denied the legitimacy of their claims to the land.[25] By paying rent, they participated in the symbolic expropriation of their land. Another issue, in which the hand of the state was clearly evident, was the insistence that all the Namiquipan lands included in the Marion measurement (10,530 hectares) be recognized as municipal lands, and therefore salable. Namiquipans at the time argued that the 1905 law should only be applied to *ejidos* 1 SGM (1,755 hectares) in extent.[26] The *jefe municipal,* no longer popularly elected but instead appointed by the *jefe politico* (political boss) of the Guerrero District with the approval of Governor Creel, wanted to alienate those 10,000 hectares under the umbrella of the 1905 Municipal Lands Law. More than 5,000 hectares of "municipal lands" were actually sold in Namiquipa between 1905 and 1910.

The Municipal Lands Law had a range of effects throughout Chihuahua. It generally tended to exacerbate rural class conflict and restrict the access of most social groups—elites and petty bourgeois excepted—to land. It had its most profound effects on communities that still enjoyed a measure of control over pueblo lands (see Lloyd 1988:90–97), since in towns and villages whose residents had already been dispossessed, there was little "municipal land" available for purchase. Particularly hard hit, then, were the former military settlement colonies. Galeana, for example, which had already lost 90 percent of its land between 1881 and 1898 (Lloyd 1988:90–91), still retained control over more than 10,000 hectares, most of which were identifiable as "municipal land." But as Lloyd notes, "Casas Grandes had the greatest number of denuncios [sales] in the entire state, followed closely by Galeana" (1988:95, n. 14).

The effects of the law were no different for Namiquipa. Of the 456 sales of municipal lands in the Guerrero District (ten *municipios*) between 1905 and 1909, 181 (totaling more than 5,000 hectares in extent) were in Namiquipa, and another 122 in Cruces (then, as now, a section of the municipality of Namiquipa). Namiquipans found themselves fighting on three fronts. First, the land of peasants who had in the past enjoyed rights to plots within what were now defined as "municipal lands" was sold from under them. Second, the Jefe Municipal and cacique Victoriano Torres, who by law had to approve all land sales, favored petty bourgeois buyers and excluded *originario* peasants from purchasing land.[27] Third, common usufruct rights to water and timber were violated as they were transformed into commodities and sold or rented by the cacique to *foráneos.*[28]

Responding to the Municipal Land Law, Namiquipans formed the Private Civil Society (La Sociedad Civil Particular, hereafter SCP) to "defend and administer" the lands of the pueblo.[29] The founding document of the SCP from May 1906 outlines a regime of land tenure. It finds the basis for the terms outlined there in the 1778 Bando and their ancestors' century of struggle to fulfill those terms. The document pointedly affirms that only Namiquipan families descended from the original colonists should enjoy rights to work the land and have access to the commons. The SCP was formed precisely to put an end to the sales of municipal lands under the 1905 law.

TABLE 1. Adjudications of Municipal Lands, Guerrero District, Chihuahua, 1905–1909

Municipality	1905	1906	1907	1908	1909	1905–1909
Cruces[a,b]	13	13	14	35	47	122[a]
Namiquipa[a,b]	1	18	80	44	38	181[a]
Bachiniva[b]	—	2	—	—	9	11
Yepomera[c]	—	21	13	6	—	40
Temosachic[c]	1	11	6	—	2	20
Matachic[c]	1	4	8	1	1	15
Tejolochachic[c]	2	24	6	3	6	41
Santo Tomás[c]	—	3	5	8	2	18
Cd. Guerrero[c]	—	—	1	1	—	2
Cocomorachic	—	—	1	—	—	1
Yepachic	—	—	—	—	5	5
Annual Totals	18	96	134	98	110	456

[a]Towns in Municipo de Namiquipa.   [b]Towns in Río Santa María Valley.
[c]Towns in Río Papigochic Valley.

According to José Rascón Iguado, son of one of the SCP's key officers, José Rascón y Tena, Victoriano Torres denounced the SCP, the leaders of which (Cornelio Espinosa and Rascón y Tena) were promptly thrown in jail in Cuidad Guerrero. In fact Torres had written a year earlier to the *jefe político* that Namiquipans complaining in 1905 about Alejandro Moya, Torres's secretary, had all participated in the agrarian revolts of a decade earlier.[30] That accusation was true, as was the fact that these individuals became the "ringleaders" of the SCP. Also true was that the SCP was powerless to stop the sales. Whereas only 1 sale was conducted in 1905 and 18 in 1906, there were 80 sales in 1907, 44 in 1908, and another 38 in 1909 in Namiquipa alone (*Anuario Estadístico;* AMN).[31]

Most sales in Namiquipa were to outsiders, petty bourgeois immigrants drawn to the region by the inexpensive lands and the opportunity to make profitable investments facilitated through their connections with the municipal and district rulers, the *jefes políticos.*[32] One stipulation of the law was that individuals could acquire only one lot of municipal land, no larger than 25 hectares of grazing land. But certain individuals using *prestanombres*—literally "name lenders," the names of friends or relatives, including distant cousins, under-age children, dead people—purchased and consolidated multiple lots of land.[33] An aggravating feature of the sales was that often, lands which Namiquipans had worked for decades, their rights to them affirmed by the 1778 Bando and the 1889 and 1893 decrees, and of which they had prior *posesión,* were sold off.

Frequently lands which had been prepared as rain-irrigated fields prior to the implementation of the law were denounced as *pastal* (pasture land) and sold to outsiders. That few Namiquipans exercised their new "right" to purchase municipal lands was the result of at least three factors. They resented having to pay for what was already theirs, and most did not have the money to do so even had they so desired. But most important was their indignation that individuals who had not defended the community from the Apaches during prior decades were effortlessly assuming control of agricultural fields. In 1908, writing to the federal government, Namiquipans pointed out their pueblo had been "the sole bulwark of civilization in these isolated regions," and the inhabitants did not abandon the pueblo, in contrast to most recent immigrants, who never sustained "that destructive struggle" against the "savages" (ATN 28-vii-1908). Going on, they remark, "We see with deep sorrow that those lands which we justly esteem to be ours, received from our fathers and fecundated with over a century's constant work, are passing into the hands of strangers through a simple petition and the payment of a few pesos" (ATN 28-vii-1908).

In 1865 the people of Galeana had written that their land "was to be bought not by gold but by torrents of blood" (ATN 1.24(06), e.3, 17-iii-1865). A century later Placido Chávez wrote of his father and uncles (leaders of the anti-Porfirian rebellion of Tomochic in 1891–92) that they "were of the humble class, they never disposed of capital; their only capital—one which was greater and more precious [than property or economic capital]—was their work, their self-esteem, and their honor, an honor without flaw or stigma" (Chávez Calderón 1964:6).

In a period of four years, more than 5,000 hectares of land in the immediate vicinity of the pueblo suddenly came under the control of families from outside the community. In addition to the multiple properties consolidated by the Comaduran, Flores, and Corral families, some people used the law as an opportunity to validate claims to hundreds of hectares of land each. These included the claims (*adjudicaciones*) of a very wealthy man who had immigrated to Namiquipa in the 1870s, his daughter and son-in-law, and Victoriano Torres himself, the *jefe municipal* and cacique for much of the decade before 1910.[34]

Namiquipans had defended their land from the Apaches for more than a century and staved off the advances of *hacendados* for half a century, but they were momentarily powerless in the face of the state. Suddenly they were on the verge of sharing the fate of millions of other rural Mexicans—to be peasants without land of their own. Nonviolent forms of resistance to agrarian dispossession and political domination were increasingly ineffective. In October of 1905, a representative of the Namiquipan peasants, Concepción Cervantes, wrote to Ricardo Flores

Magón—then attempting to organize the revolution in Mexico from overseas through the Mexican Liberal Party (Partido Liberal Mexicano, PLM)—expressing readiness to fight against "the authorities governed by the Dictatorship" of Díaz.[35] A decade later his nephew, Candelario Cervantes, would demonstrate that promise and readiness. But before discussing what happened to the land during the revolution, it is worthwhile reviewing what Namiquipans had been doing with the land up to that point.

THE MEANING OF LAND USE IN NAMIQUIPA

Before the 1910 revolution Namquipa's lands had always been on one or another kind of frontier. Initially a frontier of a "civilization" threatened by the forces of "barbarism" represented by the Apaches, it later became a frontier of socioeconomic expansion. The lands of the 1778 donation acquired a new meaning and significance within the transformed and transforming capitalist order a century later (cf. Barretta et al. 1978). As the frontier changed from a sociocultural and geographic one to a historical frontier on which contrasting developmental trajectories of elite and subaltern social groups confronted one another, the lands assumed a different role in the lives of the settlers.

During the first period, land was one of the raw materials for a new society, where the "civilized" people grazed cattle, planted crops, and built towns. Indeed, initially the settlers of Namiquipa were the beneficiaries and instruments of the process Marx wrote about as the "primitive accumulation" of capital. "The so-called primitive accumulation . . . is nothing else than the historical process of divorcing the producer from the means of production" (Marx [1867] 1906:786). During the colonial period Namiquipans were in fact *invested* with control of means of production (land); other social groups—notably landlords such as the Almoynas, and the Conchos Indians—were the ones being divorced from the means of production. (The Conchos had been "divorced" in that most incontrovertible manner, through physical extermination.) By the middle of the Porfiriato, however, the location and identity of Namiquipans as subjects in the process of primitive accumulation had been inverted. They now faced the prospect of their land—taken earlier from the Conchos and Almoynas, and for which they fought against the Apaches—being alienated.

Marx's discussion of primitive accumulation of capital in part 8 of volume 1 of *Capital* provides an accessible, resonant, and recognizable account of historical processes affecting laboring masses of the Mexican countryside during the late nineteenth century. Mario Cerutti (1989) reminds us that primitive accumulation involved more than just the celebrated "separation of producers from means of production," however. It also involved the growth and consolidation of political and economic power by a particular class, the bourgeoisie (on the Terrazas-Creels in Chihuahua, see Wasserman 1984); growth of the internal market; an amplification of available means of production—unequally distributed; and, as an outcome, a recasting of the social relations of production.

Another critical aspect of the primitive accumulation of capital in Mexico was the commodification of land. By encouraging the sale of "national" and "vacant" land, the state permitted elites to secure control of massive estates (the process of land concentration) while peasants were compelled to rent or sharecrop land they had worked in the past (rarely having enough money to purchase their own land) or sell their labor-power to the large estates. In other words, from the standpoint of the peasantry, this later moment of the primitive accumulation of capital had consequences that were both structural (separation of producers from means of production) and cultural or subjective. They had to re-orient their practice in light of the transformation of land from a subject of labor in their communities into a commodity—which they could not afford to purchase—that circulated in spheres of exchange having little to do with community life (Cardoso 1983; Marx [1857–58] 1973: 471–72; Marx [1867] 1906:784–805; D. Nugent 1988:16; Roseberry 1989:80–121).

This topic is introduced here to underline the way agrarian struggle in Namiquipa—at the end of the nineteenth century as much as throughout the twentieth—is best understood as a struggle to maintain the land as a subject of labor for the agriculturalist. It is something *more* than just an immediate, almost technical, struggle for control of a given territory or means of production. Struggle of this sort resonates in the very ways people think about themselves and conceptualize their relationships with outsiders, whether agents of the state, landlords, or petty bourgeois immigrants. This perspective may take us beyond Warman's rather limited claims about the significance of the peasant demand for "Land and Freedom" discussed in chapter 1.

After more than a century of having been worked by the original colonists and their descendants, the lands of the pueblo—the possessions and the commons—played a role in the processes of production and reproduction similar to that of the early nineteenth century for the members of the community. But in relation to the broader process of socioeconomic transformation which had redefined the frontier from a "frontier of civilization" to a "frontier of capitalism," the land assumed new and different meanings for other social groups (landlords, petty bourgeois speculators) from outside the community. Through all the military and political struggles during the first century and a half of the pueblo's existence as a settlement colony, the settlers had labored upon the land. This in turn shaped the very processes of production and reproduction—social as well as economic, ideological as well as objective—entailed in the land's assuming a particular significance for the Namiquipans, which contrasted radically to its significance to the state, the landlords, and the petty bourgeois immigrants.

Land was controlled by male heads of families of the pueblo who fought to maintain control over all the pueblo's lands collectively. Attempts by outsiders to interrupt or direct the agricultural production process by appropriating a portion of the product in the form of taxes, rents, or other more direct means of appropriation such as theft, invasion, or in "fines"levied by government officials, were systematically resisted. The fact that *fighting* was involved was no less important than that these were "agriculturalists" or agricultural "workers" who farmed their own land. In tax records and censuses from prerevolutionary Namiquipa (in the AMN and AMCG), Namiquipans are identified as *agricultores* or *labradores* to indicate "agriculturalists" or individuals who work (*labrar*) their own fields (*labores*). These are distinguished from *trabajadores* (*de raya*)—wage laborers (cf. Alonso 1992b).

At the end of the Porfiriato an important social distinction was made between *agricultor* and *trabajador de raya*.[36] In Namiquipa the ideal of socialized masculinity involved working one's own land and doing one's own work. To be a wage-slave made realization of this ideal impossible. In contemporary Namiquipa the same distinction figures in different valuations of person and work (Alonso 1992a; Nugent 1992). In addition, *agricultor* is preferred over *campesino* (peasant, with connotations of subjection, poverty, etc.) as the term individuals identify themselves by in contemporary usage.

By 1910 the situation confronting peasants in Namiquipa was not totally hopeless, as it was, say, in Galeana or Janos, where virtually all of the pueblo's lands had passed into the hands of outsiders (Lloyd 1988, 1991). But the invasion of Namiquipa through the agency of a new class of immigrants and landlords encouraged by the state was more than just physical and immediate. The state was also trying to "set the seal of general social recognition" (Engels) on the very way in which people's relationship to the land was regulated, organized, and formed. In the past Namiquipans had determined that in their own way, relying on the Bando—which was, importantly, an earlier charter issued by a different state—and the fact that they worked the land, fought the Apaches (and those landlords whose predatory expansion threatened the integrity of the pueblo's lands), and controlled their own affairs within the community. Now they could no longer do so. Consequently, the attempt by the state to reshape, codify, and regulate people's relationship to the land

became not just a crucially important site of struggle for the Namiquipans (for that, it always had been), but a site of struggle simultaneously
linked to other struggles between the community and the state *and* to a
regional and subsequently national, armed struggle aimed at destroying
the power of the state.[37]

LAND DURING THE REVOLUTION

During the early stages of the revolution in 1910, Namiquipans joined the
popular uprising which swept out of the Guerrero District of Chihuahua
in November and December of that year (Olea Arias 1961; Duarte Morales 1967; Calzadíaz Barrera 1979; Wasserman 1980:34; Katz 1981:
7–41). Namiquipans organized themselves under local, popular leadership as they had during the Apache Wars. Groups of close kin—
brothers and first cousins—fought alongside one another while fathers
and uncles supervised their action on the field of battle in a manner
analogous to the way production was organized on agricultural fields.
Both the leadership and the rank and file of armed contingents of Namiquipans in the first stage of the revolution were drawn directly from
the Sociedad Civil Particular (SCP). José Rascón y Tena, vice president
of the SCP, led the assault on the plaza of Namiquipa on November 20,
1910. José María Espinosa, son of the SCP president, Cornelio Espinosa,
led a contingent of Namiquipans that fought alongside the revolutionary
forces through the winter of 1911.

On the morning of November 20, José Rascón y Tena rode in with
his brother Pedro and other close relatives from their ranch near El Progresso, met with more armed men in the barrio of La Hacienda, and soon
took the plaza of Namiquipa in a battle during which Felix Merino, the
terracista/porfirista police commander, was killed. The first soldier from
the ranks of Namiquipan insurgents to die in battle was Rafael López;
his widow subsequently took up arms. Victoriano Torres and Pablo Porras, the caciques who had presided over sales of municipal lands after
1905, were run out of town.[38] Through the winter of 1910–11, contingents of Namiquipans—most of them descendants of the original colonists—joined the *maderista* uprising throughout western Chihuahua,
many participating in the battle of Ciudad Juárez in May 1911 immediately before the collapse of the Díaz regime.[39]

The experience of Namiquipans under outside leadership during the
1911 campaign leading up to the defeat of the Díaz army is emblematic
of the ambiguity and tension characterizing the relationship between
popular armies and the elite (largely landlord) interests promulgating
the overthrow of the Díaz government. After proposing himself as candidate for the presidency of Mexico in the 1910 elections, Francisco Ma-

dero, a Berkeley-educated landlord from an influential family with extensive landholdings and commercial interests in the cotton-growing Laguna region of southwestern Coahuila, was thrown in jail. Upon his release, Madero fled to the United States, where in October 1910 he issued an appeal to his countrymen to take up arms on November 20 against the dictatorship of Díaz (who had "won" the elections). Madero's call to arms went largely unheeded throughout Mexico, except in the state of Chihuahua, where, on November 14 in Cuchillo Parado, on the nineteenth in San Andres, and on the twentieth in towns throughout the Guerrero District, peasants took up this call. Madero himself remained in the United States for several months before entering Mexico and joining the guerilla bands operating throughout Chihuahua—but especially in the west—in February 1911.

What he found could not have pleased him. Peasants, miners, former Apache fighters, and followers of the Mexican Liberal Party (Partido Liberal Mexicano, PLM; also known as *magonistas*) from northwest Chihuahua, some of whom had participated in armed conspiracies against the government and been the objects of state repression over the previous five years,[40] were carrying red flags into battle. Madero prohibited the use of such symbols, insisting that his demands were the only permissible articulations of an anti-Díaz agenda.[41] The popular leader from Namiquipa, José María Espinosa, was stripped of his command and jailed in Ciudad Guerrero for "insubordination" in March 1911. While with his troops near the Hacienda de Rubio, not far from Namiquipa, Espinosa wanted to stop into his pueblo to change clothes and visit relatives. Madero forbade this "desertion," at which point Espinosa, who towered over the diminutive landlord and had been fighting in the sierra for months while Madero was living comfortably in the United States, is reported to have said, *"¿Quien eres tu, mocoso, para darme órdenes?"* ("Who are you, snotnose, to order me about?").[42] The other popular leaders and officers in the revolutionary army, including Francisco Villa, appealed to Madero to liberate Espinosa immediately, but to no avail, and he was remanded to jail in Ciudad Guerrero for several months (BN.AFM).

In May 1911, as the Díaz government collapsed, Namiquipans immediately petitioned revolutionary authorities to expropriate the lands alienated by the 1905 Municipal Lands Law and return them to local peasants.[43] Since their petitions were not acted on, they took matters into their own hands. In July 1911, the municipal president of Namiquipa (recently elected by the revolutionary peasants) prohibited all those who had purchased land under the 1905 law from working it.[44] As peasants ripped down the new fences enclosing over 5,000 hectares of land,[45] revolutionary authorities at the district level ordered the expropriated lands to be returned to their petty bourgeois owners and that the peasants should settle their grievances in court.[46] The superior orders were ignored.

Namiquipans' successful rescinding of the 1905–10 land sales without the official blessing of the new revolutionary leadership demonstrates their immediate reestablishment of municipal autonomy, using that political autonomy to deal first with the question of the pueblo's land. Beyond overturning sales of municipal land in the early months of the revolution, Namiquipa also assumed undisputed control of the territories being invaded by the haciendas of Santa Clara and San José de Babicora.

It is important to note Namiquipans' attitudes toward large landowners. They did not object to large private landholdings per se and indeed, as a group, were themselves *socios* or co-owners of a large property. What they objected to were invasions of their land by neighboring haciendas. Just as they tore down the Babicora fence in May 1908,[47] they did not hesitate to confiscate Santa Clara cattle found grazing in the *terrenos de común repartimiento*. What they emphasized above all in their dealings with Santa Clara and Babicora, though, was fairness and respect between the community and neighboring estates in the latter's capacity as landowners and as employers of local labor.

The landlord class was primarily resented for assuming control of the land by simply signing pieces of paper. While the audacity of such maneuvers was much admired, Namiquipans had greater respect for people who defended their land with a rifle than for those, to paraphrase Woody Guthrie, who defended it with a pen.[48] Another consideration was that landlords and wealthy people in general did not work themselves. From the perspective of *serrano* peasants, such a disengagement from the land, combined with the power to appropriate the products of the labor of others, was dishonoring for the persons who did work and dishonorable for the employers.[49]

The one family of landlords generally hated in Namiquipa on the eve of the revolution were the Terrazas, surprising in light of the former Apache fighters' respect and admiration for Don Luis and his relatives, such as Joaquin, for their roles in the Apache Wars of the nineteenth century (Katz 1988d:530; Terrazas 1905). This hatred may be related to the reversal of fortune the community suffered after Luis Terrazas turned over the governorship to Enrique Creel in 1904. During the first months of the 1910–11 uprising in Namiquipa, cattle bearing the Terrazas brands were singled out for confiscation and slaughtered to feed the families of soldiers, widows, and orphans. Müller and Hearst cattle were not so openly confiscated; if they were, the revolutionary authorities were not informed.[50]

Neighboring landlords responded differently to the early events of the revolution. The Hearst ranch continued to operate throughout the decade of 1910–20, though its livestock was raided and its buildings used by revolutionaries. According to its owners, the property decreased in value by a half between 1910 and 1920. But San José de Babicora remained intact, its administrators relying on *guardias blancas* (white guards, or private armies that worked for specific landlords), particularly active after 1915, to prevent a takeover by insurgent peasants or members of nearby communities.[51] The Müllers, by way of contrast, and closely connected to Luis Terrazas, did not press claims for the *terrenos de común repartimiento* with the revolutionary government after 1910. Then in April of 1913, local revolutionaries following orders of Francisco Villa (who had rejoined the struggle only a few weeks earlier, in the wake of the coup d'etat in which General Victoriano Huerta assumed power after murdering Francisco Madero) confiscated the Hacienda de Santa Clara in the name of the revolution (Calzadíaz Barrera 1979:102–3). While Hearst's Babicora properties were left intact, Santa Clara was put in the charge of *villistas* from Cruces and Namiquipa.

The confiscation of Santa Clara by Namiquipan *villistas* forms a footnote to Villa's policy of expropriating large estates during the years he controlled the state of Chihuahua (1913–15). Ferociously faithful to Abraham González, *maderista* leader in Chihuahua, Villa joined the revolution for the second time just after González's assassination. In March 1913 he entered Mexico from the United States with a small band of men and within a few months controlled much of the state.[52] By the end of that year the federal army no longer existed in Chihuahua, and Villa was forming his own Division of the North, many of its troops recruited in Chihuahua and Durango.

On December 12, 1913, Villa, as military governor of the state of Chihuahua, published a "Decree relating to the Confiscation of Properties," which ordered the expropriation of the lands of the Chihuahuan oligarchy. The first properties to be confiscated were "the personal property, real estate, and relevant documents of all classes belonging to [Luis] Terrazas and sons, the Creel brothers, the Falomir brothers, José Ma. Sanchez, the Cuilty brothers, the Lujan brothers, J. Francisco Molinar, and all their relatives and accomplices."[53] These properties were administered by the Office of Confiscated Goods, placed in the charge of Silvestre Terrazas.[54]

The confiscated estates were maintained intact,[55] revenues from them deriving primarily from the sale of cattle financing the revolutionary government in Chihuahua and Villa's army. No immediate action was taken towards dividing the properties and distributing land to peasants, prompting Silvestre Terrazas in the summer of 1914 to jot down a "list of matters to discuss with General Villa," the first item of which was "the means for cultivating the confiscated lands, and whether they should be rented out or given with no rent for the first year."[56]

The fact that Francisco Villa maintained the large estates in Chihuahua and did not carry out an immediate redistribution of land is cited by his detractors, radical and conservative alike, as evidence that he lacked an agrarian ideology and had little interest in carrying out an agrarian reform. But studies by González Herrera (1988), Katz (1979), and Schulze (1990) call for another interpretation. Villa relied on income from the confiscated estates to support a large professional army (Katz 1988a:244). While he recognized the *zapatista* Plan de Ayala,

> it was never implemented in the North and did not constitute the basis of Villa's agrarian plans. . . . Villa was very conscious of the need to satisfy the demands of his important and radical peasant constituency . . . [and furthermore] linked [the] expropriation [of large estates] to agrarian reform. Only Villa had promised his soldiers that they would obtain land after the victory of the Revolution. . . . [However,] it would have been counterproductive for Villa to carry out an immediate land reform [and] could easily have led to mass desertions. (Katz 1988a:241–44)

Hence Villa could not afford to distribute land in 1914–15 and continue to field his army.

Mendieta y Nuñez's discussion of Villa's Agrarian Law of May 24, 1915 (Mendieta y Nuñez 1981:183ff.), follows Antonio Díaz Soto y Gama:

> The agrarian ideal of the men of the North was and is very different compared to the manner in which those of the South understood the problem. In the South the major preoccupation was with the restitution and *dotación* [granting] of communal lands to the pueblos. . . . For the *norteños* the solution lay in the division of the enormous estates and the creation of a great number of small private properties. (Mendieta y Nuñez 1981:183–84)

Villa's Agrarian Law stipulated that no individual would be given more land than they could cultivate (Mendieta y Nuñez 1981:185), since, as Díaz Soto y Gama wrote,

> The tremendous inequality in the distribution of property has had the consequence of leaving the great majority of Mexicans, the working class, subject to and dependents of a minority of landlords; this relation of dependence has impeded the elements of the working class from exercise of their civil and political rights. (quoted in Mendieta y Nuñez 1981:186)

Some confiscated goods, however, did not figure in Silvestre Terrazas's records. These were properties, large and small, that Villa expropriated, but rather than declare them property of the revolutionary state, he put them under the direct charge of military officers and personal friends.

The Hacienda de Santa Clara was in this second category.[57] Except that it no longer advanced claims against the lands of Namiquipa, Santa Clara was managed no differently after confiscation than before. Ranch hands were employees (*trabajadores de raya*) of the hacienda, and some peasants worked the fields as *medieros* (sharecroppers).[58] The first revolutionary administrator of Santa Clara, Telesforo Terrazas,[59] from Cruces, Namiquipa, was a personal friend of Villa's who had cooperated with him in his activities as bandit and cattle salesman in the decade before 1910. An officer in Villa's army at the time he administered Santa Clara, he ran it on his own behalf. Accounts of Telesforo's regime as administrator by his contemporaries as well as by relatives still living in Cruces and Namiquipa all agree that he was "given" Santa Clara by Villa as a personal sinecure. Revolutionary peasants objected to his arbitrary and high-handed manner, and he was killed by his own men, a personal escort which included at least one first cousin and a brother-in-law or two, in 1915.

The next Namiquipan put in charge of Santa Clara was Candelario Cervantes, whose story is very different. Cervantes was a revolutionary leader in Namiquipa whose uncle, Concepción Cervantes, had been in communication with the Flores Magon organization as early as 1905. In May 1912 Candelario commanded more than five hundred men—mostly from Namiquipa—in anti-*orozquista* campaigns.[60] In January and February 1913 he single-handedly mobilized more than one hundred men in less than two weeks to defend the revolution.[61] Rising through the *villista* ranks, Candelario Cervantes was a colonel and member of Villa's elite Dorados at the time he was appointed to administer Santa Clara in 1915. That appointment must have provided a certain ironic pleasure since Cervantes had been a sharecropper on Santa Clara before 1910. Long after he was killed in battle with U.S. Army forces in May 1916, he was accused of having put his own brand on cattle belonging to Santa Clara, as Telesforo Terrazas had, but the evidence for this is unconvincing, and the accusations had more to do with posthumous character assassination, especially by the owners of Santa Clara (AMN, AMCG *passim;* on Cervantes, see Alonso 1988c:213–15).

An evocative view of what an agrarian reform in the North would consist in was advanced by Villa himself in an interview with John Reed that appears in Reed's *Insurgent Mexico,* based on his months of participant observation with the Villa army in 1913–14. Here, in the midst of a social revolution, during a break from the military campaign, Villa invokes the past of pueblos such as Namiquipa to frame "the passionate dream—the vision which animates" him to struggle to shape the future (Reed 1969:144).

When the new Republic is established there will never be any more army in Mexico. Armies are the greatest support of tyranny. There can be no dictator without an army.

We will put the army to work. In all parts of the Republic we will establish military colonies composed of the veterans of the Revolution. The State will give them grants of agricultural lands and establish big industrial enterprises to give them work. Three days a week they will work and work hard, because honest work is more important than fighting, and only honest work makes good citizens. And the other three days they will receive military instruction and go out and teach all the people how to fight. Then, when the Patria is invaded, we will just have to telephone from the palace at Mexico City, and in half a day all the Mexican people will rise from their fields and factories, fully armed, equipped and organized to defend their children and their homes.

My ambition is to live my life in one of those military colonies among my *compañeros* whom I love, who have suffered so long and so deeply with me. (Villa in Reed 1969:144–45)

Around Namiquipa from 1911 until 1920, both landlords and the state—such as it was—were in retreat. Namiquipans seized the opportunity to realize Villa's dream, in its own way scarcely distinguishable from that of Teodoro de Croix as put forth in the Bando, except that now the enemies of the pueblo were not "barbaric Indians" but barbarian landlords and capitalists. The SCP became an important organizational form internal to the community through which to actualize this dream. Beginning in 1913 (and possibly earlier), the SCP gave *originario* peasants usufruct rights to plots within the *común repartimiento* lands.[62] During the years of the revolution, many of the same personnel participated in the popularly selected *ayuntamiento* (town council) and the SCP. But it was the latter administrative body that assigned agricultural plots to farmers, looked after the *terrenos de común repartimiento,* and settled disputes raised by Namiquipans regarding *posesiones.* It is surprising there was any planting done in Namiquipa during the revolutionary decade since hundreds of men from the town were mobilized, many fighting battles far from their pueblo.

That only points to the other (external) organizational forms which Namiquipans required to sustain the political possibility of actualizing Villa's dream, namely supra-community military organizations. These they found first in the Villa army (especially as soldiers or officers in the elite Dorados of the Division of the North) and later in the Defensas Sociales. From March 1913 through much of 1916 Namiquipa was an important center of *villismo,* and Villa scored notable victories in Chihuahua even just leading guerrilla forces until his surrender and retirement to the ranch of Canutillo in 1920. He was assassinated by order of the state three years later.[63] After 1915, however, many Namiquipans no longer perceived *villismo* as a viable avenue through which to press agrarian demands. Not only did *villismo* lack a supra-local institutional framework through which to validate agrarian claims, but Villa was no longer able to guarantee protection to his adherents and the towns from which they came.[64]

But by the middle of 1916, "the Revolution" as such in Mexico, and *villismo* in particular, no longer had a center (Gilly 1983). Villa had disbanded his Division of the North in December of 1915 after his crushing defeat in a major battle outside Agua Prieta, Sonora. On March 9, 1916, Villa began four and one-half years of guerrilla warfare against revolutionary caciques in Mexico (see Osorio 1988, 1990) and against the United States with his celebrated attack on Columbus, New Mexico (see Calzadíaz Barrera 1977; Katz 1979; Harris and Sadler 1988:7–23, 101–12). While many Namiquipans (20 percent of the force of 500 men) participated in the Columbus raid, the immediate consequences for the town were devastating from the standpoint of sustaining a viable, and *villista,* resistance to outsiders of whatever provenance. Within weeks of the raid, more than 2,500 (at times as many as 5,000) U.S. Army soldiers, members of the Pershing Punitive Expedition to Mexico, camped on the outskirts of town, where they stayed from April until June 1916.[65]

U.S. soldiers searching for Villa and any of his "bandits" (i.e., Namiquipans who had participated in the Columbus raid) broke into the houses of people, took nine men from the community prisoner, and confiscated some five hundred rifles and ten machine guns hidden near the town by *villista* soldiers.[66] Nevertheless, Namiquipans were impressed that U.S. soldiers paid with gold coins for cattle, hired workers, and forage.[67] A woman whose father spent five years in jail in the United States after his capture in Cruces pointed out that he had, after all, invaded the United States and went there to kill gringos. In her opinion, U.S. Army soldiers who took him off to jail were not unjustified; what angered her more was the Cruceño neighbor who denounced her father to the U.S. soldiers.[68]

The U.S. military did not intervene in the local agrarian struggle, indeed they were hardly aware it existed. They did, however, achieve something which was to have a profound impact on local politics and the way the community subsequently negotiated its position on the agrarian question with the revolutionary state. The Punitive Expedition was instrumental in establishing a local militia in Namiquipa. This militia was formed on May 23, 1916, according to General Pershing at his "suggestion," with what the gringos misconstrued as "non-combatants" (*pacíficos*),[69] as U.S. soldiers and intelligence agents described any Mexican who did not violently resist the North American invaders.[70] But these were hardly "peaceful" and timid people.

The first chief of the local militia—later employed as a spy by the United States—was the same José María Espinosa who had led Namiquipans during the *maderista* uprising in the winter of 1910–11. Many other members of this militia old enough to have fought between 1910 and 1916 had done so. The militia was set up to defend the pueblo from "revolutionary bands" or "bandits," that is, *villistas,* and, initially, to cooperate with the gringos. As the U.S. army withdrew from the region, Namiquipans subsequently cooperated with other similar militia calling themselves Defensas Sociales.[71] While the Defensas Sociales were organized in Chihuahua to fight *villistas*—and occasionally did so—their presence in a town also discouraged *carrancista* soldiers, who routinely committed depredations against peasant communities,[72] from entering the pueblos. But local and regional *jefes* of the Defensas Sociales such as Francisco Antillon of Namiquipa and Jesús Antonio Almeida of Bachinva allied their men with, and carried out orders from, the *carrancista* general, Ignacio C. Engíquez.

Established in Namiquipa during the brief American occupation of the pueblo, the Defensas Sociales became the principal local military organization in the town for the next decade. It is largely through the Defensas Sociales that the pueblo of Namiquipa negotiated its relationship to powers outside the community after 1916. While some Namiquipans remained *villista* to their death, on the whole, *villismo* had lost its attraction for most residents of the community after the Columbus attack. This was very important in the 1920s, when a certain form of peace was reestablished in Chihuahua, and conflicts over the land of Namiquipa reemerged in the wake of a period (the revolution) during which Namiquipans had exercised through the SCP a great deal of autonomy in determining their relationship to the land because there was no outside power capable of intervening in local affairs.

For a century and a half (1778–1920s) the inhabitants of Namiquipa fought outsiders for control of the land of the pueblo. They defeated the Apaches. By 1900 they were holding their own against large estates and in that regard present a contrast to other Chihuahuan towns—even other expresidios such as Janos or Galeana—which had lost their lands to haciendas. In the decade prior to 1910 Namiquipans resisted—

though not always successfully—the incursions of immigrants and then took up arms against the Porfirian and *terracista* governments, successfully recovering from the setbacks of 1905–10. Finally, during the revolutionary period they drove many of the immigrants out, restoring their "primordial" relationship to the land.

Through all these conflicts with outsiders, Namiquipans fought to preserve a general form of landholding for the pueblo as a whole. Legal stipulations operating, encouraged, or formalized—and sometimes enforced—as a function of the state's attempt to mediate the relationship of direct agricultural producers to the land were consistently challenged. The general form, worked out through Namiquipan's interpretation and implementation of the Bando, recognized individual rights to land vested through membership in the community; collective struggle (either military or through cooperation in production processes benefiting units larger than the individual household); working the land of which one has *posesión;* and consensual recognition that control and use of the land as a whole was mediated through the interests of the community, not of any individual or household.

Until brought into direct conflict with the state after the 1905 Municipal Lands Law, Namiquipans had defended their land, using whatever means and tactics were at hand, including legal argument, passive denial of new "legal" interventions, armed struggle, isolated struggle for particular plots of land, and alliances with other pueblos against the state or particular agents of the state. During the pre-1905 period Namiquipans did not eschew invoking the power of the state either passively (during the colonial period) or actively (1880s–90s) by advancing petitions to national authorities against a range of invaders, usurpers, or forces that threatened to change the relationship of Namiquipans to the land. After 1905 the terms of struggle shifted. A few people responded positively to the radical appeal of the Partido Liberal Mexicano, which in September 1905 issued a call for a "holy war" (*una lucha santa*) against the Porfirian state (see Bartra 1977:174–75 for reproduction of this PLM document). And five years later, the majority of Namiquipans unhesitatingly threw themselves into the struggle against the state.

From the colonial period through the revolution Namiquipans never conceded to the state the power to alter the relationship of Namiquipans to the land which had been established by the 1778 Bando. The state never successfully imposed a supersession of what Namiquipans regarded as their primordial rights. The state's attempt to recast the relationship of people to land and the very definitions of "rights" and "land" in the 1880s and 1890s were simply ignored, negated by the Namiquipans' own appropriation, interpretation, and recasting of the state's edicts and rulings. The state-directed effort to alienate Namiquipans from control of the land in the 1900s was violently resisted from 1910 onward.

LAND IN A PERIOD OF TRANSITION

After 1916, the Defensas Sociales (whose members were called *socialistas*) dominated the town politically and were the community's principal link to powers outside Namiquipa. There was nothing particularly socialist about the agenda of these *socialistas*, however, nor revolutionary about their behavior. To the extent that the local project of community reconstruction and self-defense from 1916 on paralleled the earlier project of construction and defense against the Apaches, the formation of the Defensas was a throwback to the colonial period. But the very different objective circumstances framing the emergence of the Defensas Sociales in Namiquipa and the surrounding region as opponents of the Villa forces (and any other "outsiders," for that matter) indicates that this was also a period during which local leaders could negotiate the relationship of their communities to the emerging postrevolutionary state.

By 1919 Defensas Sociales controlled the region around Namiquipa. *Villistas* no longer operated in the area, and neither did *carrancista* troops harass the populace. Namiquipan *villistas* were either dead, in jail, in exile in the United States, or fighting alongside Villa elsewhere in Chihuahua, or they had joined the Defensas or just retired from the fighting.[73] *Socialista* cooperation with the Constitutionalist general, Ignacio C. Enríquez, deprived *carrancistas* from outside the region of any pretext to meddle in local affairs.

Also in 1919, the owners of Santa Clara, led by Enrique Müller's daughter, María, and her husband, Agustín Domínguez,[74] began efforts to reassume control of the hacienda. Writing to the *carrancista* military governor of Chihuahua with a complaint that armed men were occupying the hacienda, they asked that civil and military authorities effect their removal.[75] They also demanded the return of Santa Clara cattle seized by Namiquipans during the revolution.[76]

In October and November of the same year, the inhabitants of Cruces and Namiquipa formed popular juntas to conduct a survey of each pueblo's lands. Their surveys determined that since Namiquipa and Cruces were less than 8 leagues apart, Teodoro de Croix's "4 leagues to a wind" formula for each town resulted in the overlap of their 1778 grants. Namiquipans and Cruceños resolved the issue of overlapping boundaries in popular juntas. The criteria according to which the boundary between the pueblos was fixed had to do with *posesión*. Since Namiquipans had in the past used some of the "overlapping" lands, while Cruceños never had, much of the overlap went to Namiquipa, a point reflected later in the Presidential Resolutions, which established the *ejidos* of Namiquipa and Cruces in 1926.[77]

The Müllers kept up their appeals to the military governor of Chihuahua to have properties in Namiquipa, including Aranzazu and Carmen (i.e., all lands east of the Río Santa María), returned to them. Until the installation of Gen. Ignacio C. Enríquez as the first postrevolutionary constitutional governor of Chihuahua in late 1920, state authorities were incompetent to act on the Müllers' request. In 1921 the Müllers and the people of Namiquipa and Cruces, represented by Reyes Ortiz (then municipal president of Namiquipa), agreed to submit the dispute for arbitration by Governor Enríquez.[78] On March 3,1992, Enríquez delivered his judgment that Namiquipa, Cruces, and Galeana each "have legitimate right to 64 *sitios de ganado mayor*" of land, and that "the heirs of Enrique Müller have no right to the lands which fall within the area[s]" referred to.[79]

That clear, unequivocal settlement of the dispute at the state level was rejected by the Müllers, satisfied only with their argument based on owning titles to the land. Namiquipans reiterated their argument based on 143 years of uninterrupted—if not always unchallenged—possession of the land. While the dispute between *hacendados* and the *serrano* peasants remained unresolved, a potentially violent confrontation was at the same time brewing within the pueblo of Namiquipa. There a conflict emerged over whether the land of the pueblo should be administered by a popular organization (the SCP) or the municipal council, the local representative of government and the state.

During the years he was municipal president (1921 and 1922), Reyes Ortiz, who had been legal representative for Cruces and Namiquipa for more than a decade (and also had a personal conflict with Cornelio Espinosa, head of the SCP, dating back to the 1880s), took it upon himself and his *ayuntamiento* (municipal council) to administer the lands of Namiquipa. The *presidencia* assumed the authority to do what the SCP had done during most of the revolution: grant permission for individuals to work parcels and recognize or deny individuals' *posesiones*. As municipal president, though, Ortiz did more, charging rent for municipal lands. Many Namiquipans regarded Reyes Ortiz's actions as no more legitimate than the sales of municipal lands carried out between 1905 and 1910 by Victoriano Torres.[80]

Conflicts between the Ortiz administration and the SCP were mediated by Mariano Irigoyen, a deputy of the Chihuahuan Congress, and on July 30, 1921, the Municipal Council agreed to accept the SCP's authority to administer the land grant. In practice, however, Ortiz continued his prior policy. Cornelio Espinosa died in 1922, and Ortiz resigned his

post as municipal president on June 24 of the same year, probably due
to popular feeling against him. However, conflicts between the SCP and
the Municipal Council continued since Ortiz's replacement, Anastacio
Tena, continued renting "municipal land" and issuing permits for cultivation in the *terrenos de común repartimiento*, while Tena's Municipal
Council named Ortiz as Namiquipa's agrarian representative in the ongoing conflict with the owners of Santa Clara, who had chosen to ignore
Enríquez's March ruling (see Nugent and Alonso 1994).

The conflict within the pueblo and the conflict with the heirs of
Enrique Müller were both "resolved" toward the end of 1922. Anxious
to obtain legal guarantees for the community's land rights and block any
efforts by Santa Clara's owners to usurp their land, 133 Namiquipan
men (including SCP activist José Rascón y Tena) submitted a petition to
Governor Enríquez and the Comisión Local Agraria on November 18,
1922, requesting restitution of all lands from the colonial period grant
that *hacendados* threatened to invade.[81] This effort to take advantage of
the radical agrarian legislation written into the constitution of 1917 by
having the lands of Namiquipa turned into a postrevolutionary *ejido* was
soon pushed most forcefully by Reyes Ortiz, who quickly took over the
Comité Particular Administrativo of the *ejido*. As a result of the request
for an *ejido*, neither the *ayuntamiento* nor the SCP would any longer be
able to fight over which group would administer the lands and lead the
fight against the Müller and Hearst invasions. Those powers were conceded to the revolutionary state itself, by the willingness to accept as
legitimate whatever resolution of the agrarian question the Comisión
Nacional Agraria dictated.

By requesting an *ejido* on November 18, 1922, the Namiquipans lost
the struggle to determine the manner in which they would control their
own lands. Turning over all conflicts—whether internal to the pueblo
or between the pueblo and outsiders—to the state for resolution implied
acceptance of the revolutionary state's authority to override all previous
legal, political, and military tactics and initiatives they had developed
over the previous century and a half for maintaining pueblo autonomy
and popular control of the land. Forgetting popular tactics such as they
had developed against the Apaches and later used against *hacendados*
and the Porfirian state, and accepting instead terms for making their
living from the land that were dictated by the state, they set themselves
up to lose control of the land. This shift had the result that from 1922
until the present, the state secured a power it had never before enjoyed
to mediate the relationship of direct agricultural producers to their land.

4
Agrarian Reform in Western Chihuahua, 1920s

THE REVOLUTIONARY STATE AND THE AGRARIAN REFORM

The basic problem confronting the colonial state in Chihuahua at the end of the eighteenth century may be synthesized in a phrase: securing the control of a territory. Peoples inhabiting the region had to be identified and mechanisms for an orderly exploitation and transformation of the region established. The problems confronting the revolutionary state in Chihuahua in the 1920s were more complexly determined from both without and within. The limits of national territory had been redefined when the United States stole half the Mexican territory in the middle of the nineteenth century. The army of Francisco Villa surrendered in July 1920, and *carrancista* troops backed by Defensas Sociales controlled the countryside. The popular classes were exhausted by a decade of fighting, and *hacendados* were making the first tentative steps to recover—or sell off—properties in Chihuahua.

What sorts of administrative organizations could realistically be expected to function in such a period? Popular organizations? A state-controlled bureaucracy? Massive capitalist enterprises operating with relatively little state intervention? What would happen to the land in the countryside in light of the progressive agrarian policy written into the Constitution of 1917? Did the agrarian reform in Chihuahua provide a link between the years of revolution and subsequent decades of community-state relations? The postrevolutionary state's response to agrarian demands in Chihuahua alone provides examples of the variety and range of strategies implemented and advances and setbacks experienced by an equally heterogenous plurality of social groups, the compositions of which were in any event hardly stable. This is demonstrated by the fate of the large estates in Chihuahua and the lands of the peasant communities.

Carranza's (actually Luis Cabrera's) Agrarian Law of January 6, 1915, provided for the return of lands to villagers who had been illegally dispossessed. Article 27 of the Constitution of 1917 declared the state the

owner of lands and subsoil rights, of which control had been usurped
or acquired illegally between 1856 and 1915. Thanks to Villa's 1913–15
expropriations,[1] the state controlled the massive properties Luis Terrazas
had assembled between the 1860s and 1900s. In 1920 there was debate
at all levels of society regarding what to do with them.[2]

One plan involved selling the Terrazas lands as a block to a North
American developer, MacQuatters, who intended to parcel and colonize
them, possibly with North American settlers.[3] While receiving the support of Chihuahuan governor Ignacio C. Enríquez and a sympathetic
ear from President Obregón and important elements of the Comisión
Nacional Agraria (CNA), in the end this plan was not put into effect.
Instead the Mexican government purchased the lands from Terrazas and
developed them itself, here creating irrigation districts for *pequeños propietarios*, there donating lands to villagers for the establishment of *ejidos*,
elsewhere preserving them as state-owned lands. The fact that the new
revolutionary regime took the MacQuatters proposal seriously at all provides some indication of the character of the "popular" and "agrarian"
interests which immediately found a voice at the highest levels of state
power in the early 1920s.

The Terrazas-Creels got off lightly. Handsomely compensated for their
rural landholdings, they were also allowed to keep hundreds of urban
and mining properties acquired *during the course of the revolution*.[4] Other
large landowners in Chihuahua, uncertain of how the Agrarian Law
would affect their properties, arrogantly challenged the legitimacy of
the state to seize their estates, at the same time desperately racing to
sell them off before massive expropriations that were feared but never
occurred.[5]

Landholdings around Namiquipa belonged to the Müllers (Santa
Clara) to the east, the Zuloagas (southeast of the pueblo), and Hearsts
(San José de Babicora y Anexas, south and west of the pueblo). Santa
Clara was sold off in bits and pieces during the 1920s and 1930s, much
of the hacienda's southern edge purchased by Mennonite immigrants
from Canada. In 1935 a 40,000-hectare parcel was sold to a small
group of wealthy Namiquipans. Felipe Loya, Cristóbal Vásquez, and
Francisco V. Antillon, former *jefe* of the Defensas Sociales, paid for the
property with a loan advanced by Enrique Seyffert for five years at 5 percent (AGRA e.C-3521, t.1.). The Zuloaga ranching property around La
Quemada, Rubio, and San Antonio was sold to Mennonite farmers. The
Mennonites paid more than ten times the going rate for grazing land
under the mistaken notion that it was suitable for agriculture (Whetten
1948:160). Sales to Mennonites required the eviction and/or dispossession of members of farming communities that had worked the land
through the years of the revolution.[6] The American-owned Hearst ha-

cienda was maintained intact until the 1950s. Until 1934, the Agrarian Law did not permit hacienda peons to petition for lands from the estates on which they worked. Peasant and squatter communities in Babicora Baja on the plains southwest of Namiquipa and near La Quemada to the southeast, surrounded by large estates, had difficulty appealing for land.[7]

In short, with the exception of the Terrazas, Chihuahuan landowners, especially North Americans, were not immediately affected by the revolutionary Agrarian Law in the 1920s and 1930s. While they had suffered losses during the revolution, those had been losses of cattle, buildings, crops, and other movable property or resources, not definitive losses of land, which is what they feared from the revolution.[8] Records of the Mexican-American Mixed Claims Commission demonstrate that the expropriations suffered by U.S. landowners in Mexico after the revolution affected relatively few North American landholdings. The Agency of the United States for the Mixed Claims Commission studied "Agrarian Expropriations of American Owned Lands in Mexico, January 1, 1914 to June 1, 1927," finding there had been only 135 seizures totaling 284,975 hectares of U.S.-owned land in that period (WNRA RG 76, e.145, no.18). Ten of those seizures, accounting for more than a third of the land area expropriated from U.S. owners, took place in Chihuahua. Still, the figure of less than 300,000 hectares (around 100,000 in Chihuahua) represents only a small proportion of U.S.-owned properties in Mexico (see Hart 1988:73; Hart 1987).[9]

Alongside the expropriation of properties illegally acquired between 1856 and 1915, the agrarian reform was supposed to distribute land to peasants, villagers, and groups of rural workers who petitioned for lands. The latter process, however, did not get underway to any significant degree until the second half of the 1930s. It is notorious that Venustiano Carranza, promulgator of the Agrarian Law of 1915, scarcely distributed any land to peasants and in fact returned many large estates to their previous owners (Katz 1988a). President Obregón (1920–24) saw little merit in distributing land to villagers, instead seeing the future of Mexican agriculture in large-scale capitalist enterprises (Reyes et al. 1970:82ff.). Plutarco Elías Calles was no more enthusiastic than Obregón about distributing land to peasants and villagers. Although Calles initially speeded up the process of land distribution upon assuming office, by the end of his Maximato (the ten-year period ending in 1934) the pace of distribution had slowed to one scarcely greater than that achieved during Carranza's rule.[10]

There were two ways land could be distributed to peasant communities under the revolutionary agrarian legislation: by returning lands that had been taken from villagers illegally (restitución) or by the state granting land to villagers (*dotación*). The distinction between *restitución* and *dotación* is extremely important for understanding community-state relations in Mexico generally after the revolution. Since illegal dispossession was difficult to prove in light of the absence of documentation corroborating villagers' prior possession of land, the architects of the agrarian reform invented the method of *dotación* to have the legal means to distribute more land (Whetten 1948:129–30). Insofar as this is merely a procedural distinction—and the desired end of delivering land to the peasantry is the same in both events—Whetten may be correct. But the point is, Mexicans who petitioned for land often wanted *their own* land, even if they lacked the documentation to demonstrate that it was theirs in the first place. Securing a restitution was justice, while securing a *dotación* was an insult, a matter of the state posturing as a *patrón* (see A. Bartra 1985).

Some villages and groups of peasants did get land in the 1920s and early 1930s. A significant point is that many of the first redistributions were in strategically sensitive regions. The state granted land to communities whose people had waged a decade of armed struggle to resecure control of the lands, for example *zapatista* villages in Morelos (Womack 1969). But even there, popular demands for restitution of popular or communal control of land were denied; the state insisted on giving land to the villages through *dotación*. This happened in Emiliano Zapata's home town of Anenecuilco.[11] Morelenses' decade-long demonstration that a popular regime of property was possible (Gilly [1971] 1983) was negated by the postrevolutionary state. By "giving" land to the peasantry, the state was denying that peasants had any *right* to the land except that right *bestowed* by the state.

Another controversial issue is the contrast between the amount of land distributed to peasants in these years and the amount remaining in large properties in private hands.[12] Many of the millions of hectares of land given to peasants after the revolution were not suitable for agriculture (Whetten 1948:138; Stavenhagen 1970), and many more remained in private hands, more than half of that in large estates. In 1930 Mexico was still "predominantly a country of haciendas and hacendados," with 3 percent of the private properties (10,000 hectares or more) comprising more than 55 percent of the privately held land (Simpson, quoted in Reyes et al. 1970, 1:28). In 1940, when less than 1,500 private properties larger than 10,000 hectares comprised 50 percent of the privately held land in the country as a whole (Reyes et al. 1970:28), the situation was different only because by then the massive land distributions of the Cárdenas years (more than 20 million hectares between 1934 and 1940) had created a considerably expanded *ejidal* sector.

Land reform proceeded very slowly until the late 1930s. In the early years, "agrarian reform" was a *political* solution to a *political* problem that involved making concessions to and occasionally even empowering the most highly organized elements of the popular classes in the countryside. But the agrarian reform in Mexico barely began to deal with the unequal distribution of instruments and means of production in the countryside, and Mexico was still predominantly a country of large landholdings even after decades of "agrarian reform" (cf. Reyes et al. 1970; Feder 1970; Grindle 1986). What was happening in western Chihuahua after the revolution?

REVOLUTIONARY PUEBLOS AND THE STATE

As the Chihuahuan oligarchy retrenched or sold off properties in the face of the revolutionary promise to redistribute land, Chihuahuan peasants attempted to secure the benefits of that promise. Such was the case particularly in former presidios. Their inhabitants had been fighting since decades before the revolution for recognition of rights in land. But while sharing a tradition of struggle, not all these towns had arrived at the same point by the 1920s, faring unevenly in conflicts with landlords after the end of the Apache Wars.

No other town in Chihuahua retained control of as much land as did Namiquipa in the early 1920s. Janos, for example, was invaded by the United States–owned Hacienda de Corralitos; Enrique Müller's El Alamo Hueco; Los Hermanos Mápula (including a property purchased from E. Creel); and Luis García Teruel, who had earlier operated a surveying company. Galeana was carved up by a half dozen properties, including Santana del Torreón (E. Müller); Hacienda Ojo de Arrey (Ponce Hermanos); Santiago (Fco. Prieto y Hermanos); and San Miguel de Babicora, San Luis, and El Carmen (all Luis Terrazas). The total area invaded was more than 100,000 hectares. Cruces was invaded by Luis Terrazas's San Miguel de Babicora; the Hacienda Las Bocas, owned by a consortium of Chihuahuan ranchers; and Santa Clara.[13] The Müller and Hearst invasions of Namiquipa, on the other hand, had not been successful in practice, so the situation in the former presidios was not identical.

But they had several things in common. First, more than other pueblos in Chihuahua, the excolonies had suffered the effects of the 1905 Municipal Lands Law.[14] Second, these pueblos had provided the vanguard of rural Chihuahuans who armed themselves to overthrow the Díaz government in 1910 (Calzadíaz Barrera [1958] 1979; Olea Arias 1961; Duarte Morales 1968; Katz 1981:8ff.; Wasserman 1980). Third, these pueblos continued to fight through the decade of the revolution, the vindication of rights in land providing a centrally important motivation for continued mobilization (cf. Lloyd 1988 on Janos and Galeana; Alonso 1986 on Namiquipa and Cruces).

The agrarian basis of the popular mobilizations in Chihuahua has until recently been little understood or misunderstood. The northern movement(s), *villismo* in particular, were, as Alan Knight points out, for a long time routinely dismissed as "aimless mercenary rowdyism" in contrast to the coherent, communalist popular agrarian movement in the South, *zapatismo* (see Womack 1969; Gilly [1971] 1983; Warman 1988b; Aguilar Camin et al. 1979). But in the last decade convincing challenges to that caricature have been advanced.[15] In light of the information on agrarian revolts in the Guerrero District of Chihuahua presented by Ana Alonso (1986), Alan Knight wrote, "Indeed, it seems likely I was sometimes overcautious [in *The Mexican Revolution*, 1986] in my reemphasis of the peasant/agrarian factor, especially in Chihuahua" (1988:27).

Finally, the former presidios all petitioned for restitution of their lands in 1922. The petitions were seconded by the Comisión Local Agraria (CLA) in Chihuahua and, when brought before the CNA in the spring of 1926, hastily approved (CNA.RP; CNA.Actas passim). These towns appear at first glance to be the sites of "successful" agrarian struggles where the pueblos were the immediate beneficiaries of the state's radical agrarian policy.

The evidence, however, calls for differentiating between the agrarian struggles in the distinct former military settlement colonies. Janos, like Namiquipa, produced important *villista* officers, notably Porfirio Talamantes, agrarian leader in Janos before the revolution (Katz 1992:279; Lloyd 1988; ATN e.75−1407, 22-viii-1922), and so far as is known the people of Janos never betrayed Villa. But Galeana, the site of PLM agitation in the decade before the revolution, had supported Villa's fiercest enemies, the *orozquistas*. Galeanenses later failed to recover their lands under Villa since in 1914−15 he confiscated and maintained intact the very haciendas which invaded Galeana (Jane-Dale Lloyd, pers. com.; BL.AST). Namiquipa recovered control of its lands early in the revolution and, along with Cruces, was thoroughly *villista* until the spring of 1916, when members of the Pershing Punitive Expedition characterized it as "the most revolutionary *pueblo* in Mexico" (Tompkins 1934:80).[16] But it then became the site of one of the first anti-*villista* Defensas Sociales in the state, its fate closely linked to that of the Constitutionalist armies (Nugent 1985; Alonso 1988c).

In other words, in each of these pueblos "the agrarian struggle" cannot be conflated with agrarian struggles occurring elsewhere. They were not instances of a national mass movement. Rather, "the mass movement" bore the echoes of myriad diverse movements and fights, each shaped by its own history; the qualities of the land in different regions and towns; the practices developed by the inhabitants of those towns in the course of engaging the land in production; and the actions of groups which successfully or unsuccessfully dispossessed them. These were local struggles *which articulated themselves* with regional and national movements for restoration of the land and reordering of production relations. The different movements were recorded differently in the social memories of the inhabitants of the various pueblos from one place to the next, the range of experiences also reflected in distinct attitudes toward the postrevolutionary agrarian reform and the new system of *ejidos* it put into effect.

The restitutions made to these pueblos were enormous, though. Namiquipa alone recovered 12.5 percent of the land distributed *in the entire Republic* in 1926. Together, Namiquipa, Cruces, Galeana, and Janos received more than 45 percent of all land distributed in that year (Whetten 1948:125; Reyes et al. 1970, 1:86; CNA.RP passim). Further, these four pueblos received their lands as *restituciones,* a notoriously rare way of forming *ejidos* under the Agrarian Law.[17] That former presidios received land as *restitución* and not as *dotación* demonstrates the value of their colonial legacy and their tradition as homes to Apache fighters and veterans of the first stage of the revolution—points repeatedly mentioned in the Presidential Resolutions and in the Dictamen del Perito Paleografo, included in the file on Namiquipa that was reviewed by the CNA.[18] But it also underlines the state's fear that were it to deny these pueblos their land, there would be continued violence in the countryside of Chihuahua.

In a meeting of the CNA held June 23, 1926, the agricultural engineer responsible for preparing petitions from Chihuahua, Manuel Fitzmaurice, brought the files of Namiquipa and other pueblos to the agenda and argued strongly in favor of recommending restitution. Ing. Luis León, president of the CNA, was opposed. According to the minutes of the meeting, León saw in such restitutions

> a great inconvenience for the development of that region. For he [León] knows the ideology of the inhabitants of those places, who are going to want to enjoy a privileged situation, and neither apply their labor to water works nor even initiate work on the basic improvements the land requires. What those peasants do is set themselves up in distinct places, forming their ranches and under-utilizing the rest of the land.

Fitzmaurice responded that

> it is precisely for the reasons expressed by Señor Ingeniero León that he [Fitzmaurice] has formulated a memorandum . . . to the

end that if the CNA approves it, it be submitted for consideration to the President of the Republic so that he might give his opinion regarding this problem [i.e., the restitutions to Namiquipa, Cruces, Galeana, Casas Grandes, and Janos]; and that in the event that the President is opposed it would be a good idea to send some Agricultural Engineers to inform the pueblos in person that the restitutions are not going through, something which might cause many difficulties, of which the President of the Republic is doubtless aware.[19]

The language of this exchange was very muted and polite. León argued that Chihuahuan *serranos* were spoiled and idle peasants who would not develop the land. Fitzmaurice suggested that peasant demands should be met and the restitutions should go through, precisely because of their ideology; if not, there would be continued rural violence. In the end, the files were forwarded to President Calles with the recommendation that the restitutions be approved, and Calles signed resolutions to that effect for Namiquipa and Cruces on August 5, 1926.

A list of the earliest *ejidos* established in Chihuahua is a roll call of the most famous pueblos whose inhabitants fought in the revolution and, earlier still, in Apache campaigns.[20] The positive correlations between extent of popular mobilization, experience and skill in the arts of violence, and the early dates of these postrevolutionary *ejidos* indicates that granting *ejidos* was as much a military reward or trophy as it was an attempt to transform the agrarian structure of society. However, the assumption by inhabitants of the pueblos of control of the land is only partially explained by the degree of mobilization—spontaneous, popular, and aggressive—achieved during the 1910s. Another consideration is the frightening image years of popular mobilization left weighing on the minds of state functionaries—and to which Fitzmaurice alluded—in the 1920s.

Joseph and Katz have written about the vision of an uncontrolled "Nature" embodied in peasant and especially Indian uprisings in central and southern Mexico (Joseph 1988:180–84, 190–91; Katz 1988c, 1988d). Such a frightening vision has shaken the imaginations of Mexican ruling classes from the mid-nineteenth century to the present, and indeed since the colonial period. It was evident in Chihuahua before and after the revolution (see Creel 1928). A similar rhetorical figure, combining rebelliousness or political radicalism with barbarity or savagery, operates in official discourse about *magonista* uprisings in the decade before the revolution. That is surprising only because the *magonistas* articulated a sophisticated, modernist, anti-imperialist ideology and program (see Cockcroft 1968; Bartra 1977). This confused indexing of political "rebels" as "savages" also occurs in Mexican Foreign Relations Ministry documents, which uncritically quote the *El Paso Morning Times* to the effect that, "There have been rumours that the Temosachics and Yaquis might cooperate in the attack on the jail [in Casas Grandes, Chihuahua] and after releasing the prisoners take to the mountain fastness."[21] The Yaquis are native Americans who were terrorized during the Porfiriato to remove them from their fertile lands in Sonora. *Temosachic,* however, is simply a Tarahumara place-name and the name of a pueblo (of Mexicans as well as Tarahumaras) in the Guerrero District, from which many rebels came between 1880 and 1910.

The early land redistributions in Chihuahua were above all political solutions to political problems. The ways specific *ejidos* in particular regions would or would not address the agrarian question in a socially just manner figures only indirectly in many of the deliberations (CNA.Actas passim). The establishment of *ejidos* in former military settlement colonies bore echoes of the colonial period, when the Spanish Crown granted land to colonists. But if they were in one sense throwbacks to the colonial period, they were also an anticipation of the future, a future characterized by a more rigorously regulated relationship of domination and dependence between the state and the pueblos. The evident success of popular struggles for land in Chihuahua was in the end overdetermined by the peasants' new and subordinate relationship to the revolutionary state (A. Bartra 1985:20ff.). The postrevolutionary *ejidos* provided a new set of terms according to which community and state were related via the land, with the state seizing and making its own at least half of the popular slogan, "Tierra y Libertad." The way this resulted in a new conflict between community and state predicated on divergent agrarian ideologies is well illustrated by what occurred in Namiquipa in the years following the revolution.

THE FORMATION OF THE *EJIDO* IN NAMIQUIPA

At the start of the 1920s there remained two unresolved conflicts over land in Namiquipa: the old dispute with the owners of Santa Clara, and the argument within the pueblo between officers of the Municipal Council and the SCP over which group would administer the pueblo lands. Governor Enríquez's March 1922 ruling that the rights of Namiquipans to the disputed land were unquestionable and the Santa Clara claims without merit, and the Namiquipans' petition for restitution of their lands as an *ejido* in November of the same year laid the first conflict to rest. The second conflict—between an organization of state rule and a popular organization—continued into the 1920s, even as it was transformed into a conflict between the community as a whole and the national state.

It is important to distinguish between Chihuahua government officials' encouragement of the SCP and the efforts of the national state, through the CNA, to destroy it. The first is evident in the Chihuahuan government's attitude to the SCP between 1921 and 1925. In addition to the rulings favoring the SCP over the Ortiz administration in 1921, and Namiquipa over Santa Clara in 1922, after 1923 the municipal president and Municipal Council were expressly forbidden by their Chihuahuan superiors from playing an active role in the administration of Namiquipa's lands. Jesús Muchárraz, procurador general de justicia interino of Chihuahua, indicated the reasons behind the state government's position. Writing in 1925, Muchárraz commented that he had seen "testimonies of General Enríquez and the Secretaría de Fomento in which they give importance to the agreements and resolutions" of the SCP, adding that since the SCP "is a Society integrated by many Members, all agriculturalists of the region, a resolution dictated against their interests could give rise to serious conflicts and upheavals between the Government and the Society."[22]

This attitude of the Chihuahuan government to the SCP contrasts with that of the CNA, the agrarian reform apparatus of the state in the 1920s, and its regional-level branch, the CLA. In 1922, the CLA authorized the Municipal Council, headed by Ortiz, to give out land permits until the Comité Particular Administrativo (CPA), the local *ejidal* organization, could be established in Namiquipa.[23] Beginning in 1925, the CNA did everything possible to replace the SCP, an autonomous peasant organization, with the CPA, a local branch of its own administrative structure.

The petition for an *ejido* had been forwarded to the CLA to conduct a study on the basis of which the governor of Chihuahua could make a recommendation to the CNA.[24] In March 1925 the CLA recommendation (positive) was passed back to the governor's office, then occupied by Jesus Antonio Almeida. Almeida, a well-off *serrano* from Bachiniva, had been a commander of the Defensas Sociales in Chihuahua until 1920. Almeida's recommendation in favor of the Namiquipan request had the result of provoking another struggle within the town between the SCP and Reyes Ortiz. On August 29, 1925, the municipal president of Namiquipa called on the pueblo's men to attend a meeting during which they would elect representatives to the CPA, the local branch of the state's new agrarian apparatus, and receive provisional possession of Namiquipa's *ejido*.[25] Despite the president's threat that those not attending the meeting would be penalized "according to the law," fewer than forty peasants showed up.[26] Reyes Ortiz became head of the CPA.

Meanwhile the town's file was sent to the CNA in Mexico City. The petition was hastily approved in 1926 along with petitions from Cruces, Galeana, Casas Grandes, and Janos.[27] In August of that year representatives of the CNA arrived in town to "turn over" the lands to the peasants.[28] Namiquipa's was to be a staggeringly large *ejido* of almost 100,000 hectares.[29] The land was being "returned" to a community whose inhabitants had fought throughout the revolutionary decade.[30] The *ejido* would put an end to any attempt by outsiders—large landlords or petty bourgeois immigrants—to control the land. However it only was granted with strings firmly attached—to the state—a feature some Namiquipans were aware of during the summer of 1926.

The very act of forming the *ejido* in Namiquipa indexed subsequent relations between the community and the state. The ironical character of events surrounding this event embodied resonances of the conflicting popular and official agrarian ideologies apparent even in this preliminary moment. Furthermore it demonstrates Ingeniero Fitzmaurice's foresight in warning the CNA about the dangers of sending agricultural engineers to Namiquipa with bad news about the *restitución,* though for reasons quite different from those Fitzmaurice anticipated (see discussion earlier in this chapter).

On August 22, 1926, Municipal President Moncerrate García León called two hundred Namiquipan men to a meeting with agricultural engineers from the CNA, who were to give them definitive possession of the *ejido.* As Ing. Miguel Lizama later wrote, at this meeting "a disagreeable incident occurred, provoked by a certain number of the members of the so-called Civil Society . . . who refused to receive the lands in accordance with the Agrarian Law."[31] At the very moment their agrarian rights were being recognized by the state and the lands returned to them, the Namiquipans attempted to snatch defeat from the jaws of victory! After the CNA engineer Gustavo Talamantes announced he was commissioned to "turn over" the *ejido* to the pueblo, a Namiquipan, Refugio Licano, responded that "he did not recognize the Agrarian Law" (i.e., Carranza's law of January 15, 1915). Arcadio Maldonado, a former *villista* and revolutionary leader, said the *ejido* "is nice, but the pueblo fears its connection with the Agrarian Law," adding that Namiquipans were "happier with their own pieces of paper." The only individual recorded as having spoken in favor of the *ejido* at the meeting was Francisco Antillon, former chief of the Defensas Sociales in Namiquipa.[32]

As Talamantes wrote a month later,

At that meeting a group of Namiquipans led by the directors of a so-called "Civil Society" . . . made it clear they did not agree [with the *ejido*] . . . ; and furthermore explained that they had the understanding the Presidential Resolution was not necessary in order for the lands to continue to be theirs, since previous governments had also declared the lands belonged to them.[33]

Another objectionable feature of the Agrarian Law was a circular (no. 51) attached to it, ordering that *ejidatarios* give up 15 percent of their harvest to the *ejido*.

According to the CNA report, 118 of the 200 Namiquipans in attendance at the August 22 meeting were in favor of accepting possession of the *ejido*, and 83 opposed. Yet only 22 signed their names to the *acta*, confirming popular assent to the *ejido* (and several of these signed twice!). The first signature was Francisco V. Antillon's, and other of the signatories were members of Antillon's armed "Mafia," former members of the Defensas Sociales who worked as the police force in Namiquipa during the 1920s.[34] Reyes Ortiz also signed. Some of the 83 "*inconformes*" sarcastically claimed they had forgotten how to sign their names.[35]

But some did sign, just as four years earlier some had initiated the petition for restitution of Namiquipa's land. Antillon had been the leader of the Defensas Sociales in 1920 and a local protégé of Ignacio C. Enríquez. His commitment to the idea of the *ejido* probably had more to do with an interest in climbing the ladder of state politics than any strong commitment to agrarian reform in Chihuahua.

In the months that followed, Namiquipans complained to the Chihuahuan government about "irregularities" in the CPA's administration of the *ejido* and in May of 1927 called for the removal of its president, Reyes Ortiz.[36] Elections for new officers of the CPA were held in Namiquipa on February 6, 1928, and Ortiz was replaced by Adolfo Delgado, a founding member of the SCP and its interim president in 1924.[37] According to the representative of the CNA present for the election, over 60 percent of the "*ejidatarios*" attended the meeting, and all of them stated that

> they did not want the Agrarian Law, that they were better off before, that recently the extension of the land was less than what they possessed earlier, that they did not need cooperatives, that they were happy to work only with their plows. . . . Likewise they showed themselves unwilling to contribute the 15% [of their harvests to the CPA], saying that they were willing instead to pay [property] taxes, if possible $100 each, but not to pay the 15% [quota to the *ejido*]. . . .

The *ejidatarios* who knew how to sign would not sign the Certificate of Election either, saying, once again, that they did not want the Agrarian Law, explaining this once and for all, and that they would accept none of its acts.[38]

A few days later, the CNA official wrote that during this meeting the Namiquipans led by Arcadio Maldonado and Antonio Duarte, another founding member of the SCP, had spoken in "pure barbarisms to which I paid no attention," adding that by refusing to sign anything to do with the Agrarian Law, they demonstrated "a total lack of consciousness and an absolute ignorance, refusing to understand the explanations that the *suscritor* made to them; some of them said that they had forgotten their names."[39]

In disrupting these state rituals, Namiquipan men deployed an insolent humor that contested the state's rules of the game and challenged the power of inscription that codified these rules (much as earlier rebels and revolutionaries had derided the power of the official word by urinating on government documents). Their humor played with the stereotype of the illiterate, ignorant, irrational, backwards, reactionary, and recalcitrant peasant that was held by the bureaucrats of the agrarian reform. Paradoxically, through their feigned ignorance of their own names or their ability to sign them, Namiquipans refused to play the role of docile and grateful *ejidatarios*. They in fact made a mockery of these populist state rituals in which the state's authority was contingent on the pueblo's submissive authorization and literal inscription of their names to its acts. Peasants' sarcastic challenges to the state's power of codification, their claim that they were "happier with their own pieces of paper" and "better off before," and their refusal to sign or give their names were all interpreted by CNA representatives as signs of "absolute ignorance."

DEFORMATION OF THE *EJIDO*

The surprising turn of events marking the formation of the *ejido* in Namiquipa could be explained in terms of a "typically" peasant obsession with the image of limited good or the more prosaic idea that they did not realize what they were doing. Liberal and even radical social science discourse about the peasantry as political actors[40] bears many similarities to the discourse of the Mexican state as represented in the minutes of the CNA meetings and correspondence. For example, Adolfo C. Besson, organizer of the Secretaría de Agricultura y Fomento (Poder Ejecutivo) wrote in 1928 that Namiquipa was "one of the most rebellious and richest *ejidos,* where the Government could obtain great benefits" if the peasants could only be made "to understand that they should obey the Laws of the Government."[41]

But the shocking incidents of August 1926 in Namiquipa were neither isolated nor unique, nor were they predicated on the sort of "peasant" behavior commensurate with some essentialist definition of the peasantry. Rather, the actions of Namiquipans were part of a popular critique of outside—in this case, state—intervention into affairs of the community related to the pueblo's land. Positively, they presaged an alternative, popular construction of "rights" to land, a construction rooted in a colonial past but imaginatively contending with a capitalist present.

In 1928, Namiquipans objected to having to contribute 15 percent of their harvests to the *ejido,* preferring instead to pay taxes on what they called their "private properties" to the Recaudación de Rentas.[42] Threatened by any alienation of the products of agricultural labor, Namiquipans not only found the 15-percent tax excessive but resented that it went to an institution (the *ejido*) many never wanted in the first place. Significantly, signatories to the 1925 document accepting provisional possession of the *ejido* and the 1926 *acta* establishing it were among the hundreds who refused to make their "contributions" to the *ejido* in 1928.[43] Paying a fixed tax in money regardless of what was planted, or how much of which crops were planted, or *whether they planted at all* was seen as less of an intervention by the state (through the *ejido*) into the labor process.

Namiquipans had additional reasons to challenge the imposition of the Agrarian Law in the 1920s. The law itself had been formulated by *carrancistas,* whom Namiquipan *villistas* had fought against during the revolution; indeed, *carrancistas* had treated peasant communities with such little respect (appropriating crops and livestock, arresting and executing people, and raping women) that during the revolution a new term was coined: *carrancear,*—to steal.[44] The association of theft with *carrancismo* was not dispelled by the demand that the Namiquipans turn over 15 percent of their harvests to the new *ejido.* Further, the *ejido* would allow *foráneos* to receive rights to land.[45]

In the face of these provisions of the agrarian reform and the insecurity in land tenure and state domination associated with them, members of the SCP asserted they wanted to hold their lands according to their colonial charter, in which "with paternal care are fixed all the measures necessary to the formation and conservation of these pueblos" and their system of land tenure.[46] But unlike in the past, when legal titles had not been important, the SCP members now wanted to hold their individual plots as small private properties (*pequeñas propiedades*), and they appealed to the precedent set by the Bando to uphold their position.

Agrarian reform legislation in fact allowed for the recognition of some *pequeñas propiedades* within *ejidos* (Mendieta y Nuñez 1981:199–200, 214–15). Individuals were permitted to keep no more than 50 hectares of land, which had to be properly registered. *Pequeña propiedad* was heralded as the hope for Mexico's future development, but its owners were not to be peasants who lacked the proper entrepreneurial spirit (and who would, as CNA president Luis León claimed, set themselves up in their ranchos and not develop the land due to their ideology), but capitalist farmers. Significantly, neither of the two *pequeñas propiedades* legally recognized within the Namiquipan *ejido* in 1926 belonged to peasants—they were both owned by *foráneos*, Pedro Loya and José Casavantes.[47] However, the hundreds of small properties recognized by the SCP (and for which satisfactory titles did not exist) were never entered in the district Registro Público de la Propiedad. According to the Agrarian Law, those lands reverted to the *ejido*, their assignment and administration becoming the responsibility of the Comisariado Ejidal (successor to the CPA).

The concept of *la pequeña propiedad* operative in Namiquipa in the 1920s and still consensually recognized to this day is arguably a recension of the earlier notion of *posesión*.[48] By the late Porfiriato, *derechos de posesión* in Namiquipa differed from property rights only in that they were not legitimated by individual, legal titles but by permission granted by the Municipal Council, which administered the pueblo's corporate property, or, after 1906, by the SCP. But whereas property was acquired through market transactions, *posesión* was secured by virtue of membership in the community, labor on the land, and fulfillment of obligations to the pueblo. The SCP charter of 1906 articulated the same vision, and the agrarian reform implemented by the SCP in Namiquipa during the revolution echoed the conditions set out in the Bando. *Derechos de posesión* went to those who defended the land and who were *originarios*.

In practice, the Namiquipan regime of land tenure actually anticipated the postrevolutionary *ejido* system, but there was one major difference. If the subject of land rights within Namiquipan practice was a *buen vecino*, a good community member, the subject of land rights within the *ejido* system was a loyal and docile subject of the state. If the former system of land tenure was the result of a "dialectic of articulation" that had played itself out for the prior century and a half and was apprehended in local consciousness—in a manner consonant with the "internal dialectic" of community formation—as the community's own vision (Comaroff 1982b), the new regime of land tenure was experienced as an imposition from without, a form of state domination. And as demonstrated above, the historical experience of Namiquipans in prior decades had taught them they had good reason to "fear" the state.

The popular insistence on holding the land as *pequeña propiedad* was not a sign of a new (or an old) individualism (pace Díaz Soto y Gama)[49] nor of a fundamental change in the vision of land rights on the Namiquipans' part. Rather, the personal autonomy central to local ideals of masculinity, rooted in the colonization of the frontier, was an important value which inflected their notions of land tenure and the organization of work on the land. It would be a mistake to confuse this with capitalist individualism. The valuation of the person advanced by Namiquipans is informed by a sense of a collective subject, by their vision of the *patria chica* as a community of equals which is a "form and product of struggle" with outside forces (Roseberry 1991:22). Namiquipans' argument for holding individual plots as *pequeñas propiedades* formed as a strategic response to historical circumstances since the lack of "legitimate titles" had resulted in agrarian dispossession before the revolution (especially from 1905 to 1910). In the 1920s and 1930s Namiquipans came to believe that holding their individual plots as properties (rather than as *ejidal* lands) would give them greater security of land tenure, control of the production process, and autonomy from the state.

And this is precisely why the state did not want to give Namiquipans their lands as *pequeñas propiedades*. Adolfo C. Besson, quoted earlier to the effect that Namiquipan peasants should obey the laws of the government, elaborated the point with his insistence that

> this will be the only way in which some benefit can be obtained from said pueblo, because, otherwise, time will pass and the inhabitants will get more enamored of the idea that they are small property owners, and as a consequence, will refuse to recognize in all its parts what the Agrarian Law establishes for them. (AGCCA e.24/432 [721.1])

Namiquipans recognized perfectly well precisely what the Agrarian Law established for them: subordination to the state. And it is for that reason that they initially rejected it. Directly challenging the state, the system of land tenure Namiquipans elaborated in practice—indeed, by the 1980s in the very administration of the *ejido*—recognized as "properties" agricultural lands worked by Namiquipans for the century and a half before the establishment of the *ejido*. *Agricultores* in Namiquipa in the 1980s, including present and past members of the Comisariado Ejidal de Namiquipa, insisted on the existence of several hundred small private holdings *within* the *ejido*. In spite of their patent "illegality" and the fact that these *pequeñas propiedades* do not appear in the Registro Público de la Propiedad, local practice is to treat them as though they were "real" properties.

Sometime during the 1930s, the SCP ceased to function and the *ejido* took over the practical administration of Namiquipa's lands.[50] The Co-

misariado Ejidal assigned plots of land which had in the past been used
for grazing to *ejidatarios* to cultivate. Much of this land (earlier the indivisible *terrenos de común repartimiento*) was prepared for planting and
fenced off as the exploitation of *temporal* fields further from the pueblo
became more realistic. Today all of the irrigated land along the Río Santa
María and many of the fields east of the pueblo on either side of the
Arroyo de Aranzazu are regarded as "properties," while more recently
opened-up agricultural land is divided into what are regarded as "*ejidal*
plots." The basis for this distinction (which is in direct violation of the
Agrarian Law) may be found in Namiquipan agrarian ideology.

In the 1940s, the state introduced a method for distributing land to
peasants in which they became owners of their fields rather than members of *ejidos*. In *colonias agricolas*, farmers may purchase 20- to 25-
hectare lots, while *ejidatarios* only have usufruct rights to specific plots
of land, invariably less than 20 hectares of *temporal*. Another difference
is that *ejidal* plots may not be used as collateral to secure loans, and if
an *ejidatario* fails to work their land for two years in a row, the parcel
may be assigned to another *ejidatario*. That is not the case in *colonias
agrícolas*, where land is an alienable commodity. One commonly voiced
objection to *colonias agricolas* before 1991 was that *acaparamientos de tierras*—the acquisition of multiple, contiguous lots—may and frequently
do occur.[51] There are no legal leveling or equalizing mechanisms built
into the structure of land tenancy on the *colonias* preventing the establishment of *latifundios within* the *colonias*. On *ejidos*, in contrast, supposedly no *ejidatario* is allowed to control more than one *ejidal* plot, and
this appears, on the surface, to enforce a certain kind of social justice.

But the homology of contrasts between *colonias agrícolas* and *ejidos*,
on the one hand, and "the laws of the market" and legally formulated
"social justice," on the other, are as incommensurate with popular ideology as they are rare in practice. Namiquipan agriculturalists wanted to
cultivate their own land. Twenty-five hectares of *temporal* approaches
the upper limit of what one individual, with family labor and access to
a tractor that is not broken down most of the year, may be expected to
work in the 1990s. In other words, what many people today see in the
colonias is an "ideal" and socially just arrangement (including ownership of agricultural lands) stipulated by the Bando and denied them by
the *ejido*. The fact that *acaparamientos de tierras* occur just as frequently
within *ejidos* as in *colonias agrícolas*, that the "two-year rule" is either
ignored or selectively enforced, and that *ejidal* parcels circulate within
the local economy in a manner indistinguishable from "private properties" only adds more weight to the popular critique of the postrevolutionary system. In short, being an *ejidatario* and having usufruct rights
to an *ejidal* plot does not eliminate the possibility of being victimized by

"the magic of the marketplace," but it does leave the door open to a state-controlled system of exploitation.

The curious feature of postrevolutionary conflict with the state is that the long-standing Namiquipan struggle for control of agricultural and grazing land was transformed, in the new political-administrative context, into a struggle for small private properties, for *la pequeña propiedad.* The coexistence of two systems of land tenure within the *ejido* of Namiquipa in the 1980s demonstrates that Namiquipans had imaginatively subverted the distortions to the locally recognized and popularly sanctioned system of land tenure mandated by the state. Hostility to the *ejido,* and the Namiquipan's deformation of their own *ejido* (functioning in defiance of the Agrarian Law and recognizing different categories of agricultural land), did not derive from the repudiation of a system of land tenure, a form of holding and working agricultural land. For in point of fact the land tenure arrangements in Namiquipa formalized by the SCP and practiced since the time of the presidio are substantively similar to the terms of the revolutionary agrarian legislation and the *ejido* system. Rather, their hostility was based on a refusal to accept the imposition of a system of power that denied the validity of Namiquipans' historical claims to work the land. It was a rejection of the *ejido* system as an instrument of state domination in the countryside.

5
The Legacy of Agrarian Reform in Namiquipa

CUI BONO?

Before the revolution of 1910 in western Chihuahua, a rural petty bourgeoisie or an incipient "peasant bourgeoisie" (cf. Schryer 1980:7, 13; Stavenhagen 1969) was a major political force in the region. However, in Namiquipa much of the personnel of the prerevolutionary petty bourgeoisie—mostly outsiders or *foráneos*—were eliminated or driven out of the community during the revolution. Nevertheless, their "historical role" was assumed by certain factions within the community. It was not the members of the SCP (clamoring, in an apparently contradictory manner, for "property rights" in the 1920s), however, who assumed the historical role of the petty bourgeoisie of the countryside. Instead, Reyes Ortiz and leading elements of the Defensas Sociales, along with some of the better-off among the *originarios*, took up that project as their own. The interesting point is that the latter group used the postrevolutionary *ejido* as the vehicle for advancing their project.

In other words, not all Namiquipans rejected the *ejido* at its outset. The lack of consensus during the 1920s over whether the SCP or the state should administer pueblo lands indicates the presence of competing groups claiming to "speak for the pueblo" in defense of agrarian interests. But what were the competing groups saying? What were the terms in which people repudiated the postrevolutionary *ejido?* Was there a social group within Namiquipa that stood to gain from the establishment of the *ejido?*

There were indeed some people from Namiquipa who later tried to establish *colonias agrícolas;* not, however, because they were wedded to the notion of private property, but because they had been excluded, or excluded themselves, from participating in the *ejido.* Arcadio Maldonado agitated for thirty years to divide the Hearst hacienda and turn the land over to local peasants, especially former *villistas* deprived of any benefits of the agrarian reform. A native of Michoacán and later a PLM activist in Los Angeles who moved to Namiquipa shortly before 1910,

Don Arcadio joined Villa during the revolution, returning after the Americans left the region and the fighting was over. Despite his *foráneo* origins he was a member of the SCP and became a very effective spokesman for the pueblo in the 1920s, spearheading opposition to what were regarded as new and unacceptable forms of intervention by the state.

Maldonado founded a *colonia agrícola* near Namiquipa on what had been part of the Hearst estate, but only after the national government purchased San José de Babicora y Anexas from its North American owners and subdivided it for sale to Mexican farmers in the 1950s (Jordan [1956] 1981:379–81). Named División del Norte after Villa's army, veterans of the Villa movement who had not been assigned *ejidal* plots acquired small private properties in this *colonia*. The double irony was that by that time most of the veterans were too old to work the land, and adding injury to insult, they had to pay the state for the plots they acquired (Mikey Maldonado, pers. com.).

Reyes Ortiz, on the other hand, had been the legal representative for Namiquipa and Cruces in their dispute with Santa Clara for the decade preceding 1910. He fully expected to be reimbursed for his efforts. While postrevolutionary *ejidos* were intended to provide for the equal distribution of land rights to members of communities, a deal had been struck whereby once *ejidos* were secured for Namiquipa and Cruces, Ortiz would become owner of an enormous "ranch" "within" the *ejido* of Cruces. Ortiz's work at restoring the lands to the pueblos for their collective use was to be repaid by making him the owner of a large landholding within a collectively held *ejido*.

Unfortunately for Ortiz, families from Cruces who had seized control of the administrative apparatus of that *ejido* reneged on the deal. Once the *ejidos* were established in Namiquipa and Cruces, Ortiz was never able to assume control of the promised property (Rancho Colorado). He retired to his house upriver from Namiquipa and subsequently received threats on his life. During the 1930s, in Chihuahua City for the wedding of his son, he left his hotel room, went out on the street to buy a newspaper, and was last seen walking near the Plaza de Armas before he disappeared and presumably was murdered.[1]

The shifting faction fights of the 1920s were emphatically not a carryover from the prerevolutionary period but instead related to a new process of social differentiation, the locus of which was not internal to processes of production and reproduction within the community but rather a function of the community's (external) relation to the state. On the eve of the revolution the antagonistic groups in Namiquipa had been the recent immigrants to the region and the *originarios*, families of people born in the pueblo or who (like Ortiz and Maldonado) were accepted as insiders. For immigrants who purchased "municipal lands" between 1905 and 1910, land—like any other commodity—was an investment, and in turn-of-the-century Namiquipa a relatively inexpensive one at that. Their relations with one another, officials of the state, peasants, and small ranchers were governed by a calculus of sterile and alienated self-interest. These were the *"gente de razón"* of the late Porfiriato in Chihuahua.[2]

The *originarios* were more heterogeneous than the immigrants, both in background and class position, and in their attitudes toward the land and the state. They included descendants of the colonial-period settlers as well as immigrants whom had been granted membership in the community. Few had much in the way of capital or tools. Some labored on nearby haciendas as herdsmen (*vaqueros*) or sharecroppers, in more distant mines, and even in the United States. A handful of *originario* families were wealthy, owning large herds of cattle and operating flour mills and small commercial establishments. But all objected to taxes on instruments of production such as teams of animals or decrepit wagons, asserting that these were only used in the process of working on the land (AMCG passim; AMN passim). According to the ideology of the originarios there was little distinction made between land, instruments of agricultural production, and the labor expended by an individual on his own plot of land (use of the masculine article intended). These were all elements or parts of a unified process.

The early twentieth-century attitude towards the land bore echoes of the agrarian ideology articulated in Francisco Vásquez's 1808 letter responding to the González de Almoyna descendants' attempted land invasion a century earlier. It was an attitude not just toward *land* but also toward labor and the personal and social qualities of the person who works the land that distinguished *originarios* from the immigrants. Aspects of the *serrano* ideology toward capital, labor, and honor are succinctly and elegantly expressed in Plácido Chávez's description of his *serrano* forebearers, quoted above (p. 71; Chávez Calderón 1964:6).

Most of the prerevolutionary petty bourgeoisie of Namiquipa fled or was driven from the town during the early years of the revolution. The Laphond brothers, French merchants who operated a store in Namiquipa until the 1910s, moved all their commercial operations to San Antonio (now Cuauhtémoc) and Chihuahua City. Victoriano Torres, municipal president for much of the decade before 1910 and architect of the sale of Namiquipa's municipal lands, was pulled from a jail cell and executed personally by Manuel "La Mano Negra" Baca in Chihuahua City in 1914 (AJBT 5.22, fo.2336–40). One of Villa's *pistoleros* from Namiquipa, Baca did this spontaneously upon discovering Torres prisoner in a *villista* jail. His action illustrates the mutual imbrication of personal vengeance and revolutionary justice.[3] Many *originarios* also left town during the revolution to join the fighting or to go into exile but returned in the late 1910s and 1920s; most of the prerevolutionary petty bourgeoisie did not.

During the revolution, "outsiders" of whatever stripe were discouraged from intervening in the internal affairs of the pueblo. So, too, in the 1920s, the conflict between the Ortiz *ayuntamiento* (and later CPA) and the SCP was not as much about how the land would be worked or who would cultivate it as which institution would have the authority to sanction individual direct producers' relationship to the land. During the revolution and into the 1920s the SCP had formalized the principle of excluding outsiders from rights to land, the contravention of which had been the cause of suffering by the Namiquipans in the decades immediately before the revolution, when they were dispossessed by petty bourgeois immigrants. Reyes Ortiz and his allies, on the other hand, embraced the national state's regulation of the relationship of community members to the land they worked.

The petition for an *ejido* in November 1922 not only fundamentally and unalterably transformed the relationship of the community as a whole to the state, subordinating the former to the latter; it also provided an opportunity for some individuals to assume the historic role of the prerevolutionary petty bourgeoisie. The irony is that the people who found little difficulty getting in step with the "revolutionary changes" sweeping Mexican society—that is, the faction instrumental in turning Namiquipa into an *ejido*—were the ones who assumed for themselves the historical role of the prerevolutionary petty bourgeoisie. This group would use the *ejido* rather than any argument in favor of "private property" in land to guarantee that end.[4]

The process of social differentiation among *originarios* in the 1920s occurred along axes of difference laid down by the political power and apparatus of the state rather than by control of means of production. Social differentiation in the postrevolutionary decades was not to be based on differential access to means of production, but instead on differential access to circuits of power in the state. Hence, popular resistance to the *ejido* was above all a political struggle against the state centered on the meanings of land and work and not primarily a repudiation of one form of land tenure (*ejidal*, collective) in favor of another (private, individual).

THE *EJIDO* IN POPULAR IDEOLOGY

What are the different notions of agricultural land operative in Namiquipa? What are the implications of these different sets of ideas, both for the peasantry's relationship to the state and to capitalism, and for notions of personal identity? The three categories of land are *ejidal* land, capitalist property, and the "small properties" of the Namiquipans, which really involve a recension of the earlier notion of *posesión*. Working *ejidal* land implies subordination to the state, an acquiescent peasantry. Owning capitalist property is strongly linked to notions of individualism and "freedom" to exploit others. Working "small properties" that are a transformation of *posesiones* implies personal autonomy (or at least requires a struggle *for* autonomy) from *patrones* and the state, an autonomy that is central to ideals of masculinity and which is predicated on a selective tradition of resistance to what are perceived to be illegitimate forms of domination. The subject of that resistance and protagonist of that struggle, however, is a collective subject: the community, the pueblo as simultaneously people and locale.

Autonomy differs from individualism in that the concept of personhood on which the former is predicated recognizes the social and material embeddedness of identity; hence, the *buen jefe de familia* is also the *buen vecino* who fulfills obligations of both work and defense to the community and respects other *vecinos'* land rights. While the household was and remains a basic unit of production and consumption in Namiquipa, access to means of agricultural production has always been mediated by supra-household forms of organization, whether the political authority of presidial captains in the colonial period or community-level organizations after Independence such as the popular municipal councils or, after 1906, the SCP. Thus, though "production was not communal, the community constituted an important relation of production" (Roseberry 1991:22). No less important in providing the conditions for production to take place at all was collective and militant defense of the pueblo's land.

Knowledgeable Chihuahuans in the 1980s frequently described Namiquipa as "the most irregular *ejido* in the state of Chihuahua," pointing to its size and to Namiquipan rejection of state-mandated rules governing use of *ejidal* land and disposition of the products of labor upon them. In my opinion, its most anomolous feature has to do neither with its size (enormous) nor with the hundreds of small private properties maintained within the *ejido* to this day. Rather, what is most striking is that Namiquipa is not plagued, as are so many other *ejidos*, by *acaparamientos de tierras*—that is, the consolidation of large estates that exceed the legal limit in extent—*within* the collectively held lands. This is more a function of the construction and reproduction of locally meaningful practices for administering land tenure than a function of the "socially just" provisions of the *ejido*-based agrarian reform. The construction of locally meaningful practices supposes the elaboration of a symbolic system or

an imagination through which such practices are understood and transformed (cf. Marx [1867] 1906:197−98).

This makes Namiquipa special. In your garden-variety "irregular"
ejido one finds systematic violations of provisions of the Agrarian Law
relating to eligibility to cultivate, the transfer of usufruct, and limiting
the amount of cultivable land any individual may control. For examples:
the best irrigated land in the *ejido* of Galeana, Chihuahua, was "sold"
(by the *ejidal* commissioner) to Mormons in the 1960s and 1970s
(AGRA 23-399, 12-ix-1979); the *ejido* in Casas Grandes (CNA.RP Jan.
1927) was blocked by influential property owners in the region, including many Mormons, but from an earlier wave of settlement (Jesús Vargas, pers. com.); individuals assume control of multiple *ejidal* plots;
individuals lie about the size of their plots, which may be considerably
greater than the 20-hectare legal limit; plots of cultivable *ejidal* land are
purchased, rented, and sharecropped, and claims are made against them
for debts gone bad: "'Rent parcels?' groaned one Sonora peasant in
1963. 'Why here entire ejidos are rented out'" (Cockcroft 1983:170).

While some of those violations occur in Namiquipa, what qualifies it
as a "most" irregular *ejido* is that there has been very little consolidation
by individuals of extensive tracts of land (either *ejidal* or "private"). This
contrasts to the situation in *colonias agrícolas* and in *ejidos* where a handful of "*ejidatarios*" claim the best land, enclose common pastures, and
are locally regarded as *los ricos,* while poor people are systematically
excluded from the *ejidal* census, prohibited from enjoying access to cultivable land, and wind up sharecropping or working as wage laborers
for the "*ejidatarios.*"

When Galeana regained its lands in 1926, for example, the Galeanenses welcomed the *ejido* as a way of recovering control of their 1778
land grant. But Galeana is today battered by two sets of problems Namiquipans did not have to face: the sterility of the land and the presence
of foreigners within the *ejido.* Located on the lower reaches of the Río
Santa María, only 9,000 hectares (about 8 percent) of the *ejido* of Galeana is now suitable for cultivation, and that only with the introduction
of several score deep wells.[5] Within the *ejido,* a small group of Mormon
colonists from the United States invaded the *municipio,* acquiring some
of the best lands along the river from corrupt *ejidal* officers.[6] The Comisariado Ejidal functions as a *cacicazgo* in Galeana.

In the early 1980s, Ing. Victor Manuel Bueno G. wrote from the
office of the "Vieja Guardia Agrarista de Chihuahua, Chih." to the Ministry of Agrarian Reform (Secretaría de Reforma Agraria, SRA) complaining that 115 sons of *ejidatarios* and other individuals with rights in
the *ejido* enjoyed no access to cultivable lands in Galeana:

The Ejidal Commissioner [of Galeana] some time ago made himself the cacique of the region and has been frustrating the attempts at redress on the part of landless *ejidatarios*, all to the end of privileging his unconditional followers, who, without the approval of the general assembly of the *ejido*, have been extending their control of the best lands. In the same way the Ejidal Commissioner has favored a group of FOREIGN MORMONS living at the Colony called "LEBARON," which is in the middle of the *ejido*. For years the Mormons have illegally and excessively expanded their possession of irrigated land within the *ejido*, and now [the Ejidal Commissioner] is giving them land which should be destined for sons of *ejidatarios* and for *ejidatarios* themselves. (AGRA e.23-399)

Matters were only slightly different in Cruces, except the *ejido* was a *cacicazgo* from the outset. In 1931 the second elected treasurer of the *ejido* was accused of theft of public funds. The only controversy facing the people of Cruces was whether to charge him with stealing "National" funds or "community" funds.[7] During an inspection of the *ejido* conducted in 1936, agrarian reform officials found the community in the grip of a handful of wealthy ranchers, merchants, and corrupt politicians who largely exercised their authority through the municipal government (Cruces was then, as now, a municipal section of Namiquipa) but also took advantage of their position of *ejidatarios*.

The sectional president, Carmen Pérez, was "the new cacique for whom only the rich merit justice and protection"; the town secretary, Mario Rodríguez, was a holdover from Porfirian administrations; the collector of state taxes, Guadalupe Tena, discouraged *ejidatarios* from paying taxes to the *ejido;* Prisciliano Morales, the owner of a flour mill, kept 50 percent of the grain as a fee for grinding it; and Dionicio Rico, "the most important merchant and cattleman of the *ejido*," whose four hundred head of cattle grazed on the *ejidal* lands without his paying any tax at all, was a usurer, as were other individuals such as Nemecio Ortega, who "used illicit means to deprive the peasantry of their agricultural products." The report on the *ejido* of Cruces ends with the recommendation that the new caciques be kicked out of the *ejido* for being "anti-*agrarista* property-owners" (Prisciliano Morales), "anti-*agrarista* exploiters" (Guadalupe Tena), "merchants and exploiters of the peasantry" (Nemecio Ortega), or "merchants and new *caciquillos*" (Dionicio Rico and his brother Apolinar).[8]

The situation in Cruces had scarcely changed fifty years later. When asked to describe the basis of social divisions in Cruces in the 1980s, Namiquipans indicated that "*ejidatarios*" were the richest landowning group with the largest herds of cattle, while families excluded from participation in the administration of the *ejido* had few resources and little access to land if any. It was the descendants of the "merchants and new *caciquillos*" of the 1930s in Cruces who in the 1970s and 1980s controlled the irrigated land near the pueblo and claimed great expanses of grazing land in the immediate vicinity of the pueblo as their "properties." These were the lands invaded in 1983, leading to the war of the Malvinos. It is the current generation of Ricos that shot at or beat up their opponents in the pueblo. In other words, the lineaments of a process of social differentiation within the community are rooted in the introduction of a political organization for administering land, the *ejido*, introduced in the 1920s.

The large *ejidos* established in both Galeana and Cruces did not, in the end, provide new land for agricultural use. What they did provide was a framework for what became a new, revolutionary *caciquismo* that flourished within the *ejidos*. Struggles for land within the *ejidos* were shaped by the differentiation between rural social classes;[9] the instability and unevenness of the development of a practice—*temporal* agriculture—uneven and unstable from the outset; and the incommensurability of peasant aspirations and government policy.

In Namiquipa, however, people were able to cultivate considerably more land after the revolution than before, and land was not as unequally distributed as it was in Galeana and Cruces. Furthermore, while the *ejido* did provide the framework for a new *caciquismo*, those individuals who assumed control of the *ejido* used their position above all to improve their own relations with outsiders rather than to subordinate other Namiquipans. Power within the *ejido* served as a calling card providing access to political, administrative, and entrepreneurial opportunities outside the community. The *ejido* became the conduit to a power exercised *on* the community from the outside. Advocates of the *ejido* within Namiquipa seized control of an apparatus supposedly designed to channel and coordinate the collective interests of peasant agriculturalists to further their narrower and more restricted interests as *landowners, cattlemen,* and *political clients of the state.* Namiquipans who resisted the *ejido* and the superficially "*agrarista*" allies of the state and appealed instead for their "rights in property," in contrast, did so to the end of maintaining those aspects of prerevolutionary social structure that would guarantee their continued reproduction as peasants.

This popular alternative as shaped by Namiquipans has rather less to do with externally imposed or derived determinations[10] and rather more with internally controlled practices rooted in the community. The *alternative* regime of land tenure presently observed in Namiquipa is a special, but above all popular, alternative to "the rules of the game of the postrevolutionary state" (A. Bartra 1985:23). It is precisely through their response—whether of acceptance or rejection—to the state's rules of the game that Namiquipans forged their identities in the decades after the revolution.

From the perspective of Namiquipans, the *ejido* is an external administrative and institutional framework mediating the relationship of direct agricultural producers to their means of production and to the production process generally. Far from making agricultural lands available to landless peasants, the *ejido* removes land from the power of the people and the community (in a word, the pueblo) and places it in the power of the state. Not only is land alienated from pueblo control; instruments of production—credit, seed, fertilizer, water, and labor-power—and the production process as a whole—the organization and rhythm of work, the disposition of the product—are also alienated by the *ejido*. This provides a striking contrast to the official view, according to which the state donated land to a theretofore landless peasantry.[11] As one Namiquipan somewhat hyperbolically observed, "In the time of Don Porfirio we [Mexicans] were peons of the haciendas; now we are peons of the banks and of the state."[12]

The pueblo's relationship to the state is one of distinct and increasingly antagonistic social protagonists that apprehend and work upon correspondingly distinct realities (Nugent 1987). The realities upon which they work are not axiomatic expressions of structurally distinct levels within the social formation (e.g., community or pueblo as opposed to state level) but the results of different kinds of engagement the distinct social groups and classes entertain with the material at hand. In the establishment of the *ejido* in Namiquipa, the "material at hand" was identical for the architects of both official and popular views of the agrarian reform in Namiquipa. But experienced and understood differently, subjected to competing sets of interests, modulated and inflected by radically distinct forms of consciousness, that event produced divergent interpretations (see Nugent and Alonso 1994).

A critical point is that the contrast between state and popular ideologies regarding the *ejido* is not a superficial opposition masking hierarchic integration in an encompassing structure of domination/subordination. The efficacy of the state's domination of Namiquipa as an issue of politics or meaning (if the two can be abstracted apart) has been unrelentingly thrown into question by Namiquipans through their attempts (here successful, there failed) to deny that the *ejido* was ever fully implemented. From the standpoint of popular ideology, the crucial point about the *ejido* is that it signifies and materializes an illegitimate intervention of state power into the community. Consequently, rather than provide a mechanism or instrument through which integration of community to nation is possible, it provides an identifiable and tangible instrument of state power for people to struggle *against*.[13]

In one sense the *ejido* represented the vindication of Namiquipans' 150-year struggle to "make use of the fertility and beauty of the lands . . . and of the fruits of their labor and industry" (Bando): 1926 was, arguably, a replay of 1778. But in a very different sense, 1926 was a farce. How could the state give back to Namiquipans land they already had? The very act of restitution was a denial of Namiquipan history— the blood shed, the lives spent in work, the changes made to the Chihuahuan landscape—a denial that also underlined the new set of power relations into which the community was drawn through the *ejido*. After the 1920s agrarian struggle in Namiquipa assumed a new character. Where before it had been a struggle to maintain control of land, it later became a struggle to define meanings of land, different definitions having different effects on the process of working the land.

DISTRIBUTION AND USE OF LAND IN NAMIQUIPA

Namiquipans' accommodation with the *ejido* took the form of maintaining hundreds of small private properties within the borders of the *ejido*. Many properties held and worked by *originarios* in the 1920s and 1930s (as in previous decades) have since changed hands, divided among family members or in a few instances sold to immigrants to the community. With two exceptions, none of the properties has a title. But from the point of view of Namiquipans they remain *properties*, as contrasted to *ejidal* lots, whose identification as such is predicated on a popular, consensual, and locally significant historical recognition.

Not all agricultural fields within the *ejido* are recognized as properties. Beside these are *ejidal* lots consisting almost exclusively of *temporal* fields, most cultivated only since 1926. While the state reserves the right to determine (through the local Comisariado Ejidal) how *ejidal* fields are assigned, held, and worked, the practice within the community is to treat *ejidal* fields in a manner very similar to the way *pequeñas propiedades* are treated. According to the law an *ejidatario* only has usufruct rights to one *ejidal* parcel, which may not be sold, rented, or subdivided and may only be reassigned to another landless *ejidatario* in the event its previous user has neglected to exploit it for two consecutive years. But such parcels frequently change hands, like any other property that may be freely exchanged.

One example is a parcel which in the 1980s belonged to a poor farmer suffering from appendicitis. A physician performed an appendectomy for which the farmer was unable to pay, and the physician, with the complicity of local *ejido* officers, seized the man's fields in "payment" for the medical operation. Officers initially objected to approving the transfer, appealing to the wealthy doctor to seek some other settlement. But their appeals were to his person and his sentiments as friend and *compadre*. They did not use the legal argument that they lacked the authority to reassign the *ejidal* plot as payment for a debt owed by one *ejidatario* to another. Instead they authorized the reassignment of the *ejidal* lot from the farmer to the physician's daughter, an accountant.

The relative valuation of *ejidal* plots in contrast to "private properties" may result in bending the rules when previously uncultivated land is assigned to *ejidatarios*. As in other *ejidos* in the region, individual *ejidal* fields of *temporal* in Namiquipa are not supposed to exceed 20 hectares. Yet Pablo Nevares,[14] a Namiquipan *ejidatario*, told with a mixture of pride and embarrassment how he secured an *ejidal* plot of 50 or 60 hectares. He informed the *ejido* of the general location of his planned field, far from town, and an officer was sent to certify that the land was within the *ejido*, its boundaries did not intrude on any other party's land, and it was not excessively large. All this was accomplished one afternoon, and no sooner had the *ejido* officer left than Pablo moved three of the boundary markers several hundred meters. The next week he recorded the (new) location of his boundary markers with the Comisariado Ejidal.

By this means Pablo's assigned land (listed in the records of the *ejido* as consisting of 20 hectares) magically expanded to almost 60 hectares. He told this story in the context of a discussion of corruption in the *ejido*, using the assignment of *ejidal* plots as an example. But his evident shame in recognizing himself as a beneficiary of corruption was tempered by the point that no one in Namiquipa objected to his action since it was only *ejidal* land—and furthermore a considerable distance from the pueblo—not "property."

The average size of individual holdings in the *ejidal* sector for the country as a whole is a fraction of the average individual holding in the *ejido* of Namiquipa. Further, if the records of the *ejido* suggest an average holding in Namiquipa of less than 20 hectares, that figure ignores the practice of falsely recording the size of *ejidal* lots and the fact that some individuals possess more than one plot of land (frequently an *ejidal* lot and a property) or control lots officially assigned to others. For example, a father may direct the work on multiple lots assigned to his sons, or someone might work lands assigned to individuals who are not resident in the pueblo.

It is unclear how much agricultural land within the *ejido* of Namiquipa is held as "private property." One Namiquipan farmer said, "To have a property inside the *ejido* means you pay taxes twice; once to the *ejido* and once to the state tax collector," since all the "properties" fall within the boundaries of the *ejido*. It was never made clear what exactly the state tax collector did with all the money collected for these "non-existent" properties.

A statistical survey conducted by the Agricultural Technology Education Brigade of the Secretaría de Educación Pública (SEP) in 1983 provides considerable data on land use in Namiquipa.[15] Comparison of this data to other sources[16] reveals several recent tendencies in changing land use. First, the entire *municipio* consists of more than 4,000 square kilometers, or 400,000 hectares. Of this land, almost 250,000 hectares are in a dozen *ejidos*, most of that area (75 percent) in the *ejidos* of Namiquipa and Cruces. Another 70,000 or 80,000 hectares are in half a dozen *colonias agrícolas*, mostly in the old Baja Babicora, but including the 15,000-hectare Colonia Santa Clara (BETA 1983). In addition there are more than twenty Mennonite camps in the Santa Clara Valley (not included in the BETA survey). The remainder of the *municipio* is held in large and small private properties, little of it cultivated.

SRA data from the 1950s indicates that of the 200,000 hectares then in the *ejidal* sector in Namiquipa, less than 9,000 were suitable for cultivation. This is clearly an underestimation, since it refers to cultivable lands at the time the *ejidos* were first established. While, for example, only 6,000 hectares of land were cultivated within what became the *ejido* of Namiquipa in 1926, that figure had changed by the 1950s. According to the BETA survey almost 35,000 hectares—a third of the area of the *ejido*—in Namiquipa were cultivable (if not cultivated) in 1983. But we should be wary of presuming an even, constant expansion of agriculture in Namiquipa (i.e., of being enthralled by the sixfold growth of area under cultivation in the *ejido* of Namiquipa over the last six decades).

The *Manual de Estadísticas Básicas del Estado de Chihuahua* (MEBCh) data suggest that the expansion of lands under cultivation in the *municipio* as a whole stopped in the 1970s.[17] And between 1983 and 1986 progressively fewer fields were being planted as more people left the region. Finally we should bear in mind that cultivating corn and beans on fields irrigated only by seasonal rains has notoriously inconsistent outcomes. While Namiquipans recall a few good seasons in the mid-1970s, much of the 1980s was a series of agricultural disasters. But the recent downturn in the amount of land cultivated and the even more serious battering basic grain production took during the 1980s as inflation skyrocketed and guaranteed prices announced at the beginning of the growing season barely covered (or failed to cover) costs of production by the time grains were delivered to the state grain warehouses (CONASUPO) can only be understood against the backdrop of the enormity of the *ejido* Namiquipans started out with in the 1920s.

By the 1930s they "belonged" to an *ejido* in which there was an abundance of land, including virgin fields that could be assigned to future generations of cultivators. This contrasts with the situation in most *ejidos* throughout Mexico, where *dotaciones* or restitutions of land to villagers were generally scarcely sufficient to provide the basis for a means of livelihood to the inhabitants at the time of the creation of the ejido.[18]

But by the 1980s in Namiquipa, the only way to invest more individual cultivators with control of land was by fractioning existing plots and/or introducing crops that could be intensively cultivated on smaller plots of land. Such an alternative was available with apple orchards, which were established in irrigated fields alongside the Río Santa María and in outlying fields, where the cultivator could successfully sink a deep well and draw the water up. The irrigated fields alongside the river had been largely devoted to wheat until the 1970s, though there were a few orchards in Namiquipa before that time. But following the lead of some Jalisco-based fruit merchants who set up a large orchard in Namiquipa in the early 1970s, Namiquipans began to put in orchards. In 1972 there were 96,500 trees in the *municipio;* by 1980 there were 780,000, 680,000 of those in production (MEBCh 1983).

Growing apples requires a larger capital investment than cultivating corn or beans, and running an orchard ties up considerably more of the agriculturalist's resources and time. The valley of the Río Santa María in Namiquipa is hardly the optimal eco-niche for fruit trees. Some *manzaneros* (apple growers) reported expecting to secure a good harvest only once every five years. But even with the anticipation of running at a loss 80 percent of the time, the considerable, even extravagant, profits to be made from a good harvest in apples made it all worthwhile. Additionally, producing apples provides a way of avoiding state-controlled markets for agricultural staples.[19]

But why would a Namiquipan peasant, an *ejidatario* at that, go to the trouble of putting in an apple orchard on land that is part of the *ejido?* According to agrarian legislation, *ejidal* lands belong to the state and are administered by the community, and usufruct is only assigned to individual *ejidatarios* and may be revoked. The answer to that question is very simple. Namiquipans only put orchards on their small private properties, of which there are about three hundred ranging in size from 1/2 to 50 hectares (most quite small) within the borders of the *ejido.* All but two of these are "illegal," their existence an affront to the progressive social order written into the radical agrarian legislation of the 1910s and 1920s mandating the terms of a land-tenure regime within Mexican *ejidos.* With the exception of the two properties within the borders of the *ejido* recognized by the Presidential Resolution of 1926, all the others owe their origin to the work of the SCP between 1906 and 1930, which was in turn based on local arrangements and practices regarding possession and use of agricultural lands that Namiquipans had elaborated in the prior century and a half.

It is for this reason, among others, that knowledgeable Chihuahuans describe Namiquipa as "the most irregular *ejido* in Chihuahua." Elsewhere I initiated an investigation into the paradoxes of the agrarian question in Chihuahua, which are particularly evident in the action of some sectors of the Chihuahuan peasantry in the decades before 1910, in the form assumed by the agrarian reform in the decades after 1920 and in the popular response to the establishment of *ejidos* (Nugent 1990). As discussed above, there *was* an agrarian problem in Chihuahua shaping revolutionary mobilization similar to that in the center of the country. Further, some Chihuahuan communities such as Namiquipa nevertheless refused to recognize the imposition of the *ejido* or used its existence as a framework to perpetuate prior arrangements and administration of communal land. In Namiquipa, in fact, the existing land-tenure arrangements before 1905 and those formalized by the SCP during the revolution anticipated—in almost ideal-typical fashion— terms of revolutionary agrarian legislation. The theory had already been implemented in practice *before* the postrevolutionary state could claim credit for it. But what makes Namiquipa so anomalous as an *ejido* is not that many *ejidal* fields are locally recognized as properties, but rather that the *ejido* is not plagued—as are so many others—by *acaparamientos de tierras,* seizures, and consolidations of extensive properties by individuals.

In Namiquipa since the 1950s, and increasingly through the 1960s and 1970s, the Mexican state implemented programs to help farmers increase agricultural production by providing technical assistance in the countryside. The Banco Nacional de Crédito Rural (BANRURAL) and *ejidos* distribute fertilizers, agronomists do soil analyses and make recommendations to farmers regarding the most up-to-date techniques, and the Confederación Nacional Campesino (CNC) provides tractors especially for the *barbecho* (the first and very rough plowing of a field in the spring) and for opening new fields. Finally, each year the state announces guaranteed prices for basic grains, assuring that farmers will not be victimized by middlemen and speculators.

The inexpensive fertilizers, however, are available only through the Banrural or the *ejido,* and cultivators are told the kind and quantities to use as a condition for securing agricultural loans. The recommendations often have less to do with land use or the character of the soil and more with the availability of one or another combination of fertilizers. In practice the "soil analyses" are woefully inaccurate, even when they are actually conducted (see Amparan Gonzáles et al. 1987), and each spring there is a thriving black market in fertilizers. The large tractors available to peasants through programs aimed at mechanizing the *ejidal* sector in Chihuahua are maintained by state employees in garages or lots in certain communities in the *municipio* of Namiquipa. Their assignment has as much to do with payment of political favors as with specific conditions in the communities to which they are assigned. *Ejidatarios* must pay for renting the tractors and the operator's wage, but it is often difficult to get fields prepared at the time the owners of the fields require it. The 1983 BETA study counted 289 agriculturalists in La Plaza, Namiquipa, for whom there were 256 equipped tractors, but almost all of those individually owned.

Finally, guaranteed prices for corn and beans have the effect of holding down food prices in the cities rather than guaranteeing an income for farmers in the countryside. Until the 1960s, Mexico still produced enough food to feed its population and, measured in terms of value of inputs to the production process, the *ejidal* sector was no less productive than the private sector in producing basic grains (Stavenhagen 1970:249–51). That has not been the case for over two decades. While price increases for corn and beans were announced with much fanfare at the beginning of each growing season, real prices fell during the 1970s, and that tendency dramatically accelerated in the 1980s (Heath 1989; Sanderson 1986). In short, state-run programs designed to facilitate the transfer of the products of work upon the land to a national market in basic grains have the effect of depriving the direct agricultural producers of the value of their labor. The state controls the disposition of the product of labor upon the land, both *ejidal* and private, and its involvement in supervising work on the land dovetails with local perception of outsiders' intervention in local practices related to the pueblo's land. It is immaterial that the CONASUPO, price guarantees, and a state-controlled market in basic grains were designed to protect farmers from merchants, middlemen, and *coyotes* (in short, "market forces"), for the perceived effect in the countryside is that the state controls and manipulates its monopoly on the products of labor on the land.

This monopoly effects the very design of the production process—the laboring practices implemented on the fields of Namiquipa—so that the production process is no longer controlled by Namiquipans themselves, but by agents of the state: agricultural engineers, bankers, technical assistants, and evaluaters of crop yields. The local perception and reception of these "experts" is profoundly affected by the fact that the latter as a rule do not work the land themselves, and they are invariably outsiders to the community. These outsiders' involvement in transforming the land is restricted to formulating the set of terms according to which the land is worked by prescribing the timing of activities, designating the inputs to those activities, and framing them in relation to various abstractions which have little relevance or meaning within the pueblo. The farmers, in turn, must accommodate their action on the land to these demands of the state.

In short, what is at issue is again the power of outsiders to make decisions regarding use of the land. Whatever the degree to which ethnicity, education, class position, or family background have an impact on determining who is perceived to be from "inside" or "outside" the community, those determinations are finally shaped by competing definitions of the land, themselves informed by the political relationship of community and state. Regardless of how Namiquipans actually hold and use the land (as *ejidal* land, as private properties), the condition for any farmer securing assistance from the state is his or her ability to establish links with—or just tolerate—specific agents and agencies of the state. Consequently, distinctions between how different Namiquipans are able to work the land are a function of their ability to "work with" the state. *Ejidatarios* may use their relationship to officials of the state to work their land in a most un-*ejido*-like manner, just as private property owners do. By the same token, *ejidatarios* and *propietarios* alike who are recalcitrant and reluctant to admit the state's invasion of the land and of the production process have trouble working, period.[20]

Finally, in the decades since the *ejido* was established, it has become increasingly difficult for Namiquipan farmers to make a go of it simply working the land the state so generously "gave" them in 1926. To support themselves on the land many peasants have had to seek wage work outside the community, most frequently—and massively, especially since the 1940s—in the United States. The participation of Namiquipans in an international division of labor—selling their labor power at less than its value to foreign agriculture, construction, and service enterprises—is now necessary for them to maintain locally esteemed practices on the land.

6
Classes of Labor and the Status of Work

THE TRANSFORMATION OF AGRICULTURAL LABOR
IN NAMIQUIPA

Namiquipans are not a band, a tribe, or a chiefdom. They use the same language as eighty million other Mexicans and speak it very much like several million other *norteños*. They live much of their lives in the countryside but are hardly isolated and have not been for the past century. The agrarian history of Namiquipa presented in earlier chapters dealt above all with a locale. This chapter considers what the people of Namiquipa *do* in that locale, providing a narrative synopsis of practices on the land and historical formations organizing labor upon it, while examining labor itself and the way Namiquipans regard it.

Barry Carr (1973) long ago pointed to the "peculiarities" of the North. Yet a thorough analysis of "the agrarian question" in Chihuahua remains to be written.[1] By way of contrast the literature on the agrarian question in "Latin America" is voluminous, decades old, and very good (e.g., Feder 1971; Stavenhagen 1969; De Janvry 1981). Nevertheless, not all of it is useful for analyzing the North of Mexico. This gap in scholarship probably owes much to the importation of European cultural and historical baggage to the debates in Latin America, and to the tendency for continental or global approaches to bog down in scholastic controversies that have little to do with historical practice at the local level, resulting in the predominance of abstractions over people. Ambiguity regarding what is the unit of analysis remains a problem (see Comaroff 1982a, 1982b; C. Smith 1984 for useful correctives). The homogenization of Latin America in the discourse on the agrarian question (whether developmentalist or underdevelopmentalist; see Taylor 1979) renders a theoretical account of the regional peculiarities of Chihuahua extremely difficult.

From the standpoint of Mexican historiography the agrarian question in nineteenth- and twentieth-century Chihuahua was not posed in the same way it was in other parts of Mexico. Much of the arid expanse of Chihuahua was not suitable for cultivation and only transiently inhabited. The story of Chihuahua's land, especially during the second half of the nineteenth century, is the story of the greatest consolidation of landholdings in all of Mexico (Tannenbaum 1930:13–14; Hart 1988). By the 1900s, one family, the Terrazas, controlled much of the land in Chihuahua, while most of the remainder was in the hands of a dozen other families or individuals operating large cattle estates (see Wasserman 1984:48–51). The Terrazas also dominated the state economically through control of mining and banking, and assumed a political control of the state undisputed by other regional elites elsewhere in Mexico by the start of the twentieth century.

Another factor obscuring the agrarian question in Porfirian Chihuahua is the rapid and successful capitalist development there in the aftermath of the Apache Wars. Mining, timber, and cattle industries that were set up or whose operations were expanded during this period found ready markets in the southwestern United States, to which Chihuahua was connected by railroads beginning in the 1880s (Wasserman 1984; Carr 1973; Coatsworth 1974).[2]

Finally, many people in the countryside worked herding cattle (as cowboys or *vaqueros*) rather than farming. In addition, there was a wider range of opportunities for work in mines, smelters, railroads, and lumber mills, as well as on cattle haciendas. A perennial labor shortage and higher wages relative to the rest of Mexico, and the possibilities of finding work part of the year in the United States also contributed to the creation "in the north [of Mexico] of a new type of semi-industrial, semi-agricultural worker, completely unknown in the center and south of the country" (Katz 1976a:45; see also Katz 1976b; Vargas Valdez 1988).

Some of these factors and tendencies figure in later agrarian history. For example, the central problem for an agrarian reform in Chihuahua had less to do with redistributing land to the peasantry and more with breaking up the large estates (Mendieta y Nuñez 1981:184). The agrarian question was not transparently answerable through the reinstatement of a putatively prior-existing, "traditional" land-tenure regime such as village-based communal control of land. The earlier inhabitants of the region had for the most part been wiped out either by disease and "assimilation" or by wars of extermination such as were waged against the Apaches and the Yaquis (Spicer 1962). Instead the future arrangement of people on the land was the subject of debate: when the estates were broken up, what was to be the manner of their division? To whom would which lands go?

Additionally, people of the countryside, the "semi-industrial, semi-agricultural workers," enjoyed a wider range of experiences than other rural Mexicans, not only by working the land in one or another way but through having had to organize themselves and their communities in relation to the frontier and a region of North America which became—at the end of the nineteenth century—a crucible of capitalist development. But these indisputable facts, and the profound differences between the developmental trajectories of the North and the rest of Mexico, also conspire to mask the existence of a viable peasant economy in Chihuahua at the end of the nineteenth century.

1770s–1880s

Established as an outpost of "civilization" on a "barbarous" frontier, Namiquipa was continuously inhabited from the 1780s through the 1880s. Physically isolated during that century, it was also relatively isolated politically *vis-à-vis* the state, militarily by the Apaches, and socially. During this first century, regional and national elites were impotent in their efforts to penetrate the community. Most of Namiquipans' interactions were with inhabitants of neighboring pueblos, with whom they had more in common culturally and socially. Interactions with other kinds of people—whether Indians or elites—took place largely outside the community. Almost all the families of Namiquipa were existentially involved in agriculture during this period, when they were not fighting the Apaches or, less frequently, working outside the community.

At the conclusion of the Apache Wars in the 1880s, then, there existed in Namiquipa a peasant economy. Peasant farming is

> a form of production characterized by (a) the use of family labor and the integration of production and consumption within the family unit, (b) the tendency to assert a socioeconomic rationality based upon the centrality of use values—which emphasize need and not profit, as in a capitalist enterprise, (c) the control of the labor process by the producers themselves and, of course, (d) agriculture as the basic type of economic activity. (Zamosc 1986:216)[3]

Zamosc goes on to point out that looking at peasant farming as a form of production that develops (and in places disappears) historically, requires distinguishing—to invoke a Leninist idiom—the "peasant" and "landlord" "paths" from each other and from the "junker" or "farmer" path. But while Lenin postulated both peasant and junker paths leading to agrarian capitalism, Zamosc's study demonstrates one way in which that is not the inevitable course of events. The junker path may never appear, and the peasant path may be perpetuated and even in the "most advanced" capitalist societies endure in certain forms. Conditions and historical experience in Namiquipa corroborate the latter point, but some modifications to the general characterization of peasant farming in the region are still necessary.

As a result of the militarization of the pueblo, there was a *communal basis* to the defense of the land and way of life. The very existence of "the household" as site of the integration of production and consumption was dependent upon collective defense of the pueblo as a whole, collective defense assuming the function of prior condition for production to take place at all. The integration of production and consumption (in the household or in larger, more embracing units) and the socioeconomic rationality itself were profoundly shaped by the priority of communal defense of land. Additionally, "the producers" were relationally constituted as a group vis-à-vis others, whether barbarians or landlords. Namiquipan history provides examples not only of collective defense of land, but also of collective defense of the labor process in confrontation with alternatives. Those terms well describe, respectively, the conflict between the Sociedad Civil Particular and the state before and after the revolution, and between Namiquipans with "their own pieces of paper" against the *ejido* in the 1920s and 1930s.

What emerged, then, was an ideology of common defense of the pueblo and of the relationship people had to the land. Before the 1880s there was relatively little social differentiation within Namiquipa, one reason being that in light of constant Apache attacks production for profit was scarcely possible. However, several families, from within the community and from without, were notably better off than the majority of Namiquipans and had "a capital" in cattle or land.

One line of the Vásquez family (descendants of the former *alférez* of the presidio), for example, had a large herd of cattle that grazed on the *terrenos de común repartimiento*. And another, younger Francisco Vásquez in the late nineteenth century was described by an elderly informant as "the King of Namiquipa." He had several employees, kept Indian concubines, and set himself up on his rancho, where he sometimes entertained Apaches, hoping to convince them not to attack the pueblo. Prisciliano Barrera, from Casas Grandes, had made his fortune as a muleteer in Arizona and New Mexico and bought properties in Namiquipa and Cruces before 1880 (Calzadíaz Barrera 1979:300). José Casavantes, from Ciudad Guerrero, a member of one of the most important and influential families in the state (cf. Wasserman 1975 on the "Papigochic clan"; Almada 1980:290–95 on Jesús José Casavantes, Don José's father), moved to Namiquipa in the 1870s after administering a hacienda south of the pueblo. Don José owned a flour mill and a store in Namiquipa, invested in small mines in the area, owned large properties within the *municipio,* and was related through kinship or commerce to decidedly nonpeasant elements in the region.

Despite their difference from the majority of Namiquipans, individuals such as these, who lived in the pueblo during the period of Apache fighting and before the miracle of capitalist development in the region, were compelled to subordinate their interests—however alien to a "peasant socioeconomic rationality"—and structure their behavior in accordance with a fundamentally peasant economy. José Casavantes, for example, was an outsider and throughout his residence in Namiquipa could not make over his background, his status, or his interests as landowner, mill owner, investor, and so on. He was always the son of a wealthy, politically well-connected family and in Namiquipa was able to maintain a mistress and her offspring in his own house, yet he married his legitimate daughter off to a family of position in Chihuahuan society. But for many decades in his relations with Namiquipans he assumed more the roles of well-off *vecino,* broker and benign or positive *patrón,* rather than the roles of outsider, cacique, or capitalist exploiter of the community.

Like any other Namiquipan, José Casavantes had to fight the Apaches. One story I was told related how, as a young man, Don José was once humiliated by some women in the plaza who joked that he was a person of property but not a valorous man since he had not proven himself in battle against the "barbarians," as the Namiquipan men had for decades. Don José participated in the next Apache campaign. Upon returning to the pueblo, he rode into the plaza and presented the gossiping women with a trophy from battle, the testicles of an Apache warrior, which he tossed in the dust near the feet of the women.

In his function as broker for the community José Casavantes routinely interceded on behalf of Namiquipans with state authorities, supporting the former in their struggle to maintain control of the *terrenos de común repartimiento.* He was municipal president for many of the years after Namiquipa became an independent municipality in 1884 and before the local administration was seized by political clients of the Terrazas-Creel government such as Victoriano Torres at the turn of the century. In the aftermath of the armed uprising that started in Cruces on April 1, 1893, led by Simón Amaya and Celso Anaya, who "wished to depose the Supreme Power of the Nation,"[4] Casavantes prevented legal charges from being brought against Namiquipan and Cruceño rebels, allowing them to keep their guns.[5] By the end of 1894 Casavantes was accused of leading armed Namiquipans against the owners of Santa

Clara, then invading Namiquipa's land.[6] Finally, his interactions with Namiquipans were for decades guided primarily by recognition of their needs rather than a quest for profit. José Casavantes paid better wages to his workers than did other employers, distributed grains to impoverished farmers during bad years, contributed generously to collective projects such as irrigation ditches, and supported the pueblo's struggle to maintain control of the *terrenos de común repartimiento.*[7]

The initiation of violent and decisive action against Namiquipa peasants to alienate them from their land was to be the project of a later wave of nineteenth- and early twentieth-century immigrants. Namiquipans, meanwhile, imaginatively resisted the transformation of land from a subject of labor into a commodity by ignoring key aspects of the state's project for a rational division of land. Despite their attempt to subvert the new state policy (e.g., inventing a market in *"derechos"* to *terrenos de común repartimiento* while simultaneously insisting on originarios' rights to land even if they had sold their individual *derechos*), however, by the turn of the century, and especially after 1905, Namiquipans saw the best lands of the pueblo devolving to a new class of immigrants, who had a very different notion of the value of land.

1885–1910

Namiquipa is one of the few pueblos in the region not totally depopulated or abandoned during the Apache Wars. However, it was not the only rural town in Chihuahua at the end of the nineteenth century. Beginning around 1885, peasant communities in the sierra and on the margins of the sierra in Chihuahua came under attack from landlords and surveying companies. Compared to other Chihuahuan pueblos, Namiquipa was successful at preventing the owners of enormous estates from stealing the land and destroying the local economy. Nevertheless, neither the "landlord path" nor the "peasant path" were the only historical possibilities in the countryside after 1885. Petty bourgeois immigrants complicated matters, and before the revolution, Namiquipans could not keep out this new class of people, whose project involved purchasing land and instituting a new labor regime. Regional economic integration provided some of the initial conditions for the destruction of the peasant economy.

One effect on the peasant economy of the commodification of land was that some Namiquipan peasants were dispossessed, and sons of the pueblo grew up with no land of their own to work. Where in the past land had been one instrument of production among several for peasant families, there developed a market in land itself. More people did more things with the land: running cattle; growing grains for an external market; or speculating on a future value of the land, which had nothing to do with the products of labor upon it and the people engaged in the labor, but a lot do with a generalized restructuring of economic practices throughout Chihuahua. From a labor regime in which the direct producers made autonomous decisions regarding action upon the land, the labor regime in the pueblo and much of the region underwent a transformation, so that such decisions and actions were reorganized by the somewhat ephemeral demands of a market and the more concrete demands of a segment of the population which appropriated a portion of the product of peasants' labor.

By 1910 agricultural lands in Namiquipa were being worked in at least three different ways, by three different groups of people. First were those *originarios* who maintained control of their fields and worked them as in the past, relying on family labor to produce for the household. Second were the petty bourgeois immigrants who had assumed control of fields which, if they were worked at all, were worked by salaried employees or rented out to sharecroppers. Sometimes the land was left fallow, acquired only to be resold later for a profit. Third were those people who rented land from the municipal government or from landowners. These included both impoverished immigrants and *originarios* who had been dispossessed.

Whether or not they had cultivable fields, *originarios* collectively asserted and enjoyed effective control of extensive commons for wood gathering and grazing cattle, although haciendas from the east and the south threatened and occasionally invaded parts of the commons. There was a clear conflict between *originarios* and petty bourgeois immigrants over control of land. But no less important was the conflict over how the land was evaluated and worked. This was a conflict over whether land was a subject of labor or a commodity. The immigrants used their influence with and support from the state to advance their efforts to transform the labor regime (itself part of the state's project at the time) and so, too, the definition of the land.[8]

In short, the regional economic integration achieved between the Apache Wars and the revolution had the immediate effect of dispossessing some Namiquipan peasants, creating a market in land, and expanding the possibilities for sale of locally produced grains and cattle. The final result of this new invasion of the pueblo—more consequential than the previous century of invasion by *"indios bárbaros"*—was that by 1910 most of the best fields (i.e., irrigated lands and cultivable fields near the pueblo) were seized by outsiders.[9] A dramatic increase in population (see censuses in AMCG: approximately 2,000 in the *municipio* in the late 1880s, 4,000 by 1910) occurred at the same time as the opening of new *labores de temporal* (rain-irrigated fields) and as landless Namiquipans left the pueblo temporarily to labor or sharecrop on neighboring haciendas or to work for wages further from home. The peasant path was faltering, the bourgeois path was in an incipient heyday, and proletarianization best describes the possible future trajectory of Namiquipan peasants at this time.

1925–1935

During the revolution the expansion of small-scale capitalist farming was blocked. Namiquipans seized the land and restored the peasant economy, to the extent that it was possible to restore anything in the midst of a decade during which families were torn apart, many people were away fighting, and many died either in battle or from the influenza epidemic of 1918. In the early years of the revolution, it was easier to recruit fighters during the slack period of the agricultural season. That might partly explain the success of *maderista* and anti-*orozquista* mobilization in Namiquipa during the early months of the revolution (November 1910 to March 1911) by José María Espinosa[10] and in January–February 1913 by Candelario Cervantes.[11] It might also have been a factor in the difficulties Villa had recruiting soldiers in Namiquipa during the spring of 1916 (Alonso 1988c).

In the decade and a half after the revolution, when the pueblo of Namiquipa recovered its land and the people were able to work it in peace, peasant production remained the predominant form in which Namiquipans worked the land. But the peasant economy was now subjected to forces which amounted to another challenge to it. One of these, small- and large-scale capitalist agriculture, was present before the revolution. Another, the state, was novel in the manner it threatened the peasant economy.

Pressures encouraging the end of peasant production and the installation of capitalist agriculture in Namiquipa after the revolution was exercised from what, at first glance, appear strange quarters. Most of the prerevolutionary petty bourgeoisie had been eliminated or driven from the region during the decade of fighting.[12] But their historical role was assumed by people from within the community, primarily by the leadership of the successful armed faction to emerge from the revolution in Namiquipa, the Defensas Sociales, and by certain of the better-off families of *originarios*. The curious thing about this group is that at critical points (e.g., 1922, 1926) they encouraged the establishment of an *ejido* in Namiquipa. Having accomplished that, they used their positions of power within the municipal (and state) governments and within the *ejido* itself to assume control of lands which they could exploit to the

end of producing a profit. This latter goal contrasts with the more limited intentions of the postrevolutionary agrarian reform: creating a viable agricultural sector by distributing small lots of land to people
already living in the countryside.

Francisco Antillon (head of the Defensas in Namiquipa in 1920 and
first signer of the *acta* establishing the *ejido* in 1926) became a partner
in the acquisition of a 40,000-hectare parcel of Santa Clara and in the
1930s left Namiquipa, having purchased lands in an irrigation district
south of Chihuahua City. Pedro Barrera, municipal president for much
of the period from 1916 to 1940, established a cattle ranch (*El Alamo*)
within the common grazing lands of the *ejido* and later set up an apple
orchard, also within the *ejido*. That Antillon pursued his manifestly nonpeasant interests outside the *ejido*, and Barrera within, demonstrates the
range of opportunity available to this self-selected group. A more important point is that these men and others like them pegged their future
to a labor regime very different from the one that engaged most Namiquipans. They were entrepreneurs, and while they and their family
members engaged in work, the unit of production was the enterprise
(the cattle ranch, the orchard, the large irrigated field) and not the
family. They worked the land to the end of gaining a profit in capital
and directed the labor process of employees. That they, and others in
Namiquipa, used the *ejido* and their political ties to the state to realize
such ends poses the question whether the *ejido* should be regarded as
an organization for the restoration of the peasant economy, or for the
establishment of agrarian capitalism.[13]

Another challenge to the peasant economy in Namiquipa after the
revolution was the state. By approving (or ordering) the establishment
of an *ejido* in Namiquipa in 1926, it would seem the state was seeking
to guarantee the reproduction of the peasant economy. The Agrarian
Code mandated that family heads (male) have usufruct rights to agricultural fields, and that *ejidatarios* work the fields themselves. Further, it
prohibited the consolidation of large properties within *ejidos* and hence
militated against the possibility of production for profit on any grand
scale. However, there was a fairly generalized consensus within the
pueblo of Namiquipa that the state was not "giving" land to the people
who worked it, but "taking it away" from them. The state's assertion
of the legitimate authority to declare itself (and not the people) the
"owner" of the land was a personal insult to the Namiquipans (see Nugent 1990, 1991; Nugent and Alonso 1994).

In subsequent decades the state, through the *ejido*, was to exercise a
greater degree of control of the production process, even as it became
the principal organization through which production for profit (rather

than satisfaction of immediate needs) was made possible. But already in the 1925–35 period, the very denial of ownership rights to *ejidatarios* was perceived as a limit on direct agricultural producers' control of the production process, and disposition of the products of their labor.[14] More important, the *ejido* provided a model or form of landholding against which Namiquipans could construct an antithetical one, and this popular model was articulated as *la pequeña propiedad*, the small private landholding.

1940–1965

From the late 1930s until the 1960s the peasant economy in Namiquipa was bolstered by the same set of forces which provided the means of its destruction. Some of these, such as the rapid and generalized adoption of Mennonite farm machinery, enabled peasant families to reproduce themselves working marginal lands and simultaneously made the production of a significant agricultural surplus a distinct possibility for many. Another was the national market in "traditional" products from the fields such as beans and corn, which simultaneously sanctioned peasant cultivation of certain crops and encouraged the development and elaboration of "simple-commodity production" (see Bartra 1982).[15] The state's continued reliance on owners of small plots and *ejidatarios* to produce basic grains to feed the nation and expand agricultural production in the *ejidal* sector in these years was crucial. No less important was the ease with which Chihuahuans could participate in the *bracero* or "guest-worker" program in the United States between 1942 and 1964. The most distinctive feature of the *ejido* of Namiquipa, however, was that it was so large that it included sufficient lands for several generations of new farmers—sons of the original *ejidatarios*—to open up new fields.

Most postrevolutionary *ejidos* in Mexico were formed by *dotación*, granting land to groups of individuals who signed petitions for the formation of an *ejido*. Since 1920 the legal size of newly created plots has varied between 4 and 20 hectares of *temporal*, but their actual size has always averaged less than 10 hectares per family. The only provision for an *ejido's* securing new lands for the sons of a family was by petitioning for an "amplification" of the original *ejidal* grant, a process which could take decades and which did not always guarantee a positive result. Consequently, children born into *ejidos* have difficulty securing land to work within it. To remain in the countryside and work the land, they must either purchase land, form new *ejidos*, or become agricultural laborers—landless peasants. In Namiquipa until the 1960s, however, it was possible for young men to be assigned *ejidal* plots which had never before been worked. Because there was land within the *ejido* suitable for cultivation and not yet monopolized by any individual, new generations of peasants could support themselves and their families working *ejidal* lands.[16]

So in the decades between 1935 and 1965 more Namiquipans were cultivating more lands, there was an up-and-down but on the whole steady increase in agricultural production, and production was on the whole organized in very much the same manner as it had been in the 1890s. Now, however, Namiquipan agriculturalists were able to sell their agricultural surpluses (when they produced them) and thereby enter into new relationships with a variety of outsiders: merchants, middlemen, bankers, and, particularly after the 1950s, agents of the state. Direct agricultural producers still exercised control over the production process, limited only by the fact that the fields many labored upon were not their properties. Finally, while Namiquipan agriculturalists' "socioeconomic rationality" was still "based upon the centrality of use values" (Zamosc 1986:216; cf. Godelier [1969] 1974, 2:192ff.) and oriented above all toward the satisfaction of needs, they were at the same time producing commodities, if not to the socially defined end of securing a profit.

The activity of farming may be as boring to write about as it is to read about; I find it more interesting to engage in.[17] At the end of the season Namiquipan farmers had either produced enough grain to live until the end of the next growing season—consuming or selling what they had grown—or they had not. In the best of years they produced enough of certain commodities (grains) to exchange for others with which they could survive, or even improve their lives by purchasing other commodities or instruments of production, or sponsoring "rituals"—a wedding, a baptism, a dance, a round of drinks—or paying the taxman.

The majority of Namiquipans during this period owned or controlled all of their labor-power and all or almost all the means of production necessary to engage in agriculture.[18] Thus, according to a structural definition of social class of the type advocated by Gerald Cohen, they fall somewhere between "independent producers" and "peasants" (which latter category Cohen [1978: 65–68] scarcely discusses in any detail). Another way to regard them is as simple- or petty-commodity producers, which is to say the individuals labor upon their fields and organize their own productive activities, wage-labor plays an insignificant role in the process, and that portion of the final product of labor not consumed is sold to another party.

The productive activity on the land by Namiquipans, reproducing themselves and their pueblo according to a fundamentally peasant rationality, is conducted in the context of a capitalist market into which the products of their labor are introduced. In other words, their petty-commodity relations are *"production* relations [for which] [t]he essential requirement is that the product, as a commodity, is placed in circulation by the producer, who, as a controller of his means of production and the production process, is the owner of the commodity until it is exchanged" (Roseberry 1983:216). Viewed from the standpoint of the market and the socioeconomic system of which it is a part, Namiquipans are semi-independent producers of commodities—beans, corn, cattle, and labor-power. Accordingly, the labor process in Namiquipa has for decades been organized in relation to two distinct—but neither incompatible nor contradictory—logics, sets of practices, and material and ideological requirements: the peasant economy and the capitalist economy. Namiquipans are privileged to enjoy the best of two worlds as independent farmers cultivating their "own" land for their own households and free to sell not only the products of their labor but also their labor power in a capitalist market which was expanding from the 1940s onward. However, they must also endure the worst of these two worlds.

The 1930s were as difficult for Namiquipan farmers as for millions of people in the United States—New York stockbrokers and dust bowl refugees alike. Responding to immoderate price increases in the Chihuahuan countryside, the governor established *"juntas reguladoras"* (regulatory commissions) to control prices in the Guerrero District.[19] Harvests were bad, prices were high, and there was little work for agriculturalists after bad years. This changed with the United States' entrance into World War II, when the sudden demand for workers in a war-fueled economy to the north was met by the U.S. implementation of the *bracero* program (see Cockcroft 1986:64ff.), under which workers were recruited in Mexico and contracted to work in the United States, primarily in the countryside.

Namiquipans signed up for the *bracero* program en masse. The municipal government administered the list of Namiquipans who applied to work in the United States.[20] Through this program Namiquipans were able to work legally in the United States for periods ranging from several weeks to several months each year. Namiquipans preferred to work on ranches or small farms near Chihuahua, but many wound up working harvests throughout the United States, or in slaughterhouses, on railroad maintenance-of-way gangs, and in other semi-industrial jobs.

The *bracero* program established an official sanction and gave a legitimate and orderly gloss to what was fast becoming a critical feature of agricultural production in Namiquipa: the need for farmers to supplement the moderate or nonexistent incomes derived from work on their fields with wages to acquire the basic necessities for life in the pueblo. While hundreds of Namiquipans signed on as *braceros*, hundreds more went to the United States to work illegally. It was primarily men, without their families, who took advantage of formal and informal networks of contacts on *el otro lado* ("the Other Side" of the U.S.-Mexican border) to secure wage-work there.

The encouragement of circular migration for wage-work in the United States was not singularly driven from the North. First, the requirements of an income in years of bad harvests drove many men outside the pueblo temporarily. For example, in 1944, 75 percent of the maize crop failed in Namiquipa, and many men left town.[21] But a more enduring motivation was simply the rhythm of agricultural work in Namiquipa itself. People no longer were cultivating winter wheat. The growing season for corn began in April, for beans in July, and harvests were in by October or November at the latest. In other words, it is possible to be "economically active" (as the censuses put it) as an agriculturalist and be totally unoccupied in work for half the year. Coupled with the relative proximity of Namiquipa to the U.S. border, that factor has made working for wages on the Other Side feasible and desirable for decades.

Nevertheless, throughout this period (indeed until the 1990s) the Namiquipan men working in the United States, whether legally or illegally, returned to their pueblo and their lands. Their entrance into the north-of-the-border labor market was transient, the money wages earned directed toward sustaining their families in Namiquipa. From the standpoint of Namiquipans, then, what they received in wages they could save and later deploy as capital to reproduce and sustain their units of production on the land. And these were primarily in the *ejidal* or the *minifundista* sectors.[22]

The vague legality of the manner in which people worked and held their land through arrangements developed in practice by Namiquipans is highlighted in a communication of 1951 between the Comisariado Ejidal de Namiquipa and the agrarian minister for the state of Chihuahua. The Agrarian Ministry was inquiring into the situation in the various *ejidos* in the state, and the *comisario* for Namiquipa wrote back that the *ejido* is "quite large . . . with 1172 Ejidatarios included in the census," though few of them had their Certificate of Agrarian Rights.

> This Comisariado Ejidal is disposed to cooperate [with the state] so far as possible, because all the *ejidatarios* belong to our Political Institution, but it would be almost impossible, if one wanted to know, to determine the number of *ejidatarios* who have their credentials, for the simple reason that the great majority neither know about the policy nor, less, if they benefit from belonging to said Institution [no saben ni que cosa es politica y ni tampoco si les beneficia el ser miembros de dicha Institución].[23]

Popular reluctance to participate fully in the political institution which mediated their relationship to the land and organized the way they labored upon it may be understood as not only a rejection of the particular policy but also a repudiation of the state's attempt to circumscribe the political terrain organizing and invading a material terrain, namely the *pueblo's* land and the way it was worked. By the 1960s the state had in large degree redefined what it was farmers accomplished by working on the land. Rather than cultivate for local consumption, they produced commodities for sale to pay off debts to the BANRURAL. But from the standpoint of *serrano* peasants something very different was at issue: sustaining themselves as agriculturalists and feeding their families.

The Coordinadora de Uniones de Ejidos y Colonias y Comités Municipales Campesinos del Oeste del Estado [Chihuahua], C.N.C. circulated an "Informative Bulletin" during the mid-1960s describing how, at the end of a terrible year, the BANRURAL was demanding that all agricultural loans be paid back.[24] The loans were to be paid by peasants turning over all of their (limited) harvests to the state grain warehouses, the *bodegas* CONASUPO. For the agriculturalists it was less a question of paying back loans or refusing to than of surviving as farmers or not.

> Last year we worked for the development of the country, took advantage of a good season, brought in the greatest harvest in Chihuahua's history, and were able to pay off most of the credits advanced to us. This year the situation is desperate, we invested much more heavily in our lands and the credit was not enough to cover it, production is minimal, and the grains are damaged. We have two paths before us: WE PAY BACK THE LOANS OR WE FEED OUR FAMILIES.
>
> We know that the country is in crisis and more immediately are aware that all that we purchase is twice as expensive as last year. We also know that this crisis was provoked by the wealthy people who have taken their money out of the country. We know that credit will not expand and that the prices for grains only increased 30%. And if that is not enough almost all of our harvests were lost, and the little that was brought in will only in a pinch provide for our subsistence in the coming year.
>
> On the other hand . . . BANRURAL is demanding the recovery of the loans, and has sent supervisors to the *bodegas* Conasupo to order people to pay by bringing in the grain.
>
> In our assemblies we have decided to organize ourselves to protest against this situation. We want our region to be considered as it is today: as a DISASTER ZONE. That the peasant family be pro-

tected. That we be allowed to keep the little grain we produced in order to subsist until next year, which is already looking better. That we not be compelled to pay back the loans. That *we* not be made to bear the full weight of the economic crisis. (AEN e.Ejido B [1966?])

Some demands are then listed, including that the state recognize that the harvest was as bad as it was and the "crop insurance" fund cover their loans, "corrupt and despotic public employees" be identified and removed, the CONASUPO pay for grains delivered and not count them against loans, terms of credit be more favorable to agriculturalists, and the state sink thirty deep wells in the region to assure more even production from year to year.

1970–1985

The characterization advanced above of Namiquipan (men) during the period of 1940–65 probably raises more questions than it answers. But it was during that period that the effects of developments outside Namiquipa were felt more clearly within the community by these unwilling *ejidatarios*. During the 1970s and 1980s the agricultural production process in Namiquipa underwent even more profound changes related to shifts in people's orientation to the products of their labor and the popular understanding of the destiny of the products of labor. Practically, there was a movement by Namiquipans away from production of basic grains toward investment in cash crops. Experientially, it was more difficult than ever before to sustain the illusion, long dominant as a key imaginative figure in popular consciousness, that the community was an autonomous, self-reproducing whole. These shifts occurred at the same time as a manifest and absolute increase in the number of landless laborers, and a tendency in the community to direct resources (land, labor-power, capital/credit) toward the production of different commodities to free themselves from the state. Above all, the 1970s and 1980s were years of crisis. Not only have agricultural production; local, regional, and national politics; and the world economy—especially the Mexican economy—been in a state of crisis, but the legitimacy of the capitalist state in Mexico has been challenged from below.

Cultivation of seasonal (*temporal*) fields was never a reliable and consistent way of making a living working the land. The construction of waterworks in Namiquipa is a thing of the past. Most of the acequias (irrigation canals) in use today were built before the end of the nineteenth century. A few individuals successfully sank deep wells from which they draw water out with pumps, but these are used to irrigate certain fields and orchards and only indirectly constitute a benefit to the community as a whole.[25] Most farmers are at the combined mercy of increasingly less regular rains and the BANRURAL. The only definite thing one can say about agricultural production in Namiquipa since 1970 is that it has been highly variable.

During 1983 and 1984, Namiquipans talked about a bumper crop in the mid-1970s, but that decade as a whole is recalled as a period during which harvests were often minimal. Plotting the value of production for the *municipio* as a whole from 1970 to 1985 shows a steady absolute rise, but measured against the progressively accelerating increase in prices in general it shows a decline in real value.[26] By 1970 almost all of the land in the *municipio* suitable for cultivation was being cultivated. Already by the 1960s the average size of the agricultural parcel could be no larger than 20 hectares. In the *ejido* of Namiquipa in 1983, about 2,700 heads of families were cultivating almost 35,000 hectares of land, the average parcel size about 13 hectares (BETA). By 1970, of the 5,500 people in the *municipio* who worked as farmers or ranchers, slightly more than half figured in the census as *ejidatarios* (1,701) or independent producers on lands they controlled or owned (1,057); slightly less than half were salaried employees (161), day-laborers or peons (1,628), or unpaid family members (924) (National Census 1970). By the 1980s, the tendency was for landless laborers to slightly outnumber *ejidatarios* and independent producers in Namiquipa. That tendency is not more pronounced only because it is held in check by permanent and circular migration for wage-work, especially in the United States.

By the 1970s, then, there was no room for expansion of agriculture in Namiquipa, production was little more stable than it had been in the past, the number of landless agricultural laborers was increasing, and more farmers were working more, smaller plots of land. Furthermore, particularly with the onset of the economic crisis of the 1980s, the products of their labor which they were compelled to turn over to the *bodegas* CONASUPO were compensated at diminishing rates.

The only positive development during this period was the increase in apple production, a result of farmers putting orchards on virtually all of the irrigated land along the Río Santa María. Fruit trees are not new to the region. Teodoro de Croix named planting orchards as one of the tasks for the settlers in 1778, though it was never done on a large scale in Namiquipa until recently. (Bachiniva, on the upper reaches of the Río Santa María, has had extensive orchards since the early twentieth century.) Namiquipans had set up a few small orchards—100 or 200 trees on an acre or a hectare of land—by the 1960s. The first large orchard in Namiquipa was put in by a Jalisco-based company—merchants who marketed fruit in Guadalajara and Mexico City—which planted several thousand apple trees north of pueblo viejo (the old pueblo) on some "private properties" they purchased within the *ejido*. These trees were in production about the same time the paved highway spur to Namiquipa was completed, around 1970. There were fewer than 100,000 fruit trees in the *municipio* in 1975; by 1980 there were 780,000, mostly owned by Namiquipans, and more than three-quarters of those trees were in production (MEBCh; *Monografías Municipales* 1982:193).

Much of the impulse for this sudden development came from commercial enterprises based outside the community. Another group of fruit merchants from Jalisco, for example, built a large warehouse just outside Namiquipa in 1983–84 to sort, package, and ship out the local product, which they purchased from Namiquipan growers.[27] This development brought with it a new set of social problems which previously had no rooting in local society. It became realistic for more people to remain in the town as employees of capitalist enterprises controlled from the outside. Women entered the salaried work force, laboring outside the household picking apples in the orchards or packing apples in the warehouses. The buyers for the local product were frequently ruthless crooks, who would agree to purchase apples from the growers, load them onto trucks, then disappear the next day without paying the independent producers. In 1984 some foreign warehouse operators did not pay their workers minimum wage, abused the women, humiliated the men, and fired people whenever there was the slightest hint of their organizing.

However, none of this would have been possible if Namiquipans who owned (or thought they owned) land had declined to go into apple production themselves. First, because many people in Namiquipa have what they regard as properties, they are willing to make the considerable capital investments required to start an orchard. By way of contrast, no one would think of putting an orchard on an *ejidal* plot, since such a plot could be reassigned to another *ejidatario*, with no compensation for all the improvements made upon it (the trees, irrigation system, etc.). Second, and more important, they perceive setting up orchards as a way of being more independent from the state, since the products of their work (and investment) are not automatically consigned to the *bodegas* CONASUPO at prices set by the state. (Never mind that the practices of the apple merchants may be less scrupulous and fair than those of the state; in the former case there is always the possibility of personally negotiating the terms of sale, rather than their being imposed without the direct producer having any say.) Finally, there is the illusion of great profits to be made producing apples, a certain determinant of greater independence for the producer.[28]

In short, for Namiquipans the production of cash crops is more appealing than cultivation of basic grains for several reasons. It enables more people to stay in the community, working smaller plots of land. Since they recognize that in their activity as tillers of the soil (whether *ejidal* plots or *pequeñas propiedades*) they are producing commodities in any event, they might as well produce commodities whose sale is not controlled by an institution which has a monopoly on the marketing of those commodities. In short, apples have the advantage over beans and corn that, by producing them, people may free themselves from the state (even if thereby they only subject themselves to merchants).

SOCIAL CLASS OR LABOR PROCESS?

Namiquipan involvement in the production of cash crops in the 1970s and 1980s appears quite distant from the "viable peasant economy" in Namiquipa at the end of the nineteenth century described earlier. Clearly the sorts of activities people in Namiquipa now organize themselves to do, and the ways they organize themselves singly or in groups, are very different from what they were a century ago. But what are the real differences? And who are the people and groups of people in Namiquipa today who are so different from their ancestors?

One way to describe the differences between the 1880s and the 1980s in Namiquipa is in terms of the greater degree of social differentiation within the pueblo. In the 1880s Namiquipa was a community of armed peasants, well-off compared to the standards that prevailed on Porfirian haciendas and in communities of *indigenas* throughout the rest of Mexico. A few individuals and families enjoyed greater wealth, controlled more resources, and had a freer reign in the exercise of power within the community, but they were neither numerous nor so clearly differentiated from the peasant majority. A more important site of difference was between the community as a whole and outsiders, whether "barbarians" whom the Namiquipans fought to dominate or exterminate, or agents of the state and capital who sought to control and dominate, if not eliminate, the pueblo of Namiquipa.

In the 1980s, by way of contrast, there existed groups of people distinguishable in terms of different involvements with processes of production and reproduction, ranging from peasants and workers to capitalist entrepreneurs. Even those whose principal activity was in agriculture could be distinguished as capitalist entrepreneurs, peasants, simple-commodity producers, and proletarians. In addition, several groups whose primary involvement was not with agriculture are immediately recognizable: shopkeepers and artisans, bureaucrats, proletarians, and unpaid household laborers.

ON CHARACTERIZATION

In recent years it has become common to talk about rural Mexicans rather less in terms of their similarity to other historical peasantries and more in terms of rural social classes. The latter term has the value of linking these people to broader structures of power, to a world capitalist socioeconomic formation. Its use helps us detect how rural peoples participate in a form of production the logic of which has resonances far beyond the boundaries of the little community. Hence, it allows for understanding a community such as Namiquipa, for example, in relation to others in a way that reflects the people's engagement—even if only as dominated subjects—with the world rather than as "part-societies with part-cultures" (Kroeber's classic definition of peasants).

Distinct uses of the concept of social class to understand people of the countryside in Mexico generated a debate between so-called peasantists and so-called proletarianists.[29] This debate encouraged anthropologists and rural sociologists to refine their definitions of social class for the analysis of "peasants" who labor within a particular socioeconomic system, capitalism. A related development has involved the ongoing interest in peasant mobilization and participation in rebellion and revolution in the wake of new modes of production securing dominance over others within a social formation, and the ways this provides evidence of political class formation among the peasantry.[30]

In trying to understand the history of Namiquipan social class formation, I argue for maintaining some skepticism regarding the value of rigorous definitions of social class when talking about the peasantry. There has indeed been social differentiation under dependent capitalism of a more or less classical sort in Namiquipa. But the differentiated categories, particularly as they figure in social science discourse, are only marginally useful for understanding identifiable groups or individuals within the pueblo—for the inscription of caricatures rather than characterizations.

Such an unsettling, or trivial, conclusion derives largely from the tendency to essentialize attributes of "classness" or specific "class positions" in a fundamentally static and synchronic way (cf. Hobsbawm 1973; Corrigan 1975; Shanin 1987a). One alternative view that sidesteps these problems by situating social groups in historical motion is provided by the examination of political class formation. In studying Namiquipa, that would require posing questions of whether and the extent to which Namiquipans (or some among them) have developed as a "class-for-themselves," and how in this respect they have fitted into broader political struggles to change Mexican society.[31] This line of inquiry has the virtue of not being hidebound to a set of a priori criteria, but in the example of Namiquipa it would lead to the conclusion that the most revolutionary peasants pushed to the front of a popular agenda nothing less than the struggle for "private property."

That conclusion is commensurate with the material regarding struggles for land in Namiquipa presented in earlier chapters. It also highlights the contradiction revealed in that account, that in preventing control of the land by outsiders or the state through the struggle for "private properties" Namiquipans invite exploitation by capital. In other words, just as the study of social class in Namiquipa may lead to caricature rather than characterization, so the study of political class formation may leave the analysis confounded by a contradiction. Is it, then, possible to determine who these people are in terms of what they do on the land? To answer that question we must first review in greater detail specific problems that are raised by focusing on the so-called class character of the peasantry, while overlooking the cultural and political dimensions of the ways people organize their engagement with the labor process, and their relationships to other groups of people.

The debate in Mexico between *campesinistas* and *proletaristas* appears to demand an either/or answer, framed in terms of essentialist categories, to the question of whether the people of the countryside are "peasants" or "proletarians." The hardening of positions in both camps only underlines the rigidity of each of these perspectives.[32] The *proletaristas'* reticence to admit that politically dominated people in the countryside may be peasants rather than proletarians or petty bourgeois derives from their hostility to the peasantry inherited from Lenin, and clearly an element of Marxist tradition supposedly sanctified by Marx in the *Eighteenth Brumaire of Louis Bonaparte* (Alavi 1987).[33]

When he wrote about the Mexican peasantry in the 1970s, Roger Bartra drew upon parts of that earlier text (about the French peasantry in the 1840s) to deride the "petty bourgeois side" of the peasantry in Mexico and argue that soon the "proletarian side" would manifest itself (Bartra 1975b). Demonstrating that surreal intellectual contortions are not exclusively the métier of French intellectuals, this vulgar recension of "Marxism" is an example of

> a formalization of Marx's thought that brings it in line with western social science as it drives a wedge between us and Marx. Thus an epithet like *kleinstädtisch* ("small town like") acquires the fixed frenchified English [or Spanish] translation "petty bourgeois" and its precise referents in a typology of class categories are debated with scholastic fervor. (Hart 1983:116)

A more imaginative approach to the problem of characterization (are these peasants? or proletarians? or semiproletarians? or disguised proletarians? or a rural bourgeoisie?) involves the postulation of "inter-mediate" classes. An example occurs in Cockcroft's discussion of late colonial Mexico.

> "Intermediate classes" is a more accurate concept than "middle class" because various groups compose the category and are inter-mediate not because of middle levels of income, property, or power, but because they are situated in an intermediate position between major social classes that either own the means of produc-tion or apply their labor power to activate them. . . . [I]ntermediate classes do not constitute a major pole of a bipolar class contradic-tion—such as landlord-serf, bourgeoisie-proletariat, and so forth. (Cockcroft 1983:54)

Notwithstanding that this frames the issue in terms of a (single) bipolar class contradiction, therefore remaining tied to an either/or point of view, it does open up the possibility of an alternative perspective. Not only are many people "situated . . . between major social classes," but additionally, in their actions vis-à-vis the determinants of "class posi-tion" (means of production, forces of production, labor-power, relations of exploitation), people may assume a variety of different engagements. Furthermore, their engagements are partially conditioned by how the process of production is apprehended and conceived by workers them-selves: "What distinguishes the worst architect from the best of bees is this, that the architect raises his structure in imagination before he erects it in reality" (Marx [1867] 1906:198).

Formulating the problem in terms of engagement and process, rather than static a priori positionings, is better suited for developing an un-derstanding of peasants or workers in connection with their own com-munities *and* in connection with a global socioeconomic system in which they participate as social subjects, and not merely as the (inert, half-formed, exploited) inhabitants of frontier backwaters on the pe-riphery of the semiperiphery of the capitalist world-system. The larger system to which they are connected consists not of mechanically related "class positions," but of a variety of historically created relationships of power, of custom, of practice, of apprehension and conception. Their relationships are "fixed" only through the radical and in the end ab-stract theoretical maneuver which pretends to organize them concep-tually as elements of a social "science." That makes it easy to forget that it is people who are engaged in these relationships, in terms of which they not only act but also come to know themselves or redefine them-selves by conducting a similar (but distinct) set of theoretical maneu-vers.[34] But for the people, the stakes are much higher than the resolution of a theoreticist debate. It is life itself which is on the line.

Let us return, then, to the question of whether it is possible to determine who people are in terms of what they do on the land (in the workshop, in the factory or office). I maintain that question is only answerable once we arrive at the notion that it is in fact labor and work which are at issue rather than people's "class characteristics" or the degree to which they act together as a class vis-à-vis other classes (cf. Calagione and Nugent 1992). Namiquipans, for example, fight over ways of working the land. They do so, however, not because social life is structured in such a way that they are compelled to labor in one or another manner, nor because they belong to such-and-such a class with a self-evident set of interests. More important is the fact that ways of working the land are themselves the matters at stake in their struggles. Understanding how people articulate their relationships to the land, the practices they engage in upon it, and their relationships to one another as well as to outsiders requires an interrogation of notions of identity—and their meanings—that are grounded in people's experiences rather than the abstract models which social scientists can produce.

Examples of the latter would be what would result were one to distinguish contemporary groups in terms of their objective place in a network of ownership relations according to whether and how much of their labor power and their means of production they own or effectively control (Cohen 1978:65ff.). The result would be a typology of class positions consisting of something like the following: professionals, bureaucrats, shopkeepers, artisans, capitalist entrepreneurs, farmers, peasants, semiproletarians, proletarians, household laborers.

One problem with typological exercises of this sort is that it is always possible to think up intermediate "types." Another problem is that it is no less possible, indeed routine, for individuals to occupy several of these positions in the course of a lifetime, or in the course of a day. In other words, one can be a peasant in the morning, a proletarian in the afternoon, and a petty-commodity producer in the evening. The preponderance of categorical anomalies in really-existing social roles, or the tendency for individuals to occupy multiple "class positions" simultaneously, however, is evidence not so much that subjects do not "fit" as that the typology is inadequate because the distinctions it produces are not relevant to people's experience.

Like social scientists, Namiquipans use specific terms to designate specific categories of persons. Their terms, such as *trabajador* (worker, without land), *campesino* (politically dominated subject), *agricultor* (independent agriculturalist), or *rico* (wealthy individual) describe people's engagement in production and place in society. What the different terms designate, in other words, is something beyond just "native categories"

for distinguishing between rural social classes. They also indicate different qualities of personhood.

The one term that applies most accurately to the greatest number of
people in Namiquipa is *agricultor,* or agriculturalist. This is true both in
the descriptive sense, that most people engaged in agriculture participate in something more embracing and generalized than "the peasant
economy," and in the ideological sense, that most people engaged in
agricultural production self-consciously identify themselves as *agricultores* rather than as *campesinos*—and even less as *ricos.*

If *agricultor* is the privileged term according to which people identify
(and accordingly recognize) themselves, *los ricos* or *los campesinos* are
more characteristically used to identify others. For example, someone
who insists they are an *agricultor* will use the word *campesino* to describe
a less fortunate, immiserated, dominated other. In fact it is very infre-
quent to hear people identify themselves as *campesinos,* with the exception of politicians and Confederación Nacional de Campesinos (CNC)
officials or individuals whom everyone else would unhesitatingly identify as *ricos.*

What is conveyed by the *terms,* then, is not only the identification of
class position, but also different kinds of engagement with the production process as a whole. The different categories map out forms of labor
and Namiquipan regard for labor and the value of labor on the land.
Ideally, labor on the land or work is a process that the *agricultor* sets in
motion, controls from beginning to end by making autonomous decisions regarding the timing of activities and what those activities are, and
finally retains the power to dispose of the product of those actions. At
the center of this system for categorizing persons is an ideal of masculine
identity, autonomy, and engagement in the practice of working the land.

What is conveyed by Namiquipans' distinctions between *agricultor*
and *campesino* is not *only* different class positions defined in relation to
different degrees of control over the means of production and labor
power, but *also* different kinds of political domination, honor, and autonomy. People who appear to be realizing the socially recognized ideal
as *agricultores* recognize their situation as a relatively privileged one
(they are after all surviving) and that there are others (say, *campesinos*)
who are more successfully dominated than they. Or individual *ricos* try
to mask or downplay their privileged position, wealth, and power by
proclaiming a humble, dominated identity as *campesino,* which is always
preposterous.

In other words, these are categories of *status* as well as class. The way
the categories are read by Namiquipans provides knowledge not only of
class domination, but also of degrees of political domination, with relative independence providing greater social honor to the individual.

Hence, the categories are defined also in relation to perceived degrees of *independence* in the labor process *from the control of bosses* (whether *patrones* or state bureaucrats). It is this political or status dimension that is key to the contrasting meanings of *agricultor, campesino, peón, trabajador,* and so on among Namiquipans.

FUNCTIONAL DUALISM OR CULTURAL STRUGGLE?

According to the description offered earlier of the lengths Namiquipans go to to make real this socialized ideal of being independent producers on the land, they enter into relationships not only with their land, their tools, their time, their families, and their crops, but also with myriad other things and people. Namiquipan men must work outside the pueblo for at least a part of their lives, or they must work elsewhere than in their own fields; they must sell their labor-power, as well as the (agricultural) products of their work in the fields. Additionally, they must rely on institutions and organizations established or controlled by the state to prepare the fields and plant, work, and sell the product. The BANRURAL with its loan officers and agricultural engineers, the *ejido,* and the *bodegas* CONASUPO must also be engaged for any but the most impoverished *agricultor* to survive from year to year.

Viewed from the standpoint of a continental (indeed global) political economy, Namiquipan *agricultores* who sell their labor-power to capitalists in commercial agriculture, workshops, restaurants, and construction sites in the United States are arguably a "peasantized" proletariat. Capitalists may purchase their labor-power at a budget price, compensating the worker with money the value of which is not enough to cover the costs of the workers' reproduction, since the conditions for the reproduction of the work force are located in the peasant economy. This is the argument of advocates of the functional dualist hypothesis (see Kearney 1980:116; De Janvry and Garramón 1977; De Janvry 1981), according to which capitalism—particularly commercial agriculture— "requires the constant re-creation of the peasant economy" since it is "incapable of absorbing the peasant economy entirely" (Stavenhagen 1978:34–35). The conditions for the reproduction of the labor force (of capitalist enterprises) are to be found in the "subsistence" sector, the peasant economy. Capital gets off easy since It is not compelled to pay even a "living" wage to the work force. Peasant production, finally, subsidizes commercial agriculture.

This hypothesis is compelling, functionally coherent, and situates peasant agriculture in relation to a capitalist world-system. Given that Namiquipans have been selling their (undervalued) labor-power in the North American countryside for decades, it might be tempting to explain developments in Namiquipa in terms of this hypothesis. However, that would also give capital greater credit than is its due (in the conspiracy-realization department) even as it denies any agency on the part of the "peasantized" "proletariat." It may be indisputable that most of the peasantries anthropologists study "are 'precipitates' of the uneven development of capitalism and of forms of accommodation to particular directions that development may take. They emerge within a variety of social situations in response to various demands that can only be understood in terms of world-historical processes" (Roseberry 1983:208). At the same time, however, it is not to lapse into some variety of methodological individualism to insist that, as peasants, people may use the wages they receive while working in the capitalist sector to reproduce themselves, their families, and their communities in a form that is inimical to capitalism. To return again to the problem of the unit of analysis, the point is that when viewed from the standpoint of the world-system, Namiquipans and other *serrano* peasants may be attributed whatever characteristics allow them to fit neatly into the model of the system (e.g., as "disguised proletarians," as members of the Industrial Reserve Army). However, such a description says little about how they themselves view their engagement with "world-historical processes" or whether through their action they are making an accommodation to the uneven development of capitalism or resisting it.

The stubborn resiliency of what I will continue to insist on calling peasant production is not explained only by the fact that it is "functional" for capitalism or a secondary outcome of underdevelopment (e.g., as manifestation of the blockage of the development of capitalist relations of production in the periphery). It may also be explained in terms of the laboring practices and strategies of resistance of people who, in defiance of world-scale social and economic processes, seek to determine the forms and organizations through which to define, reproduce, and distinguish themselves.

The analysis of the articulation of modes of production lends some insight into how (*not* why), after all these years, the peasantry refuses to go away. The "assumption that the appearance of capitalism—whether as the result of 'internal' development as in Europe or 'external' imposition as in the case of the colonies—signaled the more or less immediate and inevitable disintegration of PCMPs ["pre-capitalist modes of production"] and the subsumption of the agents of these modes under capitalist relations of production" is no longer tenable (Wolpe 1980:2). Instead what has to be accounted for is precisely the continued reproduction of the peasantry under capitalism.

I think it is possible to view this phenomenon from the standpoint of the *agricultores,* for whom the accumulation of capital secured as wage-laborers provides the conditions for the reproduction of the peasant economy. This position is not particularly controversial, though it does introduce the issues of identity and status, which are crucial to the ideological concept of the *agricultor*. Namiquipans who work on the Other Side are aware of the manner in which they are exploited when they come to the United States to work, and they have developed a critique of the wage-system and the organization and pace of capitalist production in general in the United States (Alonso 1992a; Nugent 1992). Nevertheless, they also know that it is impossible to make a go of it simply and exclusively working their land, and so, to the end of being able to continue as *agricultores,* they sell their labor-power abroad. "The peasant economy" does not subsidize "the capitalist economy"; rather, *agricultores* use the sale of their labor-power to capitalists to subsidize their livelihood in the countryside, to sustain their identity as *agricultores,* which is to say, autonomous, independent, agricultural direct producers. Further, this humiliating and alienating activity, in which the person is exploited and denied the fruits of their labor, is an activity which is (again ideally) engaged in *outside* the pueblo.

Another challenge to the autonomy of *agricultores* involves their reliance on the institutions and organizations of the state to survive in the countryside. Here it is more difficult for Namiquipans to turn a complex of inequitable relationships to their advantage to advance their interests and consolidate their identities as *agricultores.* Failing to work with the BANRURAL may make it impossible to secure enough seed or a much-needed repair to a tractor at the right time to commence planting. After the harvest, there is no other market for the products of labor than the *bodegas* CONASUPO, where the state has a monopoly on basic grains, including their pricing and distribution. Distinct from the requirement to sell one's labor-power outside the community or contend with the circumstance that agricultural production is now (has to be) production of commodities for sale in a capitalist market, these institutions and organizations of the state are direct interventions in the process of agricultural production itself.

It is in light of these interventions by the state through the BANRURAL, the CNC, the Secretaría de Agricultura y Recursos Hidráulicos (SARH), and the *ejido* (what Roger Bartra [1982] called the "structures of mediation") that the struggle for what Namiquipans call "private property" is the most "revolutionary" struggle they can attempt to advance. "Private property" is a transformation of what, a century earlier, was referred to as land of which individuals had possession (*posesión*). Their land, or the notion of holding and working their land in a particular way, is all that they may still fight for. And the struggle for "private property"/*posesión* is not a struggle for *capitalist* property, but a struggle for control of one of multiple elements of the production process as a whole. It is a struggle for the subject of labor—land—and a struggle to preserve that subject in a particular form and, importantly, relationship to a particular subjectivity, that of the *agricultor*. What is crucial for Namiquipan *agricultores* is to be able to work in their fields and realize their identities in a manner that challenges the identifications and definitions of reality imposed from without by the state.

This way of articulating the contemporary struggle of Namiquipans is different from the issue of social class differentiation, the question of whether *agricultores* collectively constitute a "class-for-itself," or an interrogation of the relationship of class formation in Namiquipa to broader political struggles in Mexican society. The argument is that neither social differentiation (something that happens *to* people) nor class consciousness (something *imputed* to subordinated social groups) is the phenomenon to be explained. Instead what must be understood is the labor process itself (something that people *do,* are engaged in). For it is precisely this engagement in agricultural production, itself simultaneously material and ideational, which is the focus of struggle in Namiquipa today.

> Labour is, in the first place, a process in which both man and Nature participate, and in which man of his own accord starts, regulates, and controls the material re-actions between himself and Nature. He opposes himself to Nature as one of her own forces, setting in motion arms and legs, head and hands, the natural forces of his body, in order to appropriate Nature's productions in a form adapted to his own wants. By thus acting on the external world and changing it, he at the same time changes his own nature. . . .
> At the end of every labour-process, we get a result that already existed in the imagination of the labourer at its commencement. He not only effects a change of form in the material on which he works, but he also realises a purpose. (Marx [1867] 1906: 197–98)

The popular model for tenure in agricultural land in the 1920s was the small private property, *la pequeña propiedad,* and it remained so through the 1980s in what was arguably *the* revolutionary struggle in which Namiquipans were involved. This is not a struggle for capitalist property, but for control of the labor process by the direct producer. And this is an ideological struggle in the sense that "the way people conceptualize and express their relations to one another . . . [is] based on the actual ties people develop with one another in the course of organizing both the labour of production and daily life, and the social appropriation of the product" (Sider 1980:22). According to the formulation of Namiquipans, exercise of that control is internally related (Ollman

1971) to the ideological requirement that production for needs predominates over production for profit and the (material) constraint according to which production and consumption are focused in a relatively small unit, the household, the continued reproduction of which is in turn dependent on collective defense of the community as a whole. Community itself is, in this sense, a relation of production (Roseberry 1991:22). In short, the resiliency of the peasant economy in Namiquipa may be understood not only as a precipitate of capitalist underdevelopment, but also as a site of resistance to capitalism and the capitalist state.

7
Social Relations and Relations of Power: The Politics of Community-State Relations

COMMUNITY AND STATE

The emergence and transformation in Namiquipa of affinities and identities oriented to a specific locale and related to the organization of the labor process underline the way the community may figure as a relation of production. My accounts of those processes were framed by the notion that the *pueblo* of Namiquipa is a historical formation, an organized complex of material, social, and cultural forms. Similar claims may be made about the Mexican state as a relation of production (Corrigan et al. 1980). Community and state are both simultaneously material and ideological formations or organizations of power (see Abrams 1988). Furthermore, they develop in relation to one another, and neither is an autonomous process or sphere of action or representation.

If the community is not an autonomous, authentic, and bounded domain, however, neither is it simply a "little tradition" version of the state. Instead, community and state have formed in relation to one another through a "dialectic of cultural struggle" (Hall 1981:233) that has taken place in contexts of unequal power and entailed reciprocal (though never equivalent) appropriations, expropriations, and transformations. At the same time, the meanings and symbols produced and disseminated by the state are not directly reproduced within the community. The popular ideology of Namiquipans is contradictory since it embodies and elaborates dominant symbols and meanings but also challenges, rejects, revalues, and presents alternatives to them (cf. Gramsci [1929–35] 1971:333; Williams 1977:113–14).

The relationship between Namiquipa and the Mexican state has involved the parallel—and occasionally intersecting—processes of formation of community (pueblo) and state. As Namiquipans engaged the objective determinants of the community's development over time, certain characterizations have been imputed to them by the state. During several periods in the two-century-long development of this relationship, particular crystallizations of power relations within the pueblo and between the pueblo and the state were evident (see Nugent 1989a). Since the revolution, the tendency has been for the distinctly sedimented domains of power or kinds of social relations shaping the organization of the production process on the land (chapters 2 through 5) and categories of person (chapter 6) manifest in the pueblo and the state to coincide less often and less perfectly than they did in the past.

My effort to understand the development of the relationship between Namiquipa and the state over a two-hundred-year period has involved an attempt to "link histories of power and anthropologies of culture" (Cohn and Dirks 1988), while following some of the methodological guidelines set forth by Ranajit Guha (1982, 1983a) for analyzing subaltern consciousness and peasant insurgency. Namiquipan popular consciousness of having participated in a process of collective self-formation in relationship to supra-local organizations of power (i.e., the colonial, postcolonial, and capitalist states) has been examined in terms of the concrete conditions, historical events, and structures of power in relation to which popular ideology has formed. If it is possible to discover not only distinct domains of power (local, regional, national; cf. de la Peña 1981, 1989) but also the manner in which power is contested between the several domains, then what is manifest in the coming together and drawing apart of pueblo-power and state-power may be illuminated.

THE HISTORICITY OF THE ETHNOGRAPHIC PRESENT

Narratives of the past offer a perspective on the present. My account of the history of Namiquipa provides a perspective on the ethnographic present that is an alternative to the one presented in chapter 1. This is achieved not by providing a more exhaustive or carefully detailed enumeration and representation of the same "facts" presented earlier, but as a consequence of the narrative *redefining* the present, of reconstituting it in relation to prior conditions, events, processes, and changes.

The narrative offered in this book tells part of a story about Namiquipa. It advances no claims to be *the* story. Land, labor, personal identity, and revolutionary mobilization were selected and focused upon in terms of how they developed and are still changing. Emphasizing these topics (at the expense of others) required an over-layered, back-and-forth narrative that eschews linearity and unidirectional movement. One reason for adopting such a form of presentation is that this is the way people "make their own history, but not just as they please" (Marx [1852] 1963:15).

At the start of this book I underlined the bases for my initial conception of Namiquipa as a "revolutionary pueblo." Yet in trying to understand that conception of Namiquipa—whether in the 1910s or 1980s—I have had to refer to a larger and more complex process, the formation of the Mexican nation, in relation to which the historical and ideological formation of the pueblo of Namiquipa has occurred. As Adolfo Gilly wrote,

> the experiences which converged in the 1910 Revolution range from the spirit of the northern frontier to the communal traditions of southern and central Mexico; from the mass wars [of] Hidalgo and Morelos to the expulsion of French imperialism by Juárez and his men; from the shooting of Maximilian to the manifold and nameless local risings; from the external wrench of the 1847 War to the internal convulsion of the Yaqui War. There is no need to trace the economic factors behind all these events . . . , they only shape history in the last instance. Yet all those determinations were of decisive importance to the *unique* role of the Revolution in the formation and synthesization of the country. . . .
>
> In a discussion of Marx's writings on the Spanish Revolution, Michael Löwy says: 'In the end, the essential *methodological* lesson to emerge from these writings of Marx is that the historical process has been conditioned not only by the economic base, but also by past events (social, political, military) and by the revolutionary praxis of people living in the present.' *Dialectique et revolution.* (Gilly [1971] 1983:341, 396)

Gilly's highlighting of a few of the "experiences which converged" during the 1910 revolution in Mexico provides a concrete reformulation of Löwy's threefold description of "historical process" defined as the conjunction of (economic) structure, event, and action (revolutionary praxis). But it remains a perspective that is wedded to the notion of the centrality of the 1910 revolution, which is one of the major conceits of the postrevolutionary state.[1] As I tried to show for Namiquipa, though, however "revolutionary" a pueblo it was and is to this day, people's experiences during the 1910s and 1920s—when many fought for the end of dictatorship, and the town's lands were restituted by the state— were part of a much longer experience and struggle to define the meanings of land and labor. The revolution of 1910 and the resulting reformulation of the community's relationship to the state were not such "original" processes for Namiquipans.

Further, both Gilly and Löwy appear to answer in advance the question of what kind of *present* revolutionary (or nonrevolutionary) praxis occurs in. An alternative, complementary point is that "the present" is no more a fixed and eternal thing than is the economic base or the state. It is no more a space inhabited by agents-in-praxis than that praxis itself is a fixed, discrete, predictable series of unconscious actions tending toward a predetermined outcome. To paraphrase Ken Post (1978:467), it is not praxis in the abstract, but people who provide the link between structure and event in the present, thereby reshaping not only the present but also the past.

The possibility of "going back"—of allowing past experiences to (re)converge differently in relation to a new set of apprehended conditions—is what provides the condition (the determination) for the present to be continually reconstituted through the past as it is simultaneously reconstituting the past. For example, Namiquipans routinely invoked organizational tropes from the past to meaningfully order relationships to the land, each other, and outsiders in "the present." The Bando and their experience during the Apache Wars informed demands for land before the revolution (chapter 3, this volume; Gilly 1986:40); they also—among other things—inform the popular refusal to recognize the legitimacy of the state's claim to reorganize and circumscribe land-tenure arrangements in the 1920s and the 1980s. It is as a result of a particular accumulation of experience—with Teodoro de Croix and the Apaches, during the revolution, during the period of agrarian reform and the *bracereada* and the crisis of the 1980s—that the pueblo's present relationship to the state has been organized. Struggles over the meanings of land and labor and the nature or character of politics have, time and again, been axial in determining the form that organization has assumed.

Land, labor, and politics are internally related to one another within Namiquipan ideology. They are also related to the different formations of land, labor, and politics as those evolved in a region, shaped as they were by more general historical processes such as the formation of rational capitalist notions of land and labor-power as commodities, of politics as the legitimate exercise of power and violence by the state. But whatever the degree to which they were shaped by the more general historical processes, *within* Namiquipa, land, labor, and politics acquired a distinct set of meanings, different from those the state is attempting still to impose.

> All forms of external intervention necessarily enter the existing life-worlds of the individuals and groups affected and thus, as it were, pass through certain social and cultural filters. In this way, external factors are both mediated and transformed by internal structures. (Long 1984–2; see also Comaroff 1982a, 1982b).

It is my contention that popular ideology may integrate, or itself form as synthesis of, material relations of power and production. Consider, for example, the notion of distinct forms or modes of political power suggested by Partha Chatterjee:

> These modes are distinguished in terms of the *basis* of particular power relationships in the ordered and repeated performance of social activities, e.g., the particular pattern of allocation of rights or entitlements over material objects (sometimes extended to non-material objects such as knowledge) in a definite system of social production. The three modes of political power we will call the *communal*, the *feudal* and the *bourgeois* modes. (Chatterjee 1982:12)

This formulation appears in many respects similar to Eric Wolf's synthesis of much of the literature on mode of production (Wolf 1982:71ff.). Wolf writes that different modes of production are constituted by the "ways in which human beings organize their production, . . . specific, historically occurring set[s] of social relations through which human labor is deployed to wrest energy from nature by means of tools, skills, organization, and knowledge" (Wolf 1982:75). Wolf outlines a trinity of modes of production (kin-based, tributary, capitalist) roughly analogous in the sphere of production to Chatterjee's modes of power (cf. Wolf 1982:71–100; Chatterjee 1982:12–16; Chatterjee 1983).

The critical feature of both these formulations has to do neither with how one labels the different modes nor with the suggestion of an evolutionary sequence. Wolf (1982:76) is explicit on the latter point, and Chatterjee writes that different modes of power "may exist (even co-exist) in a particular state formation or structure of power relationships. . . . In agrarian societies where peasant communities are formally organized into large political units . . . these two [communal, feudal] modes of power are intertwined in the state formation" (Chatterjee 1982:12, 14). "One of the utilities of the concept of mode of production," wrote Wolf, "lies precisely in that it allows us to visualize inter-systemic as well as intrasystemic relationships. We shall use the concept to reveal the changing ways in which one mode, capitalism, interacted with other modes to achieve its present dominance" (Wolf 1982:76; see also Friedman 1974). The basic point, then, is that different modes of production and of power may coexist within particular social formations, that the distinct modes in fact develop in relation with one another.

According to Chatterjee, the communal mode of power "arises typically in societies based predominantly on agricultural production" (1982:12). The establishment of a capitalist state and the sway of the bourgeois mode of power, on the other hand, "requires . . . the destruction of the peasant communities and of the bases of peasant-communal ideology. . . . This crucial aspect of the bourgeois political revolution . . . is accomplished in the phase of the so-called primitive accumulation" (Chatterjee 1982:15–16).

While in the final analysis a truly mature capitalism may require the destruction of all alternative forms of power and production, that "maturity" is not yet evident, even in societies such as Mexico that have not been based predominantly on agriculture for a number of decades. The expansion and proliferation of "the informal economy" in the cities coupled with the range of responses and accommodations to capitalist penetration in the countryside of Mexico point to the possibility that a communal mode of power (if not of production) may in part be engendered as a result of the expansion of capitalism. In the example of Namiquipa, I would argue that this manifestation of a communal mode of power has assumed its particular form not only as a result of (or despite) the dominant mode of power (or the dominance of capitalist production), but also as a consequence of determinations shaped by the locally operative mode of power itself, its capacity to subsume influences from above or outside, even as it is formally subsumed *within* the capitalist world system.

Recall Marx's description of communal society, where there exists "the natural unity of labour with its material presuppositions, . . . [and] the individual relates to himself as proprietor, as master of the conditions of his reality . . . [and] to others as co-proprietors, as so many incarnations of the common property, or as independent producers like himself" (Marx [1857:58] 1973:471). Marx was writing about the "forms which precede capitalist production." His description applies remarkably well to popular conceptualizations of labor and membership in the community in Namiquipa in the nineteenth and twentieth centuries. The seemingly "natural" unity of labor, with its material presuppositions such as land and the products of labor upon it, was and remains an important idea informing Namiquipans' attachment to the pueblo lands (as demonstrated in chapters 2 through 5) and their self-identities (as argued in chapter 6). Of course the "naturalness" of that perceived unity is only seemingly so; it is a *historically* produced unity that has been the focus of numerous struggles—between Namiquipans and the state, *hacendados,* Apaches, and immigrants. Additionally, Marx's phrases about agriculturalists relating to each other as co-proprietors are hardly distinguishable from phrases in the founding act of the SCP in Namiquipa in 1906, nor are their meanings very different from consensually deployed terms of self-recognition such as *agricultor* (rather than *campesino*) used by inhabitants of the community today.

The crucial element here lies in the fact that *land*, which in this situation is *the fundamental basis of life and social reproduction, appears not as a product of labour but as its presupposition,* as something which must be given or found before the labour-process can commence. 'The earth is the great workshop, the arsenal which furnishes both means and material of labour, as well as the seat, the *base* of the community. They relate to it as the *property of the community,* of the community producing and reproducing itself in living labour. Each individual conducts himself only as a link, as a member of the community as *proprietor* or *possessor.* The *real appropriation* through the labour process happens under these *presuppositions,* which are not themselves the product of labour, but appear as its natural or *divine* presuppositions' [*Grundrisse,* p. 472]. Whatever *the specific institutional form of individual right or entitlement to the use of land . . . , it flows from the prior authority of the community over the entire land;* the place of the individual in the social ordering of rights is determined by his membership in the community; the collective is prior to the individual parts and its authority larger than the mere sum of the parts. (Chatterjee 1982 : 12, emphasis added except in quotation from Marx)

How, then, to resolve the contradiction between the characterization just advanced, according to which Namiquipans would be "primitive communists," with earlier statements that today the struggle for "private property" is the most "revolutionary" struggle in which Namiquipans are engaged? To achieve this we must consider more explicitly Namiquipan ideologies of land and labor, personhood and politics, community and state.

Land is one of the objects engaged in the process of production, the latter itself an element providing for the reproduction of the individual and the community. Land is not, in other words, disconnected from the individual nor from the community that engages the land—and other means of production—through its labor. This engagement is in turn predicated not only on the land's materiality (its physical qualities and location in space) or existence (as a presupposition for the labor process), but also on the relationship of power which the individual or the group has to the land and that is engaged in the process of laboring upon the land. Politics or power, then, is another presupposition—at once material and ideational—for a particular form of engagement (labor) with the land. These elements (land, labor, politics/power) are all integrated through their articulation within an ideological framework which is simultaneously shaped by material relations even as it establishes the possibilities and provides the means for the transformation of the material relations and material elements of existence, engagement, and ordering.

In Namiquipa those elements of existence, engagement, and ordering are land, labor, and politics. "The land" is the land of the pueblo, the 64 *sitios de ganado mayor* of Teodoro de Croix's donation to the settlers, the 100,000 hectares which today comprise the territory of the *ejido* of Namiquipa. An important change has occurred in the pueblo regarding the manner in which individual Namiquipan agriculturalists conceptualize their relationship to the land. While in the past the consensually validated and legitimate criteria for control of agricultural land and of the land of the pueblo as a whole was based on *posesión*, today the ideal to which some aspire and which many have realized in practice is to control a *pequeña propiedad*. Their idea of the small property is in fact a recension and transformation of the earlier idea of *posesión* and is not identical to the idea of capitalist property. But neither is it commensurate with the idea of *"ejidal* land" in the postrevolutionary period. In short, the valorization of the small property in Namiquipa is based on the popular articulation of a conception of landholding that is different from, and challenges, both what the state asserts as the official system of tenure in agricultural land for inhabitants of the *ejidal* sector and the promise of capitalism.

Labor is the productive and transformative activity of Namiquipan agriculturalists on their land, the character of which is partly a function of how individual *agricultores* conceive their relationship to the land even as it is also mediated by the manner in which they conceive their relationship to the community and to other groups in society. Unlike the *campesino*—who is subordinate to the state and/or other independent producers large and small—and the *trabajador de raya* or *jornalero* (day laborer)— subordinate to a labor regime and not even working his own land if he is engaged in agriculture—the *agricultor* is subordinate only to himself; subordinate, in other words, only to his identity in relation to his land, the action he engages in upon it, and how the products of his labor are disposed of.[2] Ideally the *agricultor* enters into this productive and transformative activity, labor, *autonomously*.

The significance of this notion of identity, today encapsulated in the descriptive term *agricultor*, has, I would maintain, been determined primarily as a result of the social relations of production as they developed historically within the community. But just as the expressions denoting the concept according to which people's relation to land are mediated have changed over time (from enjoying *posesión* to enjoying *"propiedad"*) and that change indicates a connection to a more general process which took place in the region according to which land was transformed from subject of labor to commodity, so is Namiquipan labor and its redefinition and ideological reconstitution over time connected to processes of development which take place outside the community. But while the mode of production in society as a whole has changed from being "tributary" (or "colonial" or "feudal") in character to capitalist, that great transformation has not had the effect of completely destroying the bases of "peasant-communal ideology." The great transformation in fact played a subordinate role in determining the significance of labor in Namiquipa when contrasted to the internal development of community and practices within it.

A "communal mode of power" in Namiquipa today, in other words, now coexists with the capitalist or bourgeois mode of power, which is predominant in Mexican society. The former has developed in relation to the latter. This current manifestation of a communal mode of power in Namiquipa—the historical basis of which is contradictory and predicated on the prior period of colonial expansion, so it emerges as a mystified form of conceiving of power—demonstrates how the internal development of the pueblo is dissonant with development of Mexican society as a whole.

That is not to argue that things have remained the same in Namiquipa while they became very different in the broader society, or that this coexistence provides evidence of the lack of change in the character of power predominant within the community while profound changes occurred at the regional, national, and international levels. In the late eighteenth century, the modes of power and production arguably present in Namiquipa corresponded to the intermediate terms of the two typologies: Chatterjee's "feudal mode of power," Wolf's "tributary mode of production." Since that time, the mode of power within the community viewed in relation to alternative bases of power with which the community was engaged has transformed in the direction of communal rather than bourgeois power. It now appears as a communal mode in relation or by way of contrast to the state and to capital, and its taking on this character is an outcome of the more embracing and generalized transformation of capitalist society in Mexico. But even in the face of that general historical transformation, aspects of which have provided the material and ideational repertoire in terms of which existence, engagement, and ordering are conceptualized and apprehended ideologically, people in Namiquipa have not yet embraced the identities that such a great transformation imply or, by some accounts, make inevitable.

Namiquipans are engaged in articulating and reproducing a vision for the possible construction of social life which is an alternative to that of the state and capitalism. The conflicts over and struggles for land and labor and the social changes that have come about in Namiquipa as a result of them are explainable as the outcomes of struggle and engagement in the past and the conditions for struggle and engagement in the future.

FROM CIVILIZING VANGUARD TO FRONTIER BACKWATER TO "PROBLEM" *MUNICIPIO*

Viewed from Mexico City today, Namiquipa is the *cabecera* (head, capital) of just one more "problem" *municipio*. With many inhabitants dependent on foreign wage-labor for their survival, the *municipio* battered by a recent agrarian war, and the town the site of political violence during the 1980s, this characterization is not surprising (cf. Krauze 1986; Lau Rojo 1989; *Novedades de Chihuahua,* Oct. 10, 1983; Nugent 1987). But neither is it eternal. When the *ejido* was established immediately after the revolution in 1926, Namiquipa appeared, from the capital, to be the very model of a successful agrarian community. Invading landlords were repulsed, peasants controlled the land, and the community appeared to support the revolutionary state.[3] That characterization may in turn be contrasted to the situation during the Porfiriato, when Namiquipa was a frontier backwater with communal control of extensive lands posing an obstacle to the rational, capitalist development of the North. The very existence of this military colony—a community of armed peasants—presented a challenge to the state, then attempting to break down forms of local or communal identity that stood between individual and state. During much of the previous century from 1778 through the 1870s, however, Namiquipa had been in the vanguard of civilization on the frontier of barbarism.

Those characterizations, oriented to and by the center, say something about the relationship of Namiquipa to the whole of Mexico. But would Namiquipans characterize their place within a national history and their own engagement with determinants of the community's development over the same period in the same way? If the popular view is different from that of the state, what is at stake in the relationship between the two views? Is it possible to consider the very relationship to the state as a site for the struggle for self-definition, for popular identities, by Namiquipans (cf. Lem 1989)?

It is indeed the case that Namiquipa was and is located on the frontier, in a region that has been the site of what is conceived as a struggle between "civilization" and "barbarism." Military settlement colonists and their descendants did participate in a succession of agrarian, military, and political struggles against Indians, landlords, foreign entrepreneurs, and agents of the state. Yet despite their relatively privileged position in the postrevolutionary rural social structure, Namiquipans bear a social memory and rely on idioms for representing the past that are dissonant with the officializing discourse of the revolutionary state (Alonso 1988a) and a challenge to scholarly reconstructions of that history.

My account of the relationship of Namiquipa to "the state" assumed a succession of hypostatized states, "colonial," "national," "revolutionary," and "capitalist." Relatively little attention was given to exploring the manifest ruptures and shifts that have characterized the process of state formation in Mexico. The general contours of that series of transformations were taken for granted. While processes of state formation, transformation, reformation, and even metamorphosis[4] are consequential to the issues addressed in this book, the principal item on the analytical and explanatory agenda has been the formation of community.

There do exist some useful guidelines for understanding the forms of the state in Mexico against which pueblos (or oppositional cultures; cf. Corrigan and Sayer 1985:7) have themselves formed. Enrique Semo, for example, underlined the need to appreciate the Mexican revolution of 1910–20 as one (prolonged) moment of Mexico's bourgeois revolution, only comprehensible in relation to the wars of independence from 1810 to 1821 and the wars of the reform from 1854 to 1876 (Semo 1979:136–38). The 1810 insurgency ended Spanish colonial rule in Mexico. The liberal victory over conservatives and the French invaders provided the conditions for a period of sustained, headlong capitalist development and political transformation in the cities and countryside of Mexico. The 1910 revolution ended with the reestablishment of a strong central state bureaucracy that declared itself the architect of a social revolution. The postrevolutionary state for six decades exhibited a talent for co-opting popular resistance movements through official peasant and worker organizations tied to a political party, at times resorting to violence and repression to keep popular organizations in line.

Whatever the teleological cast of this account, it does provide a framework for examining specific communities in relation to a broader set of historical processes. It identifies the colonial state, for example, and suggests that *as a particular kind of organization of power,* it is distinguishable from the immediate post-Independence "State which was only formally a State . . . [predominant during] the first moment of independent life in Mexico, generally known by the name 'the period of anarchy'" (Leal [1975] 1985:8). Those "colonial" and "national" or "anarchic" states in turn may be contrasted to the liberal state ushered in by the reforms of the mid-nineteenth century or the Porfirian state on the one hand and the postrevolutionary state on the other.[5]

Moreover, Semo's cycles-of-revolution argument provides criteria for distinguishing a sequence of distinct legitimation projects constituted by and represented in different, specific, state-created forms of knowledge in conjunction, or disjunction, with which the lives of people in the countryside are organized or destroyed. It is in relation to the different organizations of the power of the state that people in particular communities may realize, or fail to realize, their own political, social, ideological, and material possibilities. At the same time, that realization is also mediated by popular organizations of power which, in their local resonances and historically contingent elaboration, need not be identical to that of "the state" at any particular time.

It is my contention that community formation may serve as a vehicle of resistance to the state. As a form of resistance, community formation is articulated through and in relation to a distinct, though not autonomous, popular ideology (see Guha 1982; Chatterjee 1983; Asad 1987). The ways subjects of the state experience its power and challenge it give voice to terms of resistance. These are the other side of the coin to official characterizations of peasant communities (cf. A. Bartra 1985 : 21ff.) or particular communities such as Namiquipa, examples of which are the descriptions of Namiquipa as civilizing vanguard, frontier backwater, revolutionary vanguard, and problem *municipio* mentioned above. Whether community formation is *always* a form of resistance to the state, or only potentially so, may remain a subject for debate. In the example of Namiquipa, I argue that it was and continues to be so.

The distinctiveness of community formation in contrast to state formation is well illustrated by the need to develop an alternative periodization to understand the former (Nugent 1989a). The cycles-of-revolution argument provides a compelling periodization of state formation in Mexico adequate for analyzing changes at the level of the nation. But a different periodization of Namiquipan history is required to analyze the pueblo's relationship to the state processually. It is for that reason that I have proposed an alternative periodization of the history of this "revolutionary" pueblo that places greater emphasis on their experience defending (in fact *making*) the community, particularly during the nineteenth century, and rather less on their valiant role during the 1910 revolution. By looking further into the past we can find the historical basis for a popular social memory that challenges the terms laid down in official versions of history promulgated by the state.

It was the Namiquipans with whom I lived in the mid-1980s who insisted I look further into their own past. During the first few months of fieldwork I often asked Namiquipans when they had received their land. Armed with the knowledge that Namiquipa was the site of one of the largest postrevolutionary *ejidos* in Mexico, I fully expected they would answer "1926," the year the *ejido* was granted by the state. But their responses to my queries on this point invariably centered on a discussion of the colonial period and the Apache Wars. By their own account, they had received their land in 1778; it had been given them by Teodoro de Croix and not by the postrevolutionary state.

Namiquipa's location on the frontier has always been an important feature of its relationship to the state. The extermination of small groups of sedentary and semisedentary indigenes such as the Conchos, followed soon thereafter by the highly mobile and brutally efficient guerilla-style resistance to Spanish advances by the Apaches in the eighteenth and nineteenth centuries, shaped the experience of the settler colonists in a myriad of ways. To Teodoro de Croix in 1776, as during much of the prior decade to Hugo O'Conner, had fallen the task of staffing strategically placed presidios forming a line of defense against "barbarian" Indians and other colonial powers.[6] It was as an element of this defensive project that Namiquipa's relationship to the Mexican state originated.

Teodoro de Croix's Bando of 1778 stipulated the conditions according to which settlers secured rights to land and membership in the community. Their obligations basically involved taming forces of nature—whether the forests, fields, and streams of the sierra which were to be exploited and labored upon, or the "barbarians" who were to be "reduced" to "civilized" social habits or physically exterminated. With authority vested in male household heads (whether military or civilian settlers), these stipulations reinforced patriarchal control of domestic and collective dimensions of the local economy and society while simultaneously encouraging a particular notion of civility.

The colonists were manifestly aware of their historical mission in "civilizing" the frontier. A thoroughgoing historical consciousness of their role in the pacification of the North, the relationship of that project to the maintenance and reproduction of their communities, and their value and valor as people who settled and worked the land is evident in nineteenth- and early twentieth-century petitions for control of land, judicial briefs filed by the peasants against landlords invading pueblo lands, complaints by hacienda workers against supervisors, documentation of electoral fraud, and complaints about caciques, many of which were quoted in earlier chapters.[7]

As demonstrated in chapter 3, the struggle for land during the nineteenth century devolved not only to a struggle against the owners of large estates or—during certain periods—against the state itself, and against "forces of nature" broadly conceived to include "barbarians"; positively, it was a struggle for community control of land in a particular form. Whether or not the settlers and their descendants received active or passive support from the state, throughout the entire period from 1778 until after the revolution, the Bando assumed the combined functions of myth of origin and primordial charter of legitimacy for local control of land and political power. Land, power over the land, how that power was secured, what was done with the land and by whom, were all conceived of by reference to a distinctive and popularly apprehended historical experience (Nugent 1985:74–75). While initially structured in large degree by the policies and projects of the state, this historical experience was importantly modified and transformed through the popular recension of the colonial state's organization of the people-land relationship in the region.

The significance of the frontier, the struggle against barbarism, and the active tradition of rebellion in defining the relationship of Namiquipa to the state in the present is substantively similar to what it was at the end of the colonial period. However, the meanings of those three features are radically different today than they were in the late eighteenth century.

Namiquipa is still on a frontier, but it is a frontier of capitalism. The old frontier of "civilization" has been transformed into "the border" (Katz 1981:7) which Mexico shares (unequally) with the United States. Although the distinction between civilization and barbarism is still important, it is no longer deployed to link the community with the state against "barbarians" but instead to mark the difference between Namiquipa and the Mexican national state. The loci of civilization and barbarism have shifted in the popular imagination. Northern pueblos claim a greater affinity with the supposedly progressive U.S. "civilization" than with the capital of Mexico. The northern pueblos are regarded as distinctive, ethnically "purer," and more connected to the North than to the "barbarian" South (Alonso 1988b; Alonso 1992a; Nugent and Alonso 1994).

The tradition of Namiquipans and Chihuahuans generally as fighters during the revolution figures differently in official myth than it does in popular consciousness. The Guerrero District is widely recognized as "the cradle of the Revolution," and the uprising by Namiquipans and other *serrano valientes* in November 1910 did indeed herald the ten-year period of armed struggle that ensued throughout Mexico. However, among Namiquipans the only point about the revolution on which there is any consensus is that neither they nor the Mexican peasantry as a whole were the victors of that struggle. Victory went to the new state, while peasants were the spent cartridges of a bloody civil war.

The general point about the dissonance of popular and official historical reconstructions is demonstrated in the interviews with Chihuahuans conducted by teams of historians in 1973 and 1974.[8] An interview with one Victoriano Macías from October 1973 is especially compelling in this regard.[9] Born a peon on the hacienda of Santa Clara, Macías joined the Villa forces in 1913. When asked by the interviewer— an educated and very well-trained person from Mexico City—where the revolutionaries got together, Macías completely shifts the terms of discussion. "No, no, no," he says, "there was no union; each of us had their own destiny." When asked his opinion of "the" revolution, Macías again challenges the interviewer, answering, "This one we have now? That we will die of hunger! What *am* I going to suggest." Finally, when asked which revolution was better, the one he fought in or the "current" one (the interviewer referring now to quotidian life in the 1970s), he says, "The one today is heavier."

Within a decade of this interview, things had gotten still heavier. Once again in Namiquipa people were irrigating fields with their own blood. The war of Los Malvinos in the *ejido* of Cruces and the violent electoral struggle throughout the *municipio* of Namiquipa mentioned in chapter 1 offered a potent corroboration of Macías's analysis. The point is not that life was little different for people in Namiquipa in 1983 than it had been in 1910; the differences were profound. Not least was the circumstance that the state had appropriated for itself the singular claim to speak in a "revolutionary" voice. Challenges to that voice were effectively silenced throughout the 1980s. As the elderly *ejidatario* from Benito Juárez, Namiquipa, remarked in 1984, "There are no *valientes* anymore." The difference, in other words, was a qualitative one based on the capacity of the state to refashion the very terms in which people experienced everyday life. But as active participants in a rebellious tradition, Namiquipans put a different reading on that participation from the one applied from without by agents of the state.

For the past two centuries Namiquipans and other Chihuahuans have articulated elements of a vision of community which is an alternative to the one offered by the Porfirian and recent postrevolutionary states. While having profound similarities to the vision of the colonial state and bearing features that are superficially consonant with (and easily appropriated and transformed by) the early postrevolutionary state, the crucial point is that this popular vision of community has been predicated on epistemological and cultural premises distinct from those of the postcolonial, postrevolutionary, capitalist state. Further, this popular vision has come into play regardless of whether the community was in the vanguard of state formation (as during the colonial period, and perhaps the 1910–20 period) or in the subject position in a relationship of domination/subordination (Porfiriato, the present). Yet the apparent union and separation of popular and state projects is a contingent outcome of distinct historical processes of formation.

All the observable changes in the relationship of Namiquipa to the state since the revolution have tended to be in one direction, toward increasing domination of the community by the state. That is manifest in the state's success at forcing a particular form of "resolution" of conflicts over the pueblo's lands and the practical elimination of the SCP, intervening in the production process and thus altering the character of labor, and, more recently, defining the terms of political action, the limits of what is possible. Nevertheless, this has had a curious outcome since, as argued throughout this book, Namiquipans today as much as ever articulate notions of the meanings of land and labor different from those of the state, in terms of a politics of work and the person that challenges the bourgeois state. Popular ideologies of land and labor in Namiquipa today are no longer recognizable in terms the state hopes, still, to advance. But if popular and state political and ideological projects remain distinct, does that augur the ultimate demise of the peasantry or continued resistance within the pueblo? And if there is to be resistance, resistance to what?

There is an empiricist argument against the proposition that the peasantry is doomed, namely that after all these years they just won't go away. It is also possible, however, to make a positive argument, the ideological argument that they *refuse* to go away. Their persistence is an example of a development and formation parallel in space and time, if not oriented toward the same ends, to that of the state. My depiction of rural Chihuahua bears echoes of what Guha identifies as the domain of subaltern, as distinguished from elite, politics (Guha 1982:5–6). There is arguably a consistency and coherency to the alternative stream which runs through Namiquipan history. Articulated through and in relation to struggles for land and labor, this popular ideology is also articulated through historical action, the marking out of an alternative space of power, of a popular politics. This marking out is achieved both discursively and materially, through the symbolic mediation of social relations and the transformation of the world (including social relations) by action within it. Hence political struggle in Namiquipa, or struggle for power of the kind which has marked the formation of the pueblo is, and has always been, ideological or cultural struggle.

NOTES

CHAPTER ONE

1. From the adobe wall of the house, her son-in-law extracted a dumdum bullet the following day. One widely repeated claim was that the *judiciales* were armed only with blanks.

2. More than one authority has remarked on "the relation of domination and dependence established between the postrevolutionary state and urban and rural workers; the state dominates and encompasses the latter, but it is in turn dependent on them in the same way they are on it" (Gilly 1987; see also, e.g., Warman [1976] 1980; Gilly [1971] 1983; Hamilton 1982; A. Bartra 1985).

3. Cf. León-Portilla 1972 on *norteños;* Carr 1973 on the North; Lister and Lister 1966 and Jordan [1956] 1981 on Chihuahua.

4. Calzadíaz Barrera [1958] 1979; Katz 1981:7–21, 37–39; Katz 1980, 1976a, 1976b; Knight 1980; Knight 1986, 1:115–27; Wasserman 1980, 1984; Duarte Morales 1967, 1968; Tompkins 1934; Torres 1975; Olea Arias 1961; and records of the Pershing Punitive Expedition to Mexico in 1916–17 (USNA.MRB, especially U.S. Army intelligence reports in RG 393 and 395).

5. See Lau Rojo and González Hererra 1990, in which scholars working on Chihuahuan history refer to this hypothesis as a commonplace rather than a matter of controversy.

6. Cf. Katz 1980, 1981, 1992, citing material from the ATN; Calzadíaz Barrera 1969; Lloyd 1983, 1987; Alonso 1986, 1992a; Nugent 1985, 1989a.

7. See Alonso 1986, 1988b; Calzadíaz Barrera 1979; Knight 1980, 1986; Katz 1976a, 1981; Nugent 1985; and Osorio 1988 for evidence of this.

8. Cf. maps of Chihuahua produced by Celulosa de Chihuahua S.A. (1971) and the World Bank (1988) and descriptions of the Chihuahuan agricultural sector by Appendini (1983).

9. Cf. Sheridan's recent (1988) political-ecological study of agropastoralism in Cucurpe, Sonora, on the western side of the Sierra Madre. On agriculture and industry in the sierra of Chihuahua, see Lartigue (1984). Aboites (1988) analyzes irrigation districts in Chihuahua; cf. Hewitt de Alcantara (1978) on irrigation districts in Sonora, and Whiteford and Montgomery (1985) on Baja California.

10. Von Humboldt, *Political Essay on the Kingdom of New Spain,* cited in Jones 1979:14. See also Jones 1979:95; West 1949.

11. Son of the U.S. consul in Chihuahua in the mid-nineteenth century, Creel married into the most powerful family in prerevolutionary Chihuahua. He was nephew as well as son-in-law to Luis Terrazas and governor of Chihuahua in the years immediately before 1910 (Almada 1980:437ff.). His description of rural Chihuahuans, his respect for whom was considerably outweighed by his fear, is particularly valuable and interesting since he was one of the most universally reviled "Chihuahuans" in 1910.

12. This point is discussed in Nugent 1987; cf. Bartra 1975b, 1982; Margolies 1975:55ff.; Roseberry 1983:108–16, 192ff.; and the criticisms of "class reductionism" in Laclau 1978 or Kahn 1985.

13. Lister and Lister 1966; Wasserman 1984; Carr 1973; Lloyd 1987; Lartigue 1984.

14. Evidence for this is in documents in the AMN, the AMCG, and the AHSRE, which mention individuals from Namiquipa and other pueblos of the region working in the United States as long as a century ago. See also Calzadíaz Barrera [1958] 1979:300. The general observation is corroborated by Namiquipans today.

15. Alonso 1988b provides a full discussion of ethnicity in Namiquipa. Here I note only that the indigenous inhabitants of the valley, the Indios Conchos, were killed off during the colonial period, while some Tarahumaras from the Papigochic Valley settled the Santa María Valley, moving to Namiquipa and Cruces. The Tarahumaras of Chihuahua are a social group more or less apart from the predominantly Mexican (or *norteño*) society. Some Namiquipans who are willing to admit that their Spanish ancestors might have had progeny with indigenes insist there was no intermarriage with the "tame" and oppressed Tarahumaras, but only with the violent and strong Apaches (who were also the fiercest enemies of the colonial and nineteenth-century settlers), and hence that the "mestizos" of Namiquipa combine Spanish and Apache blood. There is in Namiquipa, as throughout much of the North, a generalized antipathy for people from the Center and South of the country (especially politicians and "experts"), and aspects, at least, of this antipathy have a racist, anti-*indígena* basis.

16. The observations in this paragraph are based on a reading of the APN, documents in the AMN and AMCG, and national censuses from the twentieth century.

17. *Adobón* is a brick in which the mud used for making adobes is mixed with cement and pressed into blocks, which are fired in the sun.

18. Houses with *lamina* roofs are hotter in the summer and much colder in the winter. On the other hand, they are more efficient at preventing water from entering when it rains, and they do not have the problem of dirt falling between the boards!

19. Cf. *Manual de Estadísticas Básicas del Estado de Chihuahua* 1983, which describes 79 percent of the population of the *municipio* as "agricultural workers"; *Monografías Municipales* (1982), identifying 70 percent of people of the

municipio in "agriculture, cattle, etc." Reyes (1975) found 86.7 percent of the pueblo working as "agriculturalists and ranchers."

20. Philip Corrigan introduced me to the distinction used here between *identity* (which subjects apply to themselves) and *identification* (which the state, for example, applies to its subjects).

21. In *Manual de Estadísticas Básicas del Estado de Chihuahua* 1983 the designation "rural" is applied to anyone living in the countryside or in towns with a population of fewer than five thousand persons.

22. On *ejidos* see Whetten 1948 and Mendieta y Nuñez 1981. On the establishment of *ejidos* in Chihuahua immediately after the revolution, CNA, Resoluciones Presidenciales, (AGN); CNA.Actas (AGN); AGCCA e.24/434. On the revolution in Chihuahua, Almada 1964; Katz 1976b, 1978, 1979, 1980, 1981; Knight 1980; Knight 1986, 1:115–27; Knight 1986, 2:115–29, 330–60; Wasserman 1980. On some of the peculiarities of the *ejido* of Namiquipa, see Nugent 1985:82–83; Nugent 1989b, 1991.

23. The "Simpson-Mazolli Bill" finally passed as the Immigration Reform and Control Act of 1986 under the sponsorship of congressmen Simpson and Rodino. J. Calagione is responsible for the tsunami metaphor.

24. The SAM (Mexican Food System), a state-sponsored program, was initiated in the early 1980s, after more than a decade during which Mexico was compelled to import ever greater quantities of basic grains (beans, corn). To contend with the fact that a basically agricultural society could no longer feed itself, the SAM was supposed to offer incentives to growers in both the private and *ejidal* sectors to concentrate energies in corn and bean production (see Sanderson 1986).

25. *Ejidatarios* and non-*ejidatarios* in Namiquipa were taking out loans to buy items necessary to begin agricultural work at rates varying between 25 and 48 percent; but to this must be added the corrupt practices of bank officials who would delay turning money over to peasants and often "take out" the "interest" upfront, with the result that the effective rate of interest could easily surpass 100 percent for a six-month loan. See Nugent 1987.

26. Camarena Salazar was the subject of a U.S. television network "miniseries" (starring the Cuban actor Steven Bauer) in early 1990 called "The Drug Wars." Dr. Humberto Álvarez Machain was kidnapped in Mexico and delivered to U.S. Justice Department officials in the early 1990s to stand trial in this country for the murder of Camarena Salazar. According to an Associated Press wire report, "The U.S. government has paid witnesses, some of them with criminal pasts, more than $2.7 million to testify in the trial regarding the torture-murder of U.S. drug agent Enrique Camarena Salazar" (*Arizona Daily Star*, Nov. 10, 1992).

27. Jaime Pérez Mendoza, in *Proceso* 480 (Jan. 13, 1986). Similar actions by peasants in other states, for example, Chiapas, resulted in no increase in the government's guaranteed prices.

28. Or, more precisely, it *could* have been, just as the popular mobilization throughout Mexico in 1988 *could* have been more of a turning point than it was. See *Proceso* 503–12 (June–Aug. 1986), a series of articles by Francisco Ortiz

Pinchetti and Jaime Pérez Mendoza on the "electoral" process in Chihuahua. The then recently established *El Diario de Chihuahua* printed some "news" which contradicted the official version of events. As a rule, North American newspapers tended to represent the 1986 Chihuahuan elections as a situation in which one political party (PAN) had the elections stolen from them by another (PRI) (*New York Times, Washington Post, San Diego Union, Arizona Daily Star* in July 1986). My own view is that the elections were less a matter of two battling political parties and more a matter of the people forming in opposition to the state, tactically using an existing "opposition" party (whose only appeal was that they *were* an opposition—their actual policies or pronouncements were not as critical) as a vehicle for mobilizing and channeling discontent. See interviews with Antonio Becerra Gaytan, Chihuahua state chairman of the PSUM and PSUM candidate for governor in 1986, in Ortiz's articles in *Proceso*. Becerra Gaytan's remarks, and what I saw in Chihuahua in 1986, give Marx's comment on the Paris Commune of 1871 an unnerving resonance. While completely overlooking the centrally important role assumed by women as critical agents of popular mobilization (María Teresa Guerrero, pers. com.), Lau's (1989) analysis of Chihuahua elections between 1983 and 1988 adopts a similar line of argument, explaining not "a victory for the PAN [or the right]" but "a rejection of the PRI [and the state]."

29. The PRI candidate—who won the election—was a general in the Mexican army who was not posted in Chihuahua until several weeks before filing as a candidate.

30. The Movimiento Democrático Campesino was the group which coordinated the seizure of the *bodegas* CONASUPO in Chihuahua in 1985, demanding the state pay a realistic price for grains from the countryside.

31. Cf. Stavenhagen 1970; Reyes et al. 1970; Sanderson 1984; and Appendini 1983 for discussions of the distribution of land in all of Mexico in recent decades.

32. But note, on the same page Roseberry goes on to argue that we nevertheless need to retain the concept of the peasantry, for it is "crucial for an understanding of Latin American history and for an understanding of the 'processes of proletarianization as these have developed throughout the world' (Steward et al. 1956:505)" (Roseberry 1983:208). Cf. Roseberry 1978.

33. Regional studies of marginal or intermediate social groups in rural Mexico by anthropologists, sociologists, and historians address issues raised by the fact that characteristic features of the lives of the peoples presented in their monographs defy certain of the typological specifications routinely imputed to rural Mexicans as "Indians," "peasants," "*campesinos,*" etc. (e.g., Schryer 1980; Margolies 1975; Jacobs 1982). Hewitt de Alcantara 1984, chapter 3, provides a review of the relevant literature. This has resulted in the identification of social groups such as a "peasant bourgeoisie" or relatively autonomous politico-economic domains such as a "ranchero economy," etc.; it has also occasioned the deployment of concepts like "infra-subsistence sector." The latter category in particular—which does provide an exact, empirical description of "really-existing" groups—would be comic, from a purely semantic standpoint, were it anything else than a radical indication in class terms of the degree and kind of

subordination of rural Mexicans to economic domination; or, considered as an example of the insidious manner in which genuinely radical concepts can be "tamed" by liberal discourse, a way of politely referring to starvation, ethnocide, and super-exploitation, all the while maintaining rigorous scientific concepts at a civilized (i.e., descriptive) level of remove from this murder.

34. Cf. Carnoy 1984 for a recent presentation of theories of the state, and Grindle (1986:13–18), who starts her discussion of the state and the country-side in Latin America with a breakneck review contrasting "marxist" and "de-pendentista" approaches to conceptualizations "derived from Weberian tradition" ("pluralist," "corporatist," "bureaucratic politics," and "the role of State elites" approaches). Investigations of the capitalist state useful for under-standing Mexico include Anderson 1974; Carnoy 1984; Corrigan et al. 1980; Corrigan and Sayer 1985; Jessop 1982; Marx and Engels 1975. On the early colonial period, see Gibson 1964; on the nineteenth century, Cardoso 1983; on the Porfiriato, Katz 1986; on the state and popular classes during the revolution, Gilly [1971] 1983 or Womack 1986; on the postrevolutionary state, Hamilton 1982 and Grindle 1986. Seminal discussions of the Mexican state include J. Alonso 1983; Hansen 1972; Hellman 1978; Leal [1975] 1985.

35. See Durkheim, who wrote about the state as "the very organ of social thought" or "the organ of moral discipline" (cited in Corrigan and Sayer 1985:5).

36. See Corrigan 1975 and Mohanty 1991 on the importance of under-standing the world in relational terms. Note that the preceding paragraphs were originally written *before* Arturo Warman assumed his positions first as director of the Instituto Nacional Indigenista and later as minister of agrarian reform under President Carlos Salinas de Gortari after 1988.

37. See also Joseph and Nugent 1994.

CHAPTER TWO

1. AGN.V v.20, e.4, fo.35–39, Parral, 28-i-1726, José Sebastián López de Carbajal.

2. One *sitio de ganado mayor* is equivalent to the area of a one-league square, about 1,755 hectares; one *sitio de ganado menor* is about 775 hectares; a *caba-llería* is slightly more than 42 hectares. A hectare is a square 100 meters to a side, about 2 1/2 acres.

3. The above information is from AGCCA, e.24/434, DPP, pp. 35–49, and from the AGI. Susan Deeds generously sent me copies of documents from the Archivo General de las Indias in Seville, Spain, including information on properties in eighteenth-century Namiquipa that corroborates the account of the DPP.

4. Tamarón's text refers to these as *familias de razón*, i.e., Spanish or *criollo* or Spanish-speaking and property-owning families.

5. De Croix letter to Nicholas Gil, Nov. 15, 1778, in AGCCA e.24/432 (V), p. 103.

6. A *visita* is a settlement where no priest lived and thus was visited periodi-cally and ministered to by a priest from a larger town.

7. "Stealing" children (and women) was a common practice which both

Apaches and Mexicans engaged in. It is generally agreed among many authorities—with the exception of the Apaches themselves—that Victorio, the leader of the Warm Springs Apaches in the 1870s, who led his band through the final years of his life, was born a Mexican on a hacienda in Durango. (Victorio was killed at Tres Castillos in 1880, felled by a shot from the rifle of Mauricio Corredor, a Tarahumara from the pueblo of Ariseachic. Corredor was part of a contingent composed primarily of the inhabitants of Chihuahuan sierra towns, including Namiquipa, formed in the Apache campaigns under the leadership of Joaquin Terrazas [Terrazas Sánchez 1973]. According to Apache accounts, Victorio died impaling himself on his own knife after exhausting his ammunition in the defense of his band [Ball 1970]). El Indio Ju, who led some of the Nednhi ("Mimbres"—frequently called Chiricahuas; see Ball 1980) Apaches in Chihuahua after Victorio's death, was born Lino Leyva in Namiquipa, son of a Spanish settler, Leonardo Leyva, and an Apache woman, Benigna Muños (a fact the Apaches, especially Ju's son, Ace Daklugie, hotly deny).

This curious form of "exchange" of children and women between the Apaches and the Chihuahuans is not easily explained by pointing to the need to "replenish the ranks of warriors" or "secure breeding stock." Santana Pérez, a *serrano* from the town of Yepomera, was famous for leading anti-Apache campaigns in the late nineteenth century. While gathering wood with his son one day, his son was kidnapped. Ju jumped out of the bushes and told Pérez that his son would be brought up to fight the white eyes, and that the next time he led a campaign against the Apaches, Santana Pérez should bear in mind that he might be killing his own child. Although Pérez spent years trying to recover his son, he never did (R. Osorio, pers. com.).

8. ANG.PI *listas de revista;* AGN.PI v.5 passim; AGN.PI v.13, fo.222–99 (Guizarnotegui papers).

9. All quotes are from de Croix, *Bando de 15 de Noviembre de 1778* (AEN, also quoted in DPP and elsewhere), hereafter Bando. José Muñoz Franco of Armera, Municipio Namiquipa, first showed us his typescript copy of the Bando before we found it in any archive.

10. Janos at the time was the site of a presidio. The Fourth Flying Company was assigned to Casas Grandes. Galeana was near the presidio of San Buenaventura, the troops of which were moved to the new pueblo. Cruces and Namiquipa were each assigned *piquetes* (pickets) of thirty men. Namiquipa was soon thereafter made the headquarters of the Second Flying Company, based there until the 1820s.

11. In conversation during the summer of 1985, Zacarías Márquez Terrazas, official historian of the city of Chihuahua, suggested that using the term *presidio* for Namiquipa was inappropriate. Márquez insisted on reserving the term for "real" presidios (such as Janos, Galeana, or El Norte) and not for *any* military settlement colony. However, Namiquipa was the headquarters of the Second Flying Company from 1778 until 1821, and that company was never again stationed elsewhere (see *listas de revista* in AGN.PI and AGN.CyP). Flying companies tended, in fact, to have more troops assigned to them than did presidios (see Moorhead 1975, lists of presidios and soldiers, and similar data in AGN.V and AGN.CyP), and their presence in the towns gave them a definite character,

different from strictly civilian settlements. Furthermore, Namiquipa is referred to as "the former presidio" or "the presidio" in nineteenth-century documents and in speech to this day.

12. APN passim; AGN.PI v.254, fo.111, Arispe, 11-xii-1787, Jacobo Ugarte y Loyola; cf. Moorhead 1975.

13. AGN.PI, *listas de revista,* gives numbers of soldiers in Namiquipa. Comparing those lists with data from the APN provides evidence of the two tendencies noted here.

14. AGN.PI v.254, fo.50–57, Chih., 4-i-1787, J. Ugarte y Loyola.

15. AGN.PI v.66, fo.81ff., Chih., 14-x-1791, Pedro de Nava; AGN.PI v.66, fo.146, Nam., 19-xii-1791, Teniente Pedro Bernardino González.

16. On Ojos Colorados see AGN.PI v.66, fo.289ff., various places, dates and authors, mostly March and April 1791; AGN.PI v.66, fo.358ff., Chih. 29-vii-1791; AGN.PI v.66, fo.375ff., Chih., 14-x-1791, Pedro de Nava; Griffen 1988: 72. Cf. Cordero 1796 in Matson and Schroeder (1957:352–53).

17. This statement is based on examination of the Parochial Register of Births, Marriages, and Deaths in Namiquipa from 1780 through 1820. In the earlier years, careful note is made of the ethnic background of each person born. For example, parents are named as "Español," "Mestizo," "Mulato," "Indio," "Apache," etc., or any of the gradations of caste in between (see Barnes et al. 1981:90–93 on racial terminology), but the subtlety of the distinctions progressively fades out, and by the turn of the century, ethnic distinctions disappear altogether. To what extent this change may be a function of changing attitudes toward ethnic distinctions or of the particular predilections and obsessions of individual priests—who recorded this data—is open to debate. I suspect it was more a matter of the increasing irrelevance of ethnic distinctions *within the community* during this period than anything else. See Alonso 1988b, which analyzes ethnicity and honor on the frontier.

18. On race and class on the northern frontier see Jones 1979; Alexander von Humboldt's *Political Essay on the Kingdom of New Spain* (1822); Alonso 1988b; Borah 1954.

19. The Franciscan mission of Namiquipa had been located right alongside the Río Santa María. The presidio was located one kilometer upstream on some bluffs overlooking the river, and it is there that a new church was built, construction of which was completed by 1800. The new location, on higher ground, was selected because it provided greater security for the pueblo during Apache attacks.

20. AEN, Chih., 14-xi-1807, María Salazar.

21. AEN, Nam., 30-i-1808, *capitán* of the Second Flying Company.

22. AEN, Nam., 9-i-1808, Francisco Vásquez. All following quotes from or paraphrases of Vásquez are from this document.

23. María Salazar's husband; note the legal voice of the Salazar petition is the voice of her husband, and so it is to that voice that Vásquez responds.

24. Or Hacienda del Carmen, a few miles upriver from the plaza of Namiquipa.

25. AEN, Santa Isabel, 4-vii-1808, María M. Salazar.

26. There is no evidence to suggest that the Almoynas accepted the offer of

a few *suertes* of land in Cruces. María Salazar, with her sisters, subsequently sold the titles to Aranzazu, Carmen, and Santana del Torreón to Enrique Müller. See chapter 3, "Namiquipa and the Landlords."

27. "Decreto de la Secretaría de Guerra y Marina, Sección 2ª, México, 21 Marzo 1826, Manuel Gómez Pedraza" (copy in APHS) orders presidial companies in Chihuahua to be maintained at Janos, San Eleazario, El Norte, and San Buenaventura. Cf. Griffen 1988:119ff.

28. AMCG c.5, e.66, Chih., 19-ii-1852, José Eligio Muñoz to JPG, regarding *indígenas* of Pachera whose lands were invaded by émigrés from New Mexico.

29. AMCG c.5 passim; AMCG c.7, e.78, Chih., 26-ii-1856, Juan B. Escudero to JPG, regarding *indígenas* of Santo Tomás; AMCG c.7, e.82, Santo Tomás, 10-xii-1858, PM Atenojenes Márquez to JPG; AMCG c.7, e.89, Chih., 23-ix-1862, Juan B. Escudero to JPG regarding *indígenas* of Temechic and Pachera.

30. AMCG c.11, e.138, Chih., 20-iv-1874, R. Guerrero to JPG.

31. AMCG c.7 passim.

32. AMCG c.8, e.94, Nam., 28-viii-1863, Ramón Sotelo to JPG.

33. AMCG c.8, e.94, Cruces, 15-iv-1863, Jesús María Vásquez to Juez de Cruces.

34. AMCG c.8, e.94, Nam., 7-xi-1863, Manuel Lazo to JPG.

35. Cf. AMCG c.8 passim; Almada 1955, 1980, 1982; Solis 1936:109; Actas de Adicción al Supremo Gobierno del Estado, in AMCG c.8, e.100, 13-iv-1865; Alonso 1988b:285ff.

36. On Santana Pérez, see note 7, above.

37. AMCG c.9, e.109, Nam., 15-i-1868, Manuel Lazo to JPG.

38. AMCG c.9, e.112, Chih., 23-xi-1869, J. B. Escudero to JPG, and 18-xii-1869.

39. AMCG c.9, e.112, Chih., 30-vi-1869, J. B. Escudero to JPG.

CHAPTER THREE

1. AMCG c.30, e.295, Chih., 27-vi-1893, E. Hernández to JPG.

2. CPD 1.41, c.7.16, d.346, fo.170–72, 10-ix-1889.

3. Bellingeri and Gil Sánchez 1980:315–17; Carbó and Sánchez 1983:200–202; Katz 1986, 1988b; Lloyd 1988; Meyer and Sherman 1979:458; Tannenbaum 1930:13ff.; Katz 1988d:532ff. discusses this issue in some detail, but cf. Holden 1986 for a radically different interpretation of the consequences of the operations of the surveying companies.

4. See ATN 1.71 (06), E 75669; ATN 1.24 (06), E 17.

5. AGNCh, Prot. v.74; AGCCA.DPP 24/434 (I), fo.68–71.

6. See Osorio 1988; Alonso 1986, 1988b, which demonstrate the continuities in popular mobilization in the Guerrero District from the 1880s through the 1910s.

7. There was no record of such a survey in the ATN, to the great astonishment of the archivist, who conducted an exhaustive search during the spring of 1985.

8. While both these rulings and decrees of the central government would presumably have been valid and applicable to the pueblos of Galeana, Janos,

and Casas Grandes as well, it appears as though the inhabitants of these communities were never informed (see Lloyd 1987, 1988).

9. CPD 1.41, c.7.16, d.411, fo.313–15, 9-xi-1889.

10. CPD 1.41, c.7.15, d.151, fo.263–64, 22-iv-1889.

11. CPD 1.41, c.7.16, d.346, fo.170–72, 10-ix-1889.

12. No close relation to Don Luis, but the son of the Jesús María Vásquez of Cruces in the 1860s, and maternal uncle of Pascual Orozco (Rubén Osorio, pers. comm.)

13. A pueblo near the Pacific Coast of Oaxaca. In the 1970s and 1980s Juchitán was the site of a surprisingly resilient and for a time successful popular insurgency organized by the COCEI (Coalición Obrero-Campesino-Estudiantil del Istmo, the Worker-Peasant-Student Coalition of the Isthmus of Tehuantepec).

14. CPD 1.41, c.7.16, d.339, fo.154, 5-ix-1889, emphasis added.

15. In the 1900s Namiquipans argued that the *ejido* was only a 1- or 1 1/4-league square around the pueblo. This (reduced) territory (1,750 hectares, in contrast to the more than 11,000 hectares included in the *ejido* if it is a square 2 1/2 leagues to a side) was identical to what had earlier been designated as the *fundo legal.*

16. The Registro Público de la Propiedad del Distrito Guerrero, Estado de Chihuahua, contains many entries beginning in 1900 in which the Namiquipan *derechos* (rights) are spelled out (see, e.g., RPP.CdG, Libro II). *Derechos* consisted in "a share of cultivable land, grazing land, and hillsides outside the *Ejidos* of the Pueblo, the precise size of which is unspecifiable since all of the land [of the *terrenos de común repartimiento*] is an indivisible unit" (RPP.CdG L.II, no.189 [fo.173ff.], 7-xi-1900). *Derechos* belonged only to "original" families, and there was a finite number—279—corresponding to the number of families living in Namiquipa at the time the 1893 decree was issued.

17. AMCG c.58, e.527, Nam., 24-iv-1906, PM Victoriano Torres to JPG.

18. AMCG c.44, e.397, Nam., 18-ix-1901, José Casavantes to JPG.

19. AMCG c.61, e.548, Nam., 18-ii-1907, Gertrudis Ortega to JPG.

20. RPP.CdG L.II, Nov. and Dec. 1900 passim.

21. AMCG c.50, e. 446, Chih., 13-vii-1904, J. Córtazar, Secretaría del Gobierno del Estado, Sección 1ª, Ramo Gobierno 1472, to JPG. On *posesión,* cf. AMCG c.44, e.397; c.50, e.446; c.58, e.527; c.64, e.560. On immigrants, AMCG c.44, e.397. On immigrants and conflicts with *naturales,* AMCG c.53, e.487; c.59, e.533. On collective labor and individual rights, AMCG c.61, e.548.

22. AMCG c.63, e.558, Chih. 21-iii-1908, Secª· del Gobᵒ· del Estado, Ramo de Fomento 1375, to JPG; AMCG c.65, e.567, Namiquipa, 30-v-1908, JM E. Luna to JPG; AMN c.3-bis, 29-v-1908, Hacienda Santa Ana, Francisco M. Logan (administrator) to JM Namiquipa.

23. ATN 1.24(06), e.23, 28-viii-1908; AMCG c.15, e.175; see Alonso 1988b, chapter 2, on the social organization of warfare in the colonies.

24. *Periódico Oficial de Chihuahua* 9 (Mar. 4, 1905): 7–12.

25. AMCG c.73, e.625, Nam., 17-v-1911, JM y Cmdte. Militar Cenobio Varela to JPG; AMN c.3, Nam., 8-x-1907, unsigned letter; AMN c.3, Nam., 28-iv-1906, JM Victoriano Torres.

26. ATN 1.24 (06), e.178, 20-vii-1908, complaint from the peasants of Namiquipa to Porfirio Díaz; AMN c.2-bis, e.1900–1905, 27-xii-1904, complaint from peasants of Namiquipa, transcribed to the *jefe municipal* by the *jefe político,* Urbano Zea.

27. This is evident from a review of the documentation on more than one hundred adjudications of municipal lands—including names of prospective purchasers, the location and size of lots, maps, and so on—found in the AMN.

28. For example, AMN c.3-bis from JP Urbano Zea to *jefe municipal* of Namiquipa, 25-i-1907, notifying the latter of the state government's approval of a contract between the Municipal Council and José Casavantes for the cutting of timber in *común repartimiento* lands; cf. AMCG c.56, e.508, letter from *jefe municipal* to JPG, 22-xi-1906, reported protest against the planned arrangement by Namiquipan peasants.

29. AGNCh, Prot., Nam., L.1, 26-v-1906.

30. AMCG c.53, e.487, Nam., 4-iii-1905, V. Torres to JPG.

31. In Cruces there was a slightly different rhythm, with sales progressively picking up over the five-year period. The best land in Namiquipa having been sold off, purchasers looked downriver. See Table 1.

32. *Jefes políticos* were now state government appointees, that is, minions of the Terrazas-Creel oligarchy. Despite the fact that Namiquipa was made an independent municipality in 1884, local authorities such as the municipal president and the officials who worked under them were appointed by *jefes políticos*—or installed through clearly, openly, and cynically rigged elections—from at least 1900 onward.

33. See, e.g., AMCG c.63, e.558, Chih., 9-iii-1908, Sec[a.] del Gob[o.] del Estado, Ramo de Fomento 1157 to JPG, query regarding multiple adjudications of land totaling 325 hectares to Luis J. Comaduran. In Namiquipa the Comaduran, Flores, and Corral families were the worst offenders; Annuario Estadístico, 1905–1909 passim.

34. AMN, Adjudication 1232, 24-xii-1906, for 495 hectares to José Casavantes; Adjudication 336, 18-x-1905, for more than 298 hectares to Pedro Loya and Ma. Enriqueta C. de Loya; Adjudication 925, 22-viii-1906, for 200 hectares to Victoriano Torres.

35. Bancroft Library, Berkeley, California. MB-18, box 26, folder 8-c, Nam., 13-x-1905, from Concepción Cervantes to Ricardo Flores Magón, St. Louis, Missouri.

36. The *tiendas de raya* were "company stores" used on haciendas through which debt peonage was institutionalized. While largely absent in the North of Mexico by the first decade of the twentieth century, debt peonage was still employed—particularly on Terrazas haciendas—in the state of Chihuahua (Katz 1976a:47–48).

37. For further discussion of conflict with the state and the meaning of land use in Namiquipa see Alonso 1988b and Nugent and Alonso 1994.

38. Interview with José Rascón Iguado, Cd. Chih., June 1984. Cf. AMCG c.74, e.630, Chih., 4-viii-1911, Manuel Antillon (*jefe municipal* y *comandante militar,* Nam.) to Gov. A. González, a complaint about the Porras regime in Namiquipa before 1910.

39. Duarte Morales's memoirs (1967, 1968) provide firsthand accounts of Namiquipan participation in the 1910 revolution, as does Olea Arias 1961. Olea Arias was from the nearby town of Bachiniva. Calzadíaz Barrera 1979 is based on oral histories with Namiquipan veterans. BN.AFM contains documentation on the early military campaigns in Chihuahua, including lists of soldiers, battles they fought in, and the sources of their arms. Chihuahuan *serranos* took their own weapons into battle in 1910.

40. See, e.g., AHSRE L-E 821, fo.18ff., El Paso, Texas, 26-vi-1908, Mexican consul to SRE; AHSRE L-E 821, fo.171, El Paso, 29-vii-1908, Mexican consul to SRE.

41. See, e.g., AHSRE L-E 679 R. leg.3, fo.200, El Paso, 28-ii-1911; BN.AFM, Ms.M/322, Cd. Juárez, 14-v-1911, Pascual Orozco (*hijo*).

42. Interviews with Doña Aurelia Muñoz, Nam., 1984–85.

43. AMCG c.73, e.625, Nam. 17-v-1911, various citizens.

44. AMCG c.73, e.625, Nam., 1-vii-1911, JM to JPG.

45. AMN c.5-C, e.1918, Nam., 15-x-1918, transcript of letter of complaint dated 10-x-1918 from Dolores Carrasco; and AMN c.5-C, e.1918, Nam., 21-v-1918, PM Namiquipa to governor of Chihuahua, both refer to the destruction during the revolution of fences around lands purchased under the 1905 law.

46. AMCG c.74, e.627, Nam., 17-v-1911, JM Nam. to JPyCM Cd. Guerrero; AMCG c.74, e.627, Cd. Guerrero, 20-v-1911, JPyCM to JM Namiquipa.

47. See note 22.

48.   As through this life you travel
you'll meet some funny men
some'll rob you with a six-gun
and some with a fountain pen
        Woody Guthrie, "Pretty Boy Floyd"

49. Alonso 1988d; cf. ATN, AMCG, AGCCA, and especially AJN passim. This attitude toward work on the land and the character of the person is perpetuated today in Namiquipa (see Alonso 1992a). This is not a criticism of "wealthy" people because of their wealth, but because of how that wealth was acquired. By these criteria the hardworking but poor and unsuccessful peasant, and the hardworking but wealthy and successful farmer are of the same category of person, just as the poor alcoholic who lives off the charity of the community or the wages of his family, the bureaucrat, the banker, and the landholder who rents out his fields or hires people to work them are of the same category of person.

50. AMN C.5 passim; AMCG C.74 passim.

51. See file on San José de Babicora in the Mexican and U.S. Claims Commission, WNRA RG 76, E119, Docket no. 1553, Claim on Behalf of Babicora Development Company. This property was not broken up until the 1950s.

52. Villa earlier led the riflemen of San Andres, Chihuahua, into battle on November 19, 1910, fighting for the revolution of Madero until he was jailed (and almost executed) in 1912 by Gen. Victoriano Huerta. Villa later escaped to the United States. Huerta was a holdover from the Porfirian army whom Madero

made the mistake of not decommissioning. Huerta seized power in Mexico during the United States–sponsored coup which led to the assassination of Madero in February 1913. See Katz 1981 and forthcoming.

53. BL.AST, included as an appendix to Gov. Manuel Chao's "Informe que Rende el Gobernador Militar del Estado de Chihuahua" in Mar. 1914. Cf. Wasserman 1984 and González Herrera 1988.

54. Silvestre Terrazas was a middle-class journalist who, although a distant relative of Don Luis, had edited an opposition newspaper before 1910 which chronicled the abuses of the Porfirian landlords and politicians. A committed if reformist revolutionary, Don Silvestre published the *villista* newspaper *Vida Nueva* (*New Life*) after 1913 and served as Villa's secretary and sometime governor as well as administering the Office of Confiscated Goods. Silvestre Terrazas's relationship with Villa is discussed in Katz, forthcoming. Records from the Office of Confiscated Goods are included in the papers in Terrazas's personal archive, which is now in the Bancroft Library in Berkeley, California. See also S. Terrazas 1985.

55. See Katz 1980 for an analysis of what Villa did with the confiscated goods and Katz 1979 for a description of Villa's revolutionary government in Chihuahua. Cf. González Herrera 1988 and Schulze 1990.

56. BL.AST e.1914, July–Sept. This does not demonstrate a lack of interest on Villa's part for the agrarian demands of the Chihuahuan peasantry. Villa was incapable of making a decisive land redistribution as long as he had a state to run and a military machine to finance, but the interests of landless peasants were not forgotten. See the *informe* of (*villista*) Gov. Fidel Avila of Apr. 1, 1915 (in BL.AST e. Avila, Fidel): "Entre los importantes problemas que han animado al actual Gobierno debe contarse el relativo a ejidos municipales, los que cedidos por favoritismo o por sucias combinaciones a los 'cientificos' y favoritos del régimen anterior, deben ser restituidos a los pueblos para bien de sus habitantes y tranquilidad de los pobres, que no tienen más patrimonio que el de su trabajo, con el que en otro tiempo no podian contrarrestar las maquinaciones de los ricos o de los malvados, que extorsionaron al pueblo sin consideración alguna." On *agrarista* agitation and agrarian reform in *villista* Chihuahua, see also Katz 1988a; Katz, forthcoming; González Herrera 1988; Nugent 1990; Schulze 1990.

57. Santa Clara is scarcely mentioned in the records of confiscated goods in BL.AST (cf. González Herrera 1988).

58. Interview with Victoriano Macías conducted by María Isabel Souza, Oct. 29, 1973, in La Junta, Chihuahua. AP, Instituto de Investigaciones Dr. José María Luis Mora, PHO/I/111.

59. No relation to Silvestre, nor to the family of Don Luis, and not even related to the Jesús M. Vásquez y Terrazas from Cruces who figured prominently in the 1880s and 1890s revolts, Telesforo was a member of a family which immigrated to Cruces toward the end of the nineteenth century from the Llanos de San Juan Bautista. Telesforo, his brothers, and a sister (who, according to their nephew, still living in Cruces, was the toughest of the lot) were frequently in trouble with authorities in Cruces before 1910. Telesforo was a personal friend of Villa's before the revolution, and (with Manuel Baca Valles) part of a gang which was accused of being cattle thieves and bandits before they joined

the revolution (AMN 1909 passim; interviews with Don Carlos Ruiz Terrazas, Cruces, Nam. 1985–86).

60. AHSRE L-E 816, leg.7, El Paso, 22-v-1912, Mexican consul Llorente (?) to Francisco I. Madero.

61. AMC c.7, e.1913, Nam., 2-ii-1913, Candelario Cervantes to PM Cruces; Nam., 13-ii-1913, PM Pedro Barrera (#309) to PM Cruces; Nam., 22-ii-1913, PM Pedro Barrera (#343) to PM Cruces.

62. Though most of the records of the SCP were destroyed after the revolution (interview with José Rascón Iguado, Cd. Chih., 1984), "certificates of possession" issued by the SCP beginning in 1913 are found in the AMN and AJN.

63. Katz, forthcoming, discusses this in chapters 82 and 83.

64. Katz 1988b, 1989; González 1988; cf. AJBT 3.12.785, fo.1263, Mexico D.F., 12-vi-1916, Alvaro Obregón to J. B. Treviño; AJBT 4.15.935, fo.1589, Chih., 10-x-1916, J. B. Treviño to A. Obregón.

65. See Alonso 1988c; USNA.MRB.

66. The North American accounts of the occupation of Namiquipa may be found in Tompkins 1934 and in documents in the USNA.MRB and the USMHI. Namiquipan accounts of the same period were obtained largely from interviews but also in the Suitland archive (WNRA) and AMCG.

67. USNA.MRB RG 395, E1210, 29-v-1916, George Clements, newspaper file; USNA.MRB RG 94, DF2424492, Fort Sam Houston, Texas, 1-vii-1916, to adjutant general, Washington, DC; cf. Alonso 1988c:221.

68. Interviews with Amalia Camarena de Ruiz, daughter of Tomás Camarena, in Cruces, Nam., Chih., 1985; cf. Alonso 1988c:227–28.

69. USNA.MRB RG 94, E26, D2379210, Nam., 29-v-1916, Pershing, via Funston at Fort Sam Houston, to War Department, Washington, DC.

70. USNA.MRB RG 393 passim; cf. Alonso 1988c:218.

71. See Rocha 1979; Alonso 1988c; Sepulveda 1975; AP, PHO series/I/.

72. See, e.g., AJBT 3.14.883, fo.1475–78, Satevo, Chih., 5-viii-1916, various signatures, to J. B. Treviño; or the file on San José de Babicora in the WNRA, Mexican and U.S. Claims Commission, RG 76, E119, docket no. 1553, Claim on Behalf of Babicora Development Company, in which it is clear that William Randolph Hearst's property suffered much more at the hands of *carrancista* soldiers than *villista* troops.

73. See Salazar Quintana 1988:24, which draws attention to distinguished Namiquipans who had no trouble juggling the dual roles of "valiant Villista" and member of Namiquipa's Defensa Social.

74. Enrique Müller died in 1899, leaving his estate to his children and their spouses (Gameros, Russek, and Douglas). His daughter, María Müller, took the greatest interest in preserving Santa Clara during and after the revolution because she was married to the administrator, Agustín Domínguez, and stayed on at the hacienda after her father died and her sisters had moved to the cities. Her other siblings had married into elite families of urban Mexican and North American society. Why did María Müller remain in Santa Clara and marry down, marry a hacienda administrator? Prior to the marriage, María had an illegitimate child, the result of an incestuous union with her brother. Her brother was thrown out of the family, and she was forced to marry Domínguez, a hire-

ling clearly below her class. When the child was born, María was placed in what an informant described as a "jail of water." She got incredibly fat and ever after had to be carried around by servants. The child—like Maria's brother—was sent away and raised in the United States.

75. AMN c.5-D, e.1919, Chih., 27-i-1919, Sec⁰ del Gob⁰· del Estado, to PM Namiquipa, transcript of Agustín Domínguez letter of 16-i-1919.

76. AMN c.5-D, e.1919, Chih., 21-iv-1919, Sec⁰ del Gob⁰· del Estado to PM Namiquipa, transcript of Agustín Domínguez letter of 27-iii-1919.

77. AMN c.5-D, e.1918–19, Nam., 25-viii-1919, complaint from two hundred Namiquipan men to PM; Nam., 26-x-1919, Office of the SCP, *acta* regarding survey of Cruces land; Nam., 8-xi-1919, PM Namiquipa to PS Cruces, approving survey conducted 17-x-1919 by Ing. J. M. Lizano; CNA.RP; cf. AGCCA 24/434.

78. AMC c.7, e.1921, Chih., 23-ix-1921, Sec⁰ del Gob⁰· del Estado to PM Cruces; Galeana, 7-x-1921, PM Galeana to PM Cruces, stating that the Municipal Council of Galeana, like those of Cruces and Namiquipa, accepts Governor Enríquez as mediator in conflict with the heirs of Enrique Müller. A *carrancista* general, Ignacio C. Enríquez had served in Chihuahua during the final years of the revolution. Sometime military governor of the state, he was the key link between the Defensas Sociales in Chihuahua and the *carrancista* army, enjoying close relations with Francisco V. Antillon, who took over the Defensas in Namiquipa (earlier established by José María Espinosa). Antillon was commander of the Defensas in the Guerrero District by 1920. For more information on Enríquez, see Almada 1980 and Wasserman's forthcoming study of Chihuahua from 1910 to 1940.

79. AGCCA 24/434 (III), p. 15.

80. Documentation of this controversy runs through the AMN, AGCCA, and AEN from 1921 to 1926. See Nugent and Alonso 1994.

81. AGCCA, Bienes Comunales, 24:434 (721.1), 18-xi-1922.

CHAPTER FOUR

1. The records are in BL.AST. See also González 1988; AGN.PR Sec⁰ del Gob⁰·, c.42, e.15, fo.1–228.

2. The fate of the Terrazas Estates is documented in CNA.Actas; AGN.Ptes. Obregon-Calles file 806-T-1 y Anexos; AGN.PR, Sec⁰ de Gobernación c.88, e.32; letter of Mariano Irigoyen to Chihuahuans in AMN.

3. AGN.Ptes, Obregon-Calles, 806-T-1, starting Feb. 24, 1921, and continuing through the year.

4. The Notarial Archive in Chihuahua City includes scores of *registros de título* for small properties, mines, and enterprises signed over to Enrique Creel between 1911 and 1920. See the books of the Protocolos in the AGNCh.

5. The Carranza government (1917–20) in 1918 and 1919 had kept track of estates earlier expropriated from landlords in Chihuahua, including the many Terrazas properties. Interestingly, in the lists of "antirevolutionary" landowners compiled by *carrancista* officials, no distinction was made between the Terrazas and their relatives—the old oligarchy—and *villista* generals—the popular challenge to Constitutionalist rule. See AGN.PR, Sec⁰ de Gob⁰·, c.42, e.15, fo.1–228.

6. CNA.Actas v.12 (1924–25) passim.

7. Cf. Reyes et al., 1:1970; Whetten 1948; Simpson 1937. See records of expropriated United States–owned properties in WNRA; AGNCh, AGCCA for material on "invasions" in Providencia.

8. See especially WNRA RG 76.E189, box 174, dockett no. 1553; discussion of North American properties in AHSRE e.12-27-108, fo.8; AHSRE e.16-19-154, 22-i-1916 to 22-x-1917.

9. Cf. Hart 1988 and Knight 1988 for different interpretations of the significance of North American landholdings in Mexico before and during the revolution from the standpoint of the peasantry.

10. Cf. annual figures for land distributed to peasants in Sanderson 1984; Whetten 1948:125; Reyes et al. 1970:86.

11. CNA.Actas v.8, pp. 178–79.

12. 381,926 hectares to 77,203 peasants by 1921; 2,110,612 hectares to 241,331 peasants by 1925; 5,296,906 hectares to 543,870 peasants by 1929; 7,735,417 hectares to 731,239 peasants by 1931; 11,021,397 hectares to 947,626 peasants by 1935. Cumulative totals from Reyes et al. 1970:86.

13. CNA.RP passim; AGCCA 24/434; Lloyd 1988.

14. See chapter 3, p. 69, above. *Annuario Estadístico* 1905–9; Lloyd 1988.

15. Friedrich Katz's penetrating investigation of Villa and *villismo* has been instrumental in reorienting the interpretation of northern popular movements. See González Herrera 1988; Nugent 1990; and the studies in Lau Rojo and González Herrera 1990 for examples of work influenced by this line of interpretation. Alan Knight's (1980, 1986) identification of "*serrano* movements" during the Mexican revolution provides another well-argued point of reference for this rethinking. Katz (1980) reminds us that Villa was not "rehabilitated" by the Mexican state until the 1970s.

16. See also USNA.MRB, Records of the Pershing Punitive Expedition, especially in RG 393 and 395.

17. CF. Whetten 1948:129: only 6 percent of the land distributed in Mexico between 1916 and 1940 was by the method of restitution. Sanderson 1984, whose data run almost to the present, compares:

number of recipients of land, 1916–1980

through *dotación* = 1,700,061,

by *restitución* =   29,951;

definitive resolutions approved [same period]

dotación = 21,289,

restitución =   214;

definitive resolutions as percentage of total resolutions

dotación = 79%

restitución = 17%

Total = provisional + definitive; provisional = approved by CLA and state governor but not by president; definitive = approved by president and actually delivered to communities.

18. CNA.RP passim; CNA.Actas passim; AGCCA.RPP. In the original request for restitution filed from Janos, the people only asked for 16 SGM, and requested it in the form of a *dotación*. I read many *resoluciones*, both of the CLAs

and the CNA, in which pueblos were denied *restituciónes* but granted *dotaciónes*. In Janos the case was the reverse, and further they received four times as much land as originally requested because the presidio of Janos had been donated 64 SGM in the colonial period (presidential resolution granting *ejido* to Janos, 30-xii-1926, in CNA.RP Cf. CNA.RP passim; CNA.Actas passim.

19. CNA.Actas v.14, pp. 292–94, 23-vi-1926.

20. Dates appearing after each town indicate when they received land as *ejidos:* San Isidro (17-ii-1921), Santa Isabel (29-vi-1922), San Andres (26-vii-1923), Ariseachic (12-xi-1925), Cruces and Namiquipa (5-viii-1926), Galeana (11-xi-1926), Santo Tomás (18-xi-1926), Janos (30-xii-1926), Tomochic (21-iv-1927), El Carrizal (28-vi-1927). Cf. Olea Arias 1961; Duarte Morales 1967, 1968, popular histories by revolutionary veterans, in which their memories of the men from particular locales, whose residents had actually fought and died during the revolution, provide an ultimately depressing counterpoint to the state's official history of the same events.

21. AHSRE L-E 821, fo.14, 25-vi-1908.

22. AMN, Justicia, Chihuahua, 18-ii-1925, *procurador general de justicia,* Jesús Muchárraz, to *agente subalterno del ministerio público,* Reyes Ortiz, Namiquipa. Ortiz was once again trying to discredit the SCP to the end of convincing the Chihuahuan government to curtail its activities but managed to get no support from higher-level functionaries.

23. AJN, 16-vii-1923; according to a 1919 CNA circular, municipal councils could not administer pueblo lands (AMN c.5-D, Chihuahua, 15-viii-1919, from the Secretario General, Poder Ejecutivo, Ramo de Fomento, Circular 1260, transcription of CNA circular, 11-vii-1919). For the protest against Ortiz's giving out of land permits as municipal president during 1921–22, see AMN c.7, Namiquipa, 13-viii-1924, from José Rascón y Tena, vice-president SCP, to the president and Municipal Council.

24. The CLA was the regional office of the CNA, the latter in turn responsible for evaluating requests for land and recommending to the president of the Republic what actions should be taken in regard to each petition. A typical petition for land in the 1920s went from the community or group of peasants making the request to the CLA, which made a recommendation to the state governor, whose decision could have the effect of distributing land immediately, if provisionally, before the petition was forwarded to the CNA.

25. AMN c.8, 29-viii-1925.

26. The "Acta de Deslinde" (AMN c.8-B, 1-ix-1925), ratifying the boundaries of the *ejido,* and the "Acta de Posesión Provisional" (AMN c.8-B, 1-ix-1925), ratifying acceptance of the *ejido,* were signed by only thirty-five and thirty-nine *vecinos,* respectively, not counting the names of the municipal president, representatives of the CPA, and the engineer. Only thirty-two persons voted in the election for CPA representatives (AGCCA, Bienes Comunales, e.24:432 [721.1], 27-v-1927).

27. CNA.Actas v.14. For an "ideal typical" description of the procedures through which *ejidos* are established, see Leyes y Códigos de México [1971] 1982; Mendieta y Nuñez 1981, pt. 5; Whetten 1948.

28. The agricultural engineers Gustavo Talamantes and Miguel Lizama went

to Namiquipa at the end of August 1926. Their reports are in the AGCCA, Gómez Palacio, e.24/432 (721.1).

29. Of this territory, in 1926 some 302 hectares along the Río Santa María were irrigated fields (*riegos*), and another 5,900 hectares were *temporal* (seasonal, rain-irrigated) fields. In addition there were 22,257 hectares of *monte* (mountainous terrain) and more than 65,000 hectares of *pastal* (grazing land) (AGRA). Almost half of the land classified as *pastal* in the 1920s proved suitable for cultivation in subsequent decades.

30. There were approximately two thousand inhabitants in the town of Namiquipa in 1910. Duarte Morales (1967, 1968), Olea Arias (1961), and Calzadíaz Barrera ([1958] 1979, 1967, 1972) provide the names of more than one hundred Namiquipans who fought during the revolution. Discussions with Namiquipans and a review of the archival records in Cd. Guerrero, Namiquipa, and Cruces, and court records in Mexico and the United States, verified most of these and uncovered others (AMCG; AMN; AMC; AJN; LCC; USNA).

31. AGCCA 24/432 (721.1), Lizama, 18-x-1926.

32. AGCCA e.24/432 (721.1) (V), fo.18, 22-viii-1926.

33. Ibid., fo.1, 22-ix-1926.

34. The suggestion that the group of ex-*socialistas*-turned-cops (and frequently killers as well) formed a "Mafia" in Namiquipa in the 1920s and 1930s was made by an elderly informant in 1983. Whether that was indeed the case may be a matter for debate; what is incontrovertible is that the individual making this suggestion had been all three (i.e., *socialista*, police officer, and murderer).

35. AGCCA e.24/432, fo.18 (V), 22-viii-1926. Most Namiquipan men were able to sign their names; those who could not would find someone else to sign for them or use their cattle branding marks, as one of the signatories to the August 22, 1926, *acta* did. Of the twenty-two who did sign, only seven had signed the 1925 "Certificate of Provisional Possession"; another eight of the twenty-two signed a document in 1928 affirming they were willing to pay taxes on their lands so long as those were "respected as private property" (AMN c.9, 23-ix-1928).

36. Namiquipans complained that the administration of the CPA under Ortiz was characterized by "irregularities," that he held another public post (*subagente del ministerio público*), and that "the distribution of lands he has made is not based on the law and . . . all the *ejidatarios* know nothing of his administration, only he knows what he has done" (AGCCA, Bienes Comunales, e.24:432 (721.1), 27-v-1927; Ing. Ignacio Solis to the *oficial mayor* of the CNA). Solis comments that "antiagrarista concepts are expressed" by Namiquipans, and the *oficial mayor* responded that their opinion as to the status of the lands should be ignored (AGCCA, Bienes Comunales, e.24:432 (721.1), 2-vi-1927).

37. AMN c.9, 21-?-1924. See AGCCA, Bienes Comunales, e.24:432 (721.1), Nam. 17-v-1925, petition from the officers of the SCP to the president of Mexico; the complaints against Ortiz include his charging the community of Namiquipa 1,086 pesos when he served as their agrarian representative in 1921.

38. AGCCA, Bienes Comunales, e.24:432 (721.1), Certificate of Election, 6-ii-1928.

39. AGCCA, Bienes Comunales, e.24:432 (721.1), Chih., 15-ii-1928, Alejandro Muñoz, *ayudante dibujante,* to Ing. Ignacio Solis, delegate of the CNA.

40. E.g., Foster 1967; Hobsbawm 1959, [1969] 1981; contra Hobsbawm's "primitive" and "pre-political" peasant rebels, cf. Guha 1983a and Corrigan 1975.

41. Besson in AGCCA e.24/432 (721.1); CNA.Actas passim.

42. AEN, Nam., 6-vi-1928, Adolfo Delgado, Pte. de la Cómite Particular Administrativo del Ejido de Namiquipa.

43. AMN c.9, Nam., 23-ix-1928, José Rascón y Tena, José Cervantes, Arcadio Maldonado, et al.

44. Though after 1916 many Namiquipans turned against Villa and joined Defensas Sociales to fight against him, they did not see themselves as *carrancistas* but as defenders of the *patria chica* (Alonso 1988c). Furthermore, though the *socialistas* were ostensibly allied with the *carrancista* army, that did not spare Namiquipans from abuse and murder at *carrancista* hands. See, e.g., USNA.MRB RG 395 E1187 B34 DF4963, June 30, 1916, a U.S. Military Intelligence office report that Defensas Sociales of Namiquipa prepared to resist abuses of three hundred *carrancista* soldiers operating in the area; RG 94 E26 AGO 2463934, a description of the *carrancista* flag as a skull and crossbones on a black field; or AHSRE e.16-19-154 (Jan. 1916–Oct. 1917), which provides convincing evidence that the Hearst Babicora property suffered significantly more at the hands of *carrancista* than *villista* troops.

45. AMN c.7, 13-viii-1924, from José Rascón y Tena, vice president of the SCP, to the municipal president and Council.

46. Ibid.

47. Pedro Loya actually held on to almost 300 hectares of land—six times the amount permitted by the law—and later sold these lands to a Namiquipan. (See chapter 5, "Distribution and Use of Land in Namiquipa.")

48. Jane-Dale Lloyd (pers. com.) reports a similar historical-semantic transformation among inhabitants of rural northwest Chihuahua in the same period. See also Lloyd 1987, 1988, 1991.

49. Chapter 3, this volume, "Land during the Revolution." Also, Nugent 1990:299–302; Alonso 1986; Katz 1988a:243; González Herrera 1988.

50. Available documentation sheds little light on how this came about. José Rascón y Tena's son said that *"agraristas"* (indicating that they were directly or indirectly acting in service of the state) burned the archive of the SCP at his father's ranch sometime during the 1930s (interview with José Rascón Iguado, Cd. Chih., June 1984).

51. An objection more frequently voiced by agrarian reform officials, politicians, and urban critics of the privatization of land than by *serranos.*

CHAPTER FIVE

1. This information is from an interview with his daughter in El Molino, Nam., June 1985.

2. Luis J. Comaduran was an excellent example. See, for example, his letter to the *jefe municipal* of Namiquipa complaining that the Namiquipans "les tienen envidia a los inmigrantes o 'avenidosos' que desean expulsar" (have a great deal

of resentment towards the immigrants or "newcomers" and want to kick them out) (AMCG c.59, e.533, Nam. 8-x-1907). Within less than a year, inquiries were being made from Chihuahua City questioning the legality of the Comaduran family's acquisition of 325 hectares of land in Namiquipa in February and March of 1907. AMCG c.63, e.558, Chih., Sec^a de Gob^o to JPG, Ramo de Fomento 1157, 9-iii-1908.

3. Another clear act of political/personal vengeance involved Francisco Villa, Martín López, and two or three daughters of Luis J. Comaduran at the Hacienda de San Geronimo in February of 1916. Luis J. Comaduran was a much hated cacique up and down the Santa María river valley. Villa and López raped Comaduran's daughters at San Geronimo. When their mother came to retrieve them, one chose to stay with the revolutionaries, whether with the intent of murdering Villa or López or both, or because she was captivated by their charms is unclear. Later in 1916 Luis J. Comaduran offered his services to the *carrancistas* hunting for Villa in Chihuahua and secured a rank in the Constitutionalist Army (USNA.MRB RG 393 C.2-D (files 114–18), Intelligence Section, Punitive Expedition, Daily Report 5, 17-xii-1916). See also AJBT 4.18.1078, fo.1873–74, Chih., 5-xii-1916, (*carrancista*) Mayor Alejandro Loya to general en jefe de la Divisón del Nor-Este. The general point is not that "the personal is political" but that "the political is *personal.*"

4. Excellent documentation of how the officers of neighboring *ejidos* used their positions of power to consolidate their status as petty bourgeois *within* the *ejidos* exists for Cruces during the 1920s–1930s in the AGCCA and for Galeana in the late 1970s–early 1980s in AGRA.

5. There is now a dam called El Tintero on the Río Santa María near the northern border of the *ejido* of Cruces. *Ejidatarios* from Cruces and Namiquipa fish for carp and black bass in the lake formed by this dam, the waters of which otherwise do not serve Namiquipans for anything since there is little cultivable land in the vicinity of the lake. Water from El Tintero is used to irrigate land in the *municipio* of San Buenaventura, between Cruces and Galeana, but little water flows beyond San Buenaventura except in the rainy season.

6. This is the group known in modern Utah folklore as "the Lebaron Gang." Different from the Mormon colonists who settled in Chihuahua at the end of the nineteenth century, the Lebarons are recent arrivals to Mexico, having been brought there under the direction of an aging polygamist who had been driven out of southern Utah and later Arizona in the 1960s. Today the Lebarons have a cozy, North American-style hamlet on the banks of the Río Santa María. The adult men work in the United States, and the women run the households. The men return to Mexico to supervise the commercial operations of their orchards.

7. AGCCA e.24/434 (III), p. 161. There is no indication he was ever charged with anything.

8. AGCCA e.24/434 (III), p. 188. The names have been changed in this paragraph since some of the families still exercise caciqual authority in contemporary Cruces. Indeed the "Ricos" are direct antecedents of the "Ricos" described in chapter 1.

9. For discussions of social differentiation in rural Mexico see Stavenhagen's classic studies (1969, 1970). To describe matters in northwestern Chihuahua in

the most concise, if extreme, terms, there emerged within the *ejidos* a small group of capitalist agropastoralists and larger groups of landless peasants and marginal (infrasubsistence) *ejidatarios* and farmers.

10. For example, *norteños'* "natural" affinity for private property (cf. Díaz Soto y Gama, above), or the unmediated effects of so-called primitive accumulation of capital, or even Roger Bartra's "permanent primitive accumulation" (Bartra 1975b).

11. This view is manifest in the CNA.Actas and the agricultural engineers' reports of actual "distributions"—cited above—as well as in official histories, including school textbooks, publications of the Secretaría de Educación Pública, and public announcements by the SRA.

12. Cf. Cockcroft 1986 : 15, quoting an *ejidatario* from Michoacán: "Banrural is our *patron* [boss]. We're the workers and we don't even get a wage or have a labor union. We feel more exploited by the Bank than if we were officially its employees. Our earnings in the field are far inferior to what we would earn if we worked for the bank."

13. Ana Alonso reminds me that the *ejido* may also, at times, serve as an instrument through which peasants may be "bought off" by providing an instrument for clientelist, patronage politics.

14. A pseudonym.

15. The Secretaría de Educación Pública, Brigada de Educación Technológica Aropecuaria #331 (BETA), arrived in Namiquipa in early 1983, staffed by several young engineers and a few secretaries who were hired locally. Sent to determine how Namiquipans were underutilizing resources in the region and set up programs to develop those resources, the brigade encountered great difficulty convincing Namiquipans to cooperate in development projects. It did not help the *brigadistas* that they showed up in the middle of an agrarian war. People throughout the *municipio* were reluctant to have anything to do with agents of the national state and found it difficult to distinguish between machine-gun-toting *judiciales* and engineers armed with clipboards and ballpoint pens, each in their own way scarcely distinguishable from BANRURAL officers or politicians. That they managed to carry out the survey at all in 1983 is a credit to their perseverance, and we are very grateful to them for sharing the results of their survey.

16. Specifically, a survey of the *ejidal* sector in Chihuahua in the 1950s done by a communist activist using SRA materials, and the 1983 *Manual de Estadísticas Básicas del Estado de Chihuahua* (MEBCh).

17. The total area of land usable for agriculture in 1960 was 65,253 hectares; in 1970, 95,086.3 hectares; and in 1981, 81,892 hectares (MEBCh).

18. In Mexico during the agrarian reform in 1926, the average number of hectares received per person (i.e., direct agricultural producer, or *jefe de familia*, or *ejidatario*) was 9.9 hectares, of which only 2.7 hectares were cropland. In Namiquipa there were at most perhaps three hundred potential *ejidatarios* in 1926. Assuming their restitution included a similar ratio of cultivable to non-cultivable lands, the average amount of cropland available to each Namiquipan *ejidatario* would have been on the order of more than 80 hectares, or about thirty times the national average.

19. See Alonso 1992a and Nugent 1992 on how popular perceptions of "liberating" themselves from the state masks the character of their less mediated (and even more direct) exploitation at the hands of merchants.

20. The generalized attribution of all bad elements as being from "outside" the community holds for many sorts of people, not just agents and officials of the state. In 1983 I was told Los Malvinos were all recent immigrants—outside agitators, actually—who had moved to Cruces only to seize lands which they could then sell (notice the parallel to the prerevolutionary petty bourgeoisie!). "Land invaders," in other words, are, with agents of the state, the other side of the "outsiders" coin. In fact, Los Malvinos had lived in Cruces for decades, many families since before the revolution, and had petitioned for a new *dotación* in Cruces in 1960 because the *ejido* lands were all controlled by the same *cacicazgo* as had ruled in the 1930s (AGRA, AGCCA). This was the same group still ruling in the 1980s.

CHAPTER SIX

1. Some important discussions do exist (e.g., by Marte Gómez 1966 or Mendieta y Nuñez 1981), and in the last decade scholars, inspired by the pioneering research of Friedrich Katz (1974, 1981), have done research in this area (cf. Aboites 1988; González Herrera 1988; Nugent 1990).

2. See also Lartigue's (1984) excellent study of the Sierra Tarahumara, in which the contrast is not "peasant/landlord" but between an indigenous social formation and a modern, transnational extractive industry.

3. See also Shanin [1971] 1987a.

4. Osorio 1988:150. Cf. Almada 1938:117; Almada 1955:357–58; AHSRE e.9-15-15.

5. AMCG c.33, e.315, Nam., 15-iii-1894, 29-iii-1894, 30-iii-1894, and 12-iv-1894, all from PM José Casavantes to JPG.

6. AMCG c.35, e.327, Chih., 4-i-1895, J. Cortazar to JPG.

7. AMCG, commercial censuses for late nineteenth century; AMN, material on acequias, etc.

8. While appearing to rely on a somewhat wooden and simplistic characterization of state ideology at the time, this statement is corroborated by the following quotation. In the final pages of his history of Chihuahua, Enrique Creel (1928) listed "the national dangers" and the means of saving the nation from them thus: "*Dangers*— 1. Hatred of religion. 2. Hatred of capital. 3. Hatred of foreigners. 4. Civil war. *Corrections*— 1. Peace. 2. Justice. 3. Love of capital. 4. Love of work. 5. Respect for property" (Creel 1928:79).

9. Most of the lots sold as municipal lands under the 1905 land law were sold (at a very low price) as "grazing land," though many were cultivable fields. More than 5,000 hectares in the immediate vicinity of Namiquipa were sold to outsiders/immigrants between 1906 and 1909 (dates from *Annuario Estadístico,* 1905–1909, AMN c.3, c.5 passim).

10. Olea Arias 1961; Duarte Morales 1967; Calzadíaz Barrera 1979.

11. AMC c.7, e.1913, Nam., 2-ii-1913, Candelario Cervantes to PM Cruces.

12. But not all, especially in Cruces, where, for example, the much reviled prerevolutionary cacique, Luis Chávez, still enjoyed a post in the local govern-

ment in the 1920s, and one Manuel Flores, who had been a *porfirista* judge, again assumed that position in 1920. AMN c.6, Cruces, 30-iii-1920, signatures of more than one hundred Cruceños in protest against Flores's reappointment.

13. Cf. Craig 1983 and Schryer 1980 for local-level studies from other regions of Mexico (Los Altos de Jalisco, the Huasteca) which address the issue of the alternative avenues of regional development in *ejidos* as a combined function of the politics of agrarian reform and class formation.

14. See AGCCA e.24:432 (721.1) (file on the *ejido* of Namiquipa, especially for 1925–28); AMN c.9, 23-ix-1928, José Rascón y Tena, José Cervantes, Arcadio Maldonado, and five hundred other Namiquipans in a petition; AEN 6-vi-1928, Adolfo Delgado, president of CPA, to *procurador de los pueblos*, Cd. Chih., explaining why Namiquipans oppose the Agrarian Law.

15. There is nothing particularly traditional about cultivation of corn on fields of *temporal* in Namiquipa. This is an invented tradition, today encouraged by the state. The tortilla of preference in Namiquipa—indeed throughout much of the North—is the wheat flour tortilla, not the corn tortilla. While Namiquipans have a large repertoire of uses for corn (in tortillas, for pinole, tamales, etc.), in the past it was not cultivated on the scale it is today. Wheat was cultivated in irrigated fields in the past but no longer is.

16. To this must be added the numerous *colonias agrícolas* formed on the old Hearst Babicora hacienda starting in the mid-1950s (e.g., just south of Namiquipa, División del Norte, Independencia [Cologachic], and Soto Maynez [Santa Ana]). Whatever the eventual problems resulting from consolidation of contiguous lots and formation of *latifundias* within the *colonias*, the original colonists were basically peasant agriculturalists rather than capitalist farmers.

17. Fix the tractor, borrow some tools, *barbechar* (plow), wait for rains, secure seed, purchase fertilizer, *rastrear* (harrow), wait for rains, mend the fence, *sembrar* (plant), *cultivar* (weed), wait for rains, *cultivar* (weed again), *correr los ladrones* (run off the thieves), *cortar* (cut the grain), *cosechar* (harvest), *pepenar* (pick up the leavings), *limpiar* (clean the grain), *llevar a la bodega* (deliver grain to the warehouse), etc.

18. The state's claim to own the land of the *ejido* places one set of limits on individuals' control of means of agricultural production, the unequal distribution of instruments of production within the pueblo another. The variety of terrible things that can happen to a field as a result of historical or meteorological contingencies—such as an agronomist prescribing a fertilizer inappropriate for the soil, or hail, or drought—are yet other limits on human control.

19. *Informe* of Gov. Rodrigo M. Quevedo, 16-ix-35.

20. Lists of Namiquipan *braceros* are in the AMN. E.g, in 1956 there were 815 *"aspirantes"* for participation in the *bracero* program from the *municipio*. AMN c.23-B, e.1956, 16-xi-1956.

21. AMN c.17, e.1944–45, Chih., 17-xi-1944, Ing. Esteban Uranga, Sec[a.] del Gob[o.] del Estado, to jefe, Dept[o.] Agrario.

22. Stavenhagen (1970) lumps *ejidatarios* with *minifundistas*, individuals farming plots of fewer than 5 hectares. This makes the situation in Namiquipa difficult to understand only because Namiquipans as a rule held more than 10 hectares of land, while the vast majority of rural landholders in Mexico work

plots of fewer than 5 hectares, and the major portion of privately held land is in holdings larger than 100 hectares.

23. AEN e.Ejido B, Nam., 27-iv-1951, José L. Flores (Pte. of Com°· Ejidal) to Ing. José A. Murrillo, sec°· of the ACC Agraria, Chih.

24. This *coordinadora* included the *ejidos* and *colonias* Gral. Fco. Villa, División del Norte, Socorro Rivera, and the municipal peasant committees of Ignacio Zaragoza, Madera, Gómez Farías, Temosachi, Matachi, Guerrero, Namiquipa, Bachiniva, and Gral. Trías. It reads like it could have been written in the midst of the great peasant mobilizations of the mid-1980s, but it is certainly ten or twenty years older, since it was found in 1984 among one of several boxes of papers from the *ejido* rotting in a storage shed where they had been put by a former *comisario ejidal* after he left office more than a decade earlier (taking much of the archive with him).

25. The state offered to finance wells, but until 1986 the offer was made only to groups of ten farmers with contiguous fields exceeding 100 hectares in total extent who agreed to share the water. Such a well was built near El Terrero, but the participants in the collective project later fought. It is now in disuse. A successful water co-op of this type was functioning in El Picacho (Ejido Guadalupe Victoria) south of Namiquipa. Within the *ejido* of Namiquipa on the plain directly to the east of the pueblo, there were three electrically powered pumps pulling water out of deep wells by 1983. The first of these was built by a wealthy Namiquipan who controlled a large plot of land (the former Loya property) and many cattle after the revolution; the other two were financed by the individuals' having worked for years (in one case decades) in the United States, one as an agricultural laborer, another as a diesel mechanic in the Alaskan fisheries. The former diesel mechanic's adult sons now work in Alaska.

26. Compare figures for minimum wages, which increased tenfold between 1969 and 1982 (and again more than four times between 1982 and 1985) and guaranteed agricultural prices from 1960 to 1982 (Sanderson 1986:203).

27. This company was notorious for not paying its local debts. Their warehouse was destroyed in a fire—supposedly started in the faulty refrigeration plant—which many people believe the owners set to collect the insurance.

28. Though this is, again, largely illusory. The (ecological) fact of the matter is, Namiquipa is far from the ideal eco-niche for apples. Late spring frosts frequently hit after the trees have flowered. Orchards require expensive irrigation systems. Hail storms in the late summer invariably damage the almost ripened fruit unless the grower has constructed an expensive system of nets to protect the trees. But "doing well" with apples, if only once every five years, can mean incredible profits, which are almost invariably reinvested by Namiquipans to buy more trees or more land, nets to protect from hail, a new tractor or truck.

29. E.g., Esteva 1980 versus Bartra 1974; cf. Lucas de Rouffinglac 1985 and Redclift 1980 for (admittedly partisan) reviews of the debate.

30. Cf. influential studies by Wolf (1969b) or Paige (1975), for example, or some of the anthologies assembled by Teodor Shanin ([1971] 1987b) and his collaborators (Alavi and Shanin 1982; Archetti et al. 1987) or case studies such as Zamosc (1986) on the peasant movement in Colombia.

31. Studies that pose such questions for Mexico include Gilly [1971] 1983 and Semo 1983.

32. E.g., Lucas de Rouffinglac (1985:xvi): "The peasant class is a working class-in-itself [and] also forms a class-for-itself," versus Otero 1986: "The semiproletariat is the most dynamic class in Mexico today."

33. The reference here is to the celebrated "Potato Thesis" (Michael Ducey, a history student at the University of Chicago in 1986, introduced me to that expression) in Marx ([1852] 1963:123–24), according to which, "The smallholding peasants form a vast mass, . . . but without entering into manifold relations with one another. . . . In this way, the great mass of the French nation is formed by simple addition of homologous magnitudes, much as potatoes in a sack form a sack of potatoes." See Roseberry (1991:19): "One of the first tests one might apply in evaluating the degree of orthodoxy in a Marxist is whether or not this passage has been memorized." Also see Roseberry 1983:224–26 for an alternative reading of the passage in which the Potato Thesis is advanced.

34. Cf. passage from Post 1978 quoted above, p. 36: people are "the link between structures and history."

CHAPTER SEVEN

1. Those passages by Gilly (and Löwy) were published in 1983—in other words, before both the dramatic neo-*cardenista* mobilizations of 1988 throughout Mexico that were, in my opinion, in part an attempt by many people in the society to reclaim "the revolution" for themselves, and also before President Carlos Salinas de Gortari's explicit repudiation of the spirit of the Mexican revolution, which had been such a crucial element of the PRI/state's ideology until the 1990s.

2. Use of the gender-specific terms "he," "himself," and "his" in this paragraph is intentional: the concept of *agricultor* is implicated in a profoundly masculine notion of identity. See Alonso 1992a and Nugent and Alonso 1994.

3. Never mind that within the community a very different reading was put on that period. See chapter 4, this volume; Nugent 1989b; Nugent and Alonso 1994.

4. See, e.g., Hamilton 1982; Grindle 1986; Alonso 1983; Cockcroft 1983; Hansen 1972; Hart 1978; Hellman 1978; Leal [1975] 1985; R. Bartra 1985; Gilly 1985.

5. Semo notes the irony of the capitalist state in twentieth-century Mexico celebrating its "revolutionary" origins (1979:135).

6. It is ironic to note that that during this early period of "nation-building," the task of securing the northern frontier of "New Spain" (later "Mexico") was placed in the hands of two individuals with decidedly non-Spanish names: Hugo O'Conner, who reinforced "the Line" of presidios in the 1770s, and Teodoro de Croix, the first governor and commanding general of the *provincias internas*.

7. See above, especially the 1807 González de Almoyna descendants versus Francisco Vasquez dispute, discussed in chapter 2 (AEN); Namiquipa and Galeana petitions preceding the Díaz decree of 1889, in AMCG and AGCCA; Namiquipa, Janos, Galeana, and Cruces papers in ATN; documents cited by expert

paleographer (DPP) in AGCCA; suits against the administrator of Santa Clara in AJN; Santana Pérez Plan (AGN.RMGR); Lauro Aguirre Plan (CRO/AHSRE); Plácido Chávez (1964); Foundation of SCP in 1906 (AGNCh); letters from José Rascón y Tena in AMN, AMCG, 1922–29; Olea Arias (1961); Duarte Morales (1967, 1968); José María Espinosa play (1895?).

8. See the AP, Instituto de Investigaciones Dr. José María Luis Mora, especially PHO/I/111–13, 120, 127, 147, 149, 150, all of which were done in towns near Namiquipa.

9. Interview with Victoriano Macías, conducted by María Isabel Souza, Oct. 29, 1973, La Junta, Chih.; AP, Instituto de Investigaciones Dr. José María Luis Mora, PHO/I/111.

BIBLIOGRAPHY

A NOTE ON ARCHIVAL SOURCES
Mexico City

In Mexico City during 1985 I consulted the Archivo General de la Nación (National Archives), in the old penitentiary of Lecumberri, the very prison in which Adolfo Gilly had written *La revolución interrumpida* a decade and a half earlier. Particularly valuable were the following *ramos:* Provincias Internas, Virreynato, Cárceles y Presidios (for the colonial period), Período Revolucionario, Comisión Nacional Agraria, and Presidentes (for the early twentieth century). The Biblioteca Nacional (National Library), on the same block as our residence in Mexico City (the Hotel Monte Carlo), was an equally valuable source of information on Namiquipa during the colonial period. In addition to the Archivo Franciscano (Archive of the Religious Order of St. Francis) it has an excellent collection of eighteenth-century manuscripts (Manuscritos). Some of the Francisco I. Madero's papers from 1910–11, including lists of armaments and soldiers who participated in the first *maderista* uprising, are in the National Library as well.

The Colección Porifiro Díaz (papers of President Porfirio Díaz), at the Universidad Iberoamericana, along with the Archivo Histórico de la Secretaría de Relaciones Exteriores (Historical Archive of the Ministry of Foreign Relations), include a wealth of data useful for understanding Namiquipa in the late nineteenth century. In the Biblioteca e Hemeroteca Nacional, at the Universidad Nacional Autónoma de México, is the Archivo Jacinto B. Treviño. Treviño was the *carrancista* general in charge of the state of Chihuahua for much of 1916. The Archivo de la Palabra (the Archive of the Spoken Word), in the Instituto Dr. José María Luis Mora, holds the results of a project in the oral history of the revolution in Chihuahua, including a fantastic collection of interviews conducted in the early 1970s with veterans of the revolution.

I found abundant and detailed information on the agrarian history of western Chihuahua in the twentieth century in the Archivo General de Reforma Agraria (Archive of the Ministry of Agrarian Reform). Ana Alonso was able to work in the Archivo de Terrenos Nacionales, the Sección Histórico of the AGRA, and she shared the incredible documentation this collection holds on agrarian conflicts during the nineteenth century.

Durango

The best source for understanding the conflict between Namiquipans and the postrevolutionary state in the 1920s and 1930s is the Archivo General del Cuerpo Consultativo Agrario, located in Gómez Palacio, Durango. This archive contains records of virtually all the correspondence between Namiquipans and agrarian reform officials in those decades, including the Dictamen del Perito Paleografo.

Chihuahua

Guerrero City (formerly called Papigochic) was the district capital of western Chihuahua during the nineteenth century and through 1910. The Archivo Municipal de Ciudad Guerrero, in the Presidencia Municipal (town hall) of Guerrero, provided the most thorough documentation on Namiquipa during the Apache Wars, through the last tumultuous decades of the Porfiriato and the revolutionary decade. The Registro Público de la Propiedad for the district, also in the Presidencia, contains information on transfers of land around the turn of the century.

In Chihuahua City, the state capital, the most diverse, and for an understanding of specific local developments, the most detailed, archive is the Colección de Rubén Osorio. Dr. Osorio has amassed a superb collection of photocopies, documents, and transcripts of his own interviews with people from throughout Chihuahua. Also in Chihuahua City I consulted the Archivo General de Notarías del Estado de Chihuahua and the Registro Público de la Propiedad, Estado de Chihuahua, Sección Antigua, in the Government Palace for information on property holdings and purchases of "National" lands in the region around Namiquipa. The Centro de Investigación y Documentación del Estado de Chihuahua, a library of the Universidad Autónoma de Chihuahua, has census data and official state government documents and reports alongside a superb collection of secondary sources.

Namiquipa

The *Archivo Parroquial de Namiquipa* (Iglesia de San Pedro de Alcantara de Namiquipa) includes records of births, marriages, and deaths from 1780 until the present. The Archivo Municipal de Namiquipa (Presidencia Municipal, Namiquipa) was our major source after the Guerrero archive. While there was little from the first half of the nineteenth century (Governor Creel ordered that all municipal archives throughout the state remit their holdings to the capital, where presumably they were burned in the fire that gutted the government offices in the 1940s), some records (on local elections, land petitions, and of course *animales mostrencos* [stray animals]) did remain, and this was an especially rich source for the period from the 1890s onward. The 1910–20 period was thin, though, since some of General Francisco Villa's troops burned what they could find of the archive in 1917. The Archivo Municipal was particularly useful for the years after 1920, when internal affairs in Namiquipa were no longer administered from the district capital.

The Archivo del Juzgado de Namiquipa (AJN) , now in the Presidencia Municipal of Namiquipa, contains judicial records of the juez menor (county judge) from the 1880s through the 1950s. (While some of the early court records were included with the Presidencia papers in 1983, a large part of what presently comprises the AJN was archived only when we discovered that the judge was on the verge of burning about twenty boxes of "old papers" [the existence of which he had earlier denied] to destroy life-threatening "microbes.")

The Archivo Municipal de Cruces, in Cruces, Municipio de Namiquipa, contained some useful information, particularly on the revolutionary years. The Archivo Ejidal de Namiquipa, in the office of the *ejido* of Namiquipa, was a particularly useful source. Finally, the Brigada de Educación Tecnológica Agropecuaria (BETA) #331, a rural development group sent to Namiquipa by the Secretaría de Educación Pública (Ministry of Public Education) shared with us the results of their own sociological survey of all the communities in the *municipio* of Namiquipa.

UNITED STATES

Documentary Relations of the Southwest, at the Arizona State Museum on the campus of the University of Arizona in Tucson, has cross-referenced indexes and summaries of documents concerning northwestern Mexico during the colonial period from a wide range of archives in Mexico and the United States. The Arizona Historical Society (until recently the Arizona Pioneer Historical Society), also in Tucson, has some documentation pertaining to the fate of former presidios during the nineteenth century. The Special Collections department of the University of Texas-El Paso Library is especially valuable for its mcirofilms of Chihuahua newspapers from the first two decades of the twentieth century and official state publications. The Bancroft Library at the University of California, Berkeley, has documents on the revolution in Chihuahua, including the Archive of Silvestre Terrazas.

At the United States Military History Institute in Carlisle, Pennsylvania, are some of the papers of some of the U.S. soldiers who participated in the Pershing Punitive Expedition to Mexico in 1916. The records of the Punitive Expedition are for the most part lodged in the Military Reference Branch of the United States National Archives in Washington, D.C. The richest sources of information were in Record Group 94 (Correspondence of the Adjutant General's Office), RG 393 and 395 (Military Intelligence Section). Also useful are the State Department's reports of conditions along the U.S.-Mexican border (RG 812).

I also visited the Luna County Courthouse in Deming, New Mexico, where *villistas* captured during the Columbus raid or kidnapped in Mexico by U.S. troops in the months following (this occurred in Namiquipa) were initially brought to trial. Finally, the Washington National Records Administration in Suitland, Maryland, now includes the records of the Mexican and U.S. Special and Mixed Claims Commissions.

ARCHIVES AND PRIMARY SOURCES
MEXICO CITY

Archivo de la Palabra, Instituto de Investigaciones Dr. José María Luis Mora
Archivo de Terrenos Nacionales, Sección Histórico of the AGRA
Archivo General de la Nación
  Ramo Cárceles y Presidios
  Ramo Comisión Nacional Agraria
  Ramo Período Revolucionario
  Ramo Presidentes
  Ramo Provincias Internas
  Ramo Virreynato
Archivo General de Reforma Agraria, Secretaría de la Reforma Agraria
Archivo Histórico de la Secretaría de Relaciones Exteriores
Archivo Jacinto B. Treviño, Biblioteca e Hemeroteca Nacional, Universidad Nacional Autónoma de México
Biblioteca Nacional
  Archivo Franciscano
  Archivo Francisco I. Madero
  Manuscritos
Colección Porfirio Díaz, Universidad Iberoamericana

DURANGO

Archivo General del Cuerpo Consultativo Agrario, Gómez Palacio, Durango

CHIHUAHUA

Archivo General de Notarias del Estado de Chihuahua, Palacio de Gobierno, Cd. Chihuahua
Archivo Municipal de Ciudad Guerrero, Presidencia Municipal, Cd. Guerrero, Chihuahua
Centro de Investigación y Documentación del Estado de Chihuahua, Universidad Autónoma de Chihuahua
Colección Particular de Dr. Rubén Osorio, Cd. Chihuahua
Registro Público de la Propiedad, Distrito Guerrero
Registro Público de la Propiedad, Estado de Chihuahua, Sección Antigua, Cd. Chihuahua

NAMIQUIPA

Archivo del Juzgado de Namiquipa, Presidencia Municipal
Archivo Ejidal de Namiquipa, in the office of the *ejido*
Archivo Municipal de Cruces, Cruces, Mpio. Namiquipa
Archivo Municipal de Namiquipa, Presidencia Municipal
Archivo Parroquial de Namiquipa, Iglesia de San Pedro de Alcantara de Namiquipa
Brigada de Educación Tecnológica Agropecuaria #331 (Secretaría de Educación Pública)

UNITED STATES

Arizona Pioneer Historical Society, Tucson, Arizona
Bancroft Library, University of California, Berkeley
Documentary Relations of the Southwest, Arizona State Museum, University of
    Arizona, Tucson, Arizona
Luna County Courthouse, Deming, New Mexico
United States Military History Institute, Carlisle, Pennsylvania
United States National Archives, Military Reference Branch, Washington, D.C.
University of Texas-El Paso Library, Special Collections
Washington National Records Administration, Suitland, Maryland

PERIODICALS

Arizona Daily Star
Diario de Chihuahua
New York Times
Nexos
Novedades de Chihuahua
Periódico Oficiál de Chihuahua
Proceso

BOOKS AND ARTICLES

Aboites, Luis. 1988. *La irrigación revolucionaria.* México: SEP/CIESAS.
Abrams, Philip. 1982. *Historical sociology.* Ithaca: Cornell University Press.
———. [1977] 1988. Notes on the difficulty of studying the state. *Journal of Historical Sociology* 1 (1): 58–89.
Aguilar Camin, Héctor. 1977. *La frontera nómada.* México: Siglo XXI.
Aguilar Camin, Héctor, et al., eds. 1979. *Interpretaciones de la revolución mexicana.* México: Editorial Nueva Imagen.
Alavi, Hamza. 1982. State and class under peripheral capitalism. In H. Alavi and T. Shanin (eds.), *Introduction to the sociology of "developing societies."* New York: Monthly Review Press.
———. 1987. Peasantry and capitalism: A Marxist discourse. In T. Shanin (ed.), *Peasants and peasant societies.* Oxford: Basil Blackwell.
Alavi, Hamza, and Teodor Shanin, eds. 1982. *Introduction to the sociology of "developing societies."* New York: Monthly Review Press.
Almada, Francisco. 1938. *La rebelión de Tomochi.* Chihuahua: Sociedad Chihuahense de Estudios Históricos.
———. 1955. *Resumen de la historia del estado de Chihuahua.* México: Libros Mexicanos.
———. 1964. *La Revolución en el estado de Chihuahua.* Chihuahua: Biblioteca del Instituto Nacional de Estudios Históricos de la Revolución Mexicana.
———. 1980. *Gobernadores del estado de Chihuahua.* Chihuahua: Centro Librero La Prensa.
———. 1982. *Diccionario de historia, geografía y biografía de Chihuahua.* Chihuahua: Gobierno del Estado.
Alonso, Ana María. 1986. The hermeneutics of history: Class struggle and revo-

lution in the Chihuahuan sierra. Paper presented to a history department seminar, University of Chicago, Feb. 1986.

———. 1988a. The effects of truth: Representations of the past and the imagining of community. *Journal of Historical Sociology* 1 (1): 33–57.

———. 1988b. *Gender, ethnicity and the constitution of subjects: Accommodation, resistance and revolution on the Chihuahuan frontier.* Ph.D. diss., University of Chicago.

———. 1988c. U.S. military intervention, the Villista movement and the *Defensas Sociales.* In D. Nugent (ed.), *Rural revolt in Mexico and U.S. intervention.* San Diego: Center for U.S.-Mexican Studies.

———. 1988d. "Progress" as disorder and dishonor: Discourses of *serrano* resistance. *Critique of Anthropology* 8 (1): 13–33.

———. 1992a. Work and *gusto:* Gender and re-creation in a North Mexican pueblo. In John Calagione, Doris Francis, and Daniel Nugent (eds.), *Worker's expressions: Beyond accommodation and resistance.* Albany: State University of New York Press.

———. 1992b. Gender, power, and historical memory: Discourses of serrano resistance. In Judith Butler and Joan Scott (eds.), *Feminists theorize the political.* New York and London: Routledge.

Alonso, Jorge, ed. 1983. *El estado Mexicano.* México: CIESAS.

Althusser, Louis. 1970. *For Marx.* New York: Vintage.

———. 1971. *Lenin and Philosophy.* New York: Monthly Review Press.

Amparan González, Miguel, Gabriel Borunda Olivas, and Simon Verduzco. 1987. La democracia y la lucha por los precios de garantía: Nueva perspectiva del movimiento campesino en Chihuahua. Paper presented to the First Congress on Agrarian Problems in the Northwest of Mexico and the Southwest United States, Culiacán, Sinaloa, Jan. 1987.

Anderson, Benedict. 1983. *Imagined communities.* London: Verso/New Left Books.

Anderson, Perry. 1974. *Lineages of the absolutist state.* London: New Left Books.

Anuario Estadístico del Estado de Chihuahua. Chihuahua: Imprenta del Gobierno, Secretaría de Gobernación, Sección Estadística, 1906, 1908, 1909, 1910, 1913.

Appendini, Kirsten. 1983. La polarización de la agricultura mexicana: Un análisis a nivel de zonas agrícolas en 1970. In Gonzalo Rodríguez Gigena (ed.), *Economía mexicana, series temática: Sector agropecuario.* México: Centro de Investigación y Docencia Económicas A.C.

Archetti, Eduardo, Paul Cammack, and Bryan Roberts, eds. 1987. *The sociology of "developing societies": Latin America.* London: Macmillan Education.

Asad, Talal. 1987. Are there histories of people without europe? *Comparative Studies in Society and History* 29 (3): 594–607.

Ball, Eve. 1970. *In the days of Victorio.* Tucson: University of Arizona Press.

———. 1980. *Indeh.* Provo: Brigham Young University Press.

Barnes, Thomas, Thomas Naylor, and Charles Polzer. 1981. *Northern New Spain: A research guide.* Tucson: University of Arizona Press.

Barretta, Silvio R. Duncan, and John Markoff. 1978. Civilization and barbarism:

Cattle frontiers in Latin America. *Comparative Studies in Society and History* 20 (4): 587–620.

Bartra, Armando, ed. 1977. *Regeneración, 1900–1918: La corriente más radical de la revolución mexicana de 1910 a través de su periodico de combate.* Articles by Ricardo Flores Magón, Práxedis Guerrero, Juan Sarabia, Enrique Flores Magón, Librado Rivera, and others. Mexico: Era.

———. 1985. *Los herederos de Zapata.* México: Era.

Bartra, Roger. 1974. *Estructura agraria y clases sociales en México.* México: Era.

———, ed. 1975a. *Caciquismo y poder político en el México rural.* México: Siglo XXI.

———. 1975b. Peasants and political power in Mexico: A theoretical approach. *Latin American Perspectives* 2 (2): 125–45.

———. 1982. Capitalism and the peasantry in Mexico. *Latin American Perspectives* 9 (3): 36–47.

———. 1987. *La jaula de la melancólia.* México: Grijalbo.

Bellingeri, Marco, and Isabel Gil Sánchez. 1980. Las estructuras agrarias bajo el Porfiriato. In Ciro Cardoso (ed.), *México en el siglo XIX (1821–1910): História económica y de la estructura social.* México: Nueva Imagen.

Bennett, Wendell, and Robert Zingg. 1935. *The Tarahumara.* Chicago: University of Chicago Press.

Borah, Woodrow. 1954. Race and class in Mexico. *Pacific Historical Review* 23 (4): 331–42.

Branford, Sue, and Bernardo Kucinski. [1987] 1988. *The debt squads: The U.S., the banks and Latin America.* London: Zed.

Calagione, John, and Daniel Nugent. 1992. Worker's expressions: Beyond accommodation and resistance on the margins of capitalism. In John Calagione, Doris Francis, and Daniel Nugent (eds.), *Worker's expressions: Beyond accommodation and resistance.* Albany: State University of New York Press.

Calzadíaz Barrera, Alberto. 1967. *Hechos reales de la Revolución.* Vol. 2. 3d ed. México: Editorial Patria.

———. 1969. *Víspera de la Revolución (Abuelo Cisneros).* México: Ed. Patria.

———. 1972. *Hechos reales de la Revolución.* Vol. 3, El fin de la División del Norte. 2d ed. México: Ed. Patria.

———. 1977. *Hechos reales de la Revolución.* Vol. 6, Por qué Villa atacó Columbus: Intriga internacional. 1st ed. México: Ed. Patria.

———. [1958] 1979. *Hechos reales de la Revolución.* Vol. 1. 4th ed. México: Ed. Patria.

Carbó, Margarita, and Andrea Sánchez. 1983. México bajo la dictadura porfiriana. In Enrique Semo (ed.), *México: Un pueblo en la historia.* Vol. 2. México: Nueva Imagen/Universidad Autónoma de Puebla.

Cardoso, Ciro, ed. 1983. *México en el siglo XIX (1821–1910): História económica y de la estructura social.* México: Nueva Imagen.

Carnoy, Martin. 1984. *The state in political theory.* Princeton: Princeton University Press.

Carr, Barry. 1973. Las peculiaridades del norte mexicano: Ensayo de interpretación. *História Mexicana* 22 (3): 321–46.

————. 1980. Recent regional studies of the Mexican Revolution. *Latin American Research Review* 15 (1): 3–14.

Castoriadis, Cornelius. 1976. The Hungarian source. *Telos* 9(3): 4–22.

Cerutti, Mario. 1989. El noreste mexicano en el siglo XIX. Ph.D. diss., University of Leiden, Netherlands.

Chatterjee, Partha. 1982. Agrarian relations and communalism in Bengal, 1926–1935. In Ranajit Guha (ed.), *Subaltern studies. Vol. 1, Writings on South Asian history and society,* 9–38. Delhi: Oxford University Press.

————. 1983. More on modes of power and the peasantry. In Ranajit Guha (ed.), *Subaltern Studies. Vol. 2,* 311–49. Delhi: Oxford University Press.

Chávez Calderón, Plácido. 1964. *La defensa de Tomochi.* México: Editorial Jus.

Clifford, James, and George Marcus, eds. 1986. *Writing culture.* Berkeley: University of California Press.

Coatsworth, John. 1974. Railroads, landholding and agrarian protest in the early Porfiriato. *Hispanic American Historical Review* 54 (1): 48–71.

————. 1984. *El impacto económico de los ferrocarriles en el Porfiriato.* México: ERA.

Cockcroft, James. 1968. *Intellectual precursors of the Mexican Revolution, 1900–1913.* Austin: University of Texas Press.

————. 1983. *Mexico: Class formation, capital, accumulation and the state.* New York: Monthly Review Press.

————. 1986. *Outlaws in the promised land.* New York: Grove Press.

Cohen, Gerald. 1978. *Karl Marx's theory of history: A defense.* Princeton: Princeton University Press.

Cohn, Bernard. 1980. History and anthropology: The state of play. *Comparative Studies in Society and History* 22 (2): 198–221.

————. 1985. The command of language and the language of command. In R. Guha (ed.), *Subaltern Studies.* Vol. 4. Delhi: Oxford University Press.

Cohn, Bernard, and Nicholas Dirks. 1988. Beyond the fringe: The nation state, colonialism and the technologies of power. *Journal of Historical Sociology* 1 (2): 224–29.

Comaroff, John L. 1982a. Class and culture in a peasant economy: The transformation of land tenure in Barolong. In R. P. Webner (ed.), *Land reform in the making.* London: Rex Collings.

————. 1982b. Dialectical systems, history and anthropology: Units of study and questions of theory. *Journal of Southern African Studies* 8 (2): 143–72.

Compendio Estadístico del Estado de Chihuahua 1958–1959. n.d. Bound typescript. Ed. Ing. Leopoldo Hurtado Olin. UNAM library.

Córdova, Arnaldo. 1973. *La ideología de la Revolución Mexicana.* México: Siglo XXI.

Cornelius, Wayne. 1986. Political liberalization and the 1985 elections in Mexico. In P. Drake and E. Silva (eds.), *Elections and democratization in Latin America, 1980–1985.* La Jolla, CA: Center for Iberian and Latin American Studies and Center for U.S.-Mexican Studies.

Corrigan, Philip. 1975. On the politics of production: A comment on "Peasants and Politics" by Eric Hobsbawm. *Journal of Peasant Studies* 2 (3): 341–49.

Corrigan, Philip, and Derek Sayer. 1985. *The great arch: English state formation as cultural revolution.* Oxford: Basil Blackwell.

Corrigan, Philip, Harvie Ramsay, and Derek Sayer. 1980. The state as a relation of production. In P. R. D. Corrigan (ed.), *Capitalism, state formation and Marxist theory: Historical investigations.* London: Quartet Books.

Craig, Ann. 1983. *The first* Agraristas, Berkeley: University of California Press.

Cramaussel, Chantal. 1990. *Primera página de historia colonial chihuahuense: La provincia de Santa Bárbara en Nueva Vizcaya, 1563–1631.* Juárez: Universidad Autónoma de Ciudad Juárez.

Creel, Enrique. 1928. *El estado de Chihuahua: Su historia, geografía y riquezas naturales.* México: Tip. El Progresso.

De Janvry, Alain. 1981. *The agrarian question and reformism in Latin America.* Baltimore: Johns Hopkins University Press.

De Janvry, Alain, and Carlos Garramón. 1977. The dynamics of rural poverty in Latin America. *Journal of Peasant Studies* 4 (2): 206–16.

de la Peña, Guillermo. 1981. *A legacy of promises.* Austin: University of Texas Press.

———. 1989. Local and regional power in Mexico. Texas Papers on Mexico no. 88-01. Austin: Mexican Center of the Institute of Latin American Studies.

de Souza, Joao Francisco. 1987. Investigación participativa, producción de conocimiento y subjeto histórico. Paper presented to the Taller de Investigación Acción Participativa, Managua, Nicaragua, Nov. 1987.

Díaz Polanco, Hector. 1982. Indigenismo, populism and Marxism. *Latin American Perspectives* 9 (1) [33]: 42–61.

Duarte Morales, Teodosio. 1967. *El rugir del cañon.* Ed. B. Herrera. Juárez.

———. 1968. *Villa y Pershing: Memorias de la Revolución.* Ed. B. Herrera. Juárez.

Emmanuel, Agghiri. 1972. White settler colonialism and the myth of investment imperialism. *New Left Review* 73: 35–57.

Engels, Friedrich. [1884] 1942. *The origin of the family, private property and the state.* Trans. from the 4th German ed. New York: International Publishers.

Ennew, Judith, Paul Hirst, and Keith Tribe. 1977. "Peasantry" as an economic category. *Journal of Peasant Studies* 4 (4): 295–322.

Escudero, José Agustín. 1834. *Noticias estadísticas del estado de Chihuahua.* México: Imprenta del Puente de Palacio y Flamencos #1.

———. 1839. *Observaciones sobre el estado actual del departamento de Chihuahua y los medios de ponerlo a cubierto de las incursiones de los bárbaros.* México: Impreso por Juan Ojeda.

Esteva, Gustavo. 1980. *La batalla en el México rural.* México: Siglo XXI.

Feder, Ernest. 1971. *The rape of the peasantry.* New York: Doubleday.

Foster, George. 1967. Peasant society and the image of limited good. In Jack M. Potter, May Díaz, and George Foster (eds.), *Peasant society: A reader.* Boston: Little, Brown and Company.

Foster-Carter, Aidan. 1978. Can we articulate "articulation"? In John Clammer (ed.), *The new economic anthropology.* London: Macmillan. Also appeared as "The Modes of Production Controversy" in *New Left Review* 107.

Frank, Andre Gunder. 1967. *Capitalism and underdevelopment in Latin America.* New York: Monthly Review Press.

Friedman, Jonathan. 1974. Marxism, structuralism and vulgar materialism. *Man* 9 (3): 444–69.

Friedrich, Paul. [1970] 1977. *Agrarian revolt in a Mexican village.* Chicago: University of Chicago Press.

Gerhard, Peter. 1982. *The northern frontier of New Spain.* Princeton: Princeton University Press.

Geuss, Raymond. 1981. *The idea of a critical theory: Habermas and the Frankfurt School.* New York: Cambridge University Press.

Gibson, Charles. 1964. *The Aztecs under Spanish rule.* Berkeley: University of California Press.

Gilly, Adolfo. [1971] 1983. *The Mexican Revolution.* London: New Left Books.

———. 1985. *La larga travesía.* México: Editorial Nueva Imagen.

———. 1986. La División del Norte y Pancho Villa: El tiempo de los héroes y los mitos. In his *Arriba los de abajo: Perfiles mexicanos.* México: Océano.

———. 1987. Citas en los pies, ideas en la cabeza. *Nexos* 110 (Feb. 1987).

Gledhill, John. 1985. The peasantry in history. *Critique of Anthropology* 5 (1): 33–56.

Godelier, Maurice. [1969] 1974. *Rationalité et irrationalité en economie.* 2 vols. Paris: Maspero.

Gómez, Marte R. 1966. *La reforma agraria en las filas villistas, años 1913 a 1915 y 1920.* México: Biblioteca del Instituto Nacional de Estudios Históricos de la Revolución Mexicana.

González Herrera, Carlos. 1988. El villismo frente al problema agrario. *Cuadernos del Norte* 1 (3): 18–25.

Gramsci, Antonio. [1929–35] 1971. *Selections from the prison notebooks.* Trans. and ed. Q. Hoare and G. Nowell-Smith. New York: International Publishers.

Griffen, William. 1988. *Apaches at war and peace: The Janos presidio, 1750–1858.* Albuquerque: University of New Mexico Press.

Grindle, Merilee. 1986. *State and countryside: Development policy and agrarian politics in Latin America.* Baltimore: Johns Hopkins University Press.

Guha, Ranajit. 1982. On some aspects of the historiography of colonial India. In R. Guha (ed.), *Subaltern Studies.* Vol. 1. Delhi: Oxford University Press.

———. 1983a. *Elementary aspects of peasant insurgency in colonial India.* Delhi: Oxford University Press.

———. 1983b. The prose of counterinsurgency. In R. Guha (ed.), *Subaltern Studies.* Vol. 2. Delhi: Oxford University Press.

Hall, Stuart. 1981. Notes on the difficulty of studying "The Popular." In Raphael Samuels (ed.), *People's history and socialist theory.* London: Routledge and Kegan Paul.

Hamilton, Nora. 1982. *The limits of state autonomy.* Berkeley: University of California Press.

Hansen, Roger. 1972. *The politics of Mexican development.* Baltimore: Johns Hopkins University Press.

Harris, Charles, and Louis Sadler. 1988. *The border and the Revolution.* Silver City, NM: High-Lonesome Books.

Hart, John M. 1978. *Anarchism and the Mexican working class, 1860–1931.* Austin: University of Texas Press.

―――. 1987. *Revolutionary Mexico: The coming and process of the Mexican revolution*. Berkeley: University of California Press.

―――. 1988. U.S. economic hegemony, nationalism and violence in the Mexican countryside, 1876–1920. In D. Nugent (ed.), *Rural revolt in Mexico and United States intervention*. San Diego: Center for U.S.-Mexican studies.

Hart, Keith. 1983. The contribution of Marxism to economic anthropology. In Sutti Ortiz (ed.), *Economic anthropology: Topics and theories*. Monographs in Economic Anthropology, no. 1. Lanham, MD: Society for Economic Anthropology/University Press of America.

Heath, John Richard. 1989. The dynamics of Mexican agricultural development: A comment on Bartra and Otero. *Journal of Peasant Studies* 16 (2): 276–85.

Hellman, Judith. 1978. *Mexico in crisis*. New York: Holmes & Meier.

Hernández Padilla, Salvador. 1984. *El magonismo: Historia de una pasión libertaria, 1900–1922*. México: Era.

Hevia, James. 1990. "Making China perfectly equal." *Journal of Historical Sociology* 3 (4): 379–400.

Hewitt de Alcantara, Cynthia. 1978. *La modernización de la agricultura mexicana*. México: Siglo Veintiuno.

―――. 1984. *Anthropological perspectives on rural Mexico*. London: Routledge and Kegan Paul.

Hilton, Rodney. 1976. *The transition from feudalism to capitalism*. London: New Left Books.

Hindess, Barry, and Paul Hirst. 1975. *Pre-capitalist modes of production*. London: Routledge and Kegan Paul.

―――. 1977. *Mode of production and social formation*. London: Routledge and Kegan Paul.

Hobsbawm, Eric. 1959. *Primitive rebels*. Manchester: Manchester University Press.

―――. 1973. Peasants and politics. *Journal of Peasant Studies* 1 (1): 3–22.

―――. 1975. Reply [to Corrigan 1975]. *Journal of Peasant Studies* 2 (3): 349–51.

―――. [1969] 1981. *Bandits*. New York: Pantheon Books.

Holden, Robert. 1986. The Mexican state manages modernization: The survey of public lands in six states, 1876–1911. Ph.D. diss., University of Chicago.

―――. n.d. Warfare, settlers and settlement on the northern frontier of New Spain and Mexico.

Jacobs, Ian. 1982. *Ranchero revolt*. Austin: University of Texas Press.

Jessop, Bob. 1982. *The capitalist state*. New York: New York University Press.

Jones, Okah L. 1979. *Los paisanos*. Norman: University of Oklahoma Press.

Jordan, Fernando. [1956] 1981. *Crónica de un país bárbaro* 6th ed. Chihuahua: Centro Librero La Prensa.

Joseph, Gilbert. 1982. *Revolution from without*. New York: Cambridge University Press.

―――. 1988. The United States, feuding elites and rural revolt in Yucatán. In D. Nugent (ed.), *Rural revolt in Mexico and United States Intervention*. San Diego: Center for U.S.-Mexican Studies.

Joseph, Gilbert, and Daniel Nugent. 1994. Popular culture and state formation in revolutionary Mexico. In G. Joseph and D. Nugent (eds.), *Everyday forms of state formation: Revolution and the negotiation of rule in modern Mexico*. Durham, NC: Duke University Press. Forthcoming.

Kahn, Joel. 1985. Peasant ideologies in the Third World. *Annual Review of Anthropology* 14.

Katz, Friedrich. 1974. Labour conditions on Porfirian haciendas: Some trends and tendencies. *Hispanic American Historical Review* 54 (1): 1–47.

———. 1976a. *La servidumbre agraria en México en la época porfiriana*. México: Era.

———. 1976b. Peasants and the Mexican Revolution of 1910. In Joseph Spielberg and Scott Whiteford (eds.), *Forging nations*. East Lansing: Michigan State University Press.

———. 1978. Pancho Villa and the attack on Columbus, New Mexico. *American Historical Review* 83 (1): 101–30.

———. 1979. Villa: Reform governor of Chihuahua. In George Wolfskill and Douglas Richmond (eds.), *Essays on the Mexican Revolution*. Austin: University of Texas Press.

———. 1980. Pancho Villa, peasant movements and agrarian rebellion in northern Mexico. In David Brading (ed.), *Caudillo and peasant in the Mexican Revolution*. New York: Cambridge University Press.

———. 1981. *The secret war in Mexico*. Chicago: University of Chicago Press.

———. 1986. The Porfiriato. In Leslie Bethell (ed.), *The Cambridge history of Latin America*. Vol. 5. Cambridge: Cambridge University Press.

———. 1988a. From alliance to dependency: The formation and deformation of an alliance between Francisco Villa and the United States. In D. Nugent (ed.), *Rural revolt in Mexico and U.S. Intervention*. San Diego: Center for U.S.-Mexican Studies.

———, ed. 1988b. *Riot, rebellion, and revolution: Rural social conflict in Mexico*. Princeton: Princeton University Press.

———. 1988c. Rural uprisings in preconquest and colonial Mexico. In Friedrich Katz (eds.), *Riot, rebellion, and revolution: Rural social conflict in Mexico*. Princeton: Princeton University Press.

———. 1988d. Rural rebellions after 1810. In Friedrich Katz (ed.), *Riot, rebellion, and revolution: Rural Social Conflict in Mexico*. Princeton: Princeton University Press.

———. 1992. Los motivos agrarios de la revolución en Chihuahua. In Ricardo Avila Palafox, Carlos Martínez Assad, and Jean Meyer (eds.), *Las formas y las políticas del dominio agrario: Homenaje a François Chevalier*. Guadalajara: Editorial Universidad de Guadalajara.

———. *Pancho Villa*. New York: Alfred Knopf. Forthcoming.

Kearney, Michael. 1980. Agribusiness and the demise or the rise of the peasantry. *Latin American Perspectives* 7 (4): 115–24.

Knight, Alan. 1980. Peasant and caudillo in revolutionary Mexico, 1910–1917. In David Brading (ed.), *Caudillo and peasant in the Mexican Revolution*. New York: Cambridge University Press.

———. 1985a. The political economy of revolutionary Mexico, 1900–1940. In Chris Abel and Colin Lewis (eds.), *Latin America, economic imperialism and the state: The political economy of the external connection from Independence to the present,* 288–317. London: Athlone Press.

———. 1985b. The Mexican Revolution: Bourgeois? nationalist? Or just a "Great Rebellion"? *Bulletin of Latin American Research* 4 (2): 1–37.

———. 1986. *The Mexican Revolution.* 2 vols. New York: Cambridge University Press.

———. 1988. The United States and the Mexican peasantry c. 1880–1940. In D. Nugent (ed.), *Rural revolt in Mexico and U.S. intervention.* San Diego: Center for U.S.-Mexican Studies.

Krauze, Enrique. 1986. Chihuahua, ida y vuelta. *Vuelta* 115 (June).

Laclau, Ernesto. 1978. *Política e ideología en la teoría Marxista.* México: Siglo XXI.

Larrain, Jorge. 1979. *The concept of ideology.* London: Hutchinson.

Lartigue, François. 1984. *Indios y bosques.* México: La Casa Chata.

Lau Rojo, Rubén. 1989. *Las elecciones en Chihuahua, (1983–1988).* Special issue of *Cuadernos del Norte.*

Lau Rojo, Rubén, and Carlos González Herrera, eds. 1990. *Actas del Primer Congreso de Historia Regional Comparada, 1989.* Juárez: Universidad Autónoma de Ciudad Juárez.

Leal, Juan Felipe. [1975] 1985. *México: Estado, burocracia y sindicatos.* México: El Caballito.

Lem, Winnie. 1989. History and identity: Historical consciousness in rural Languedoc.

León-Portilla, Miguel. 1972. The norteño variety of Mexican culture. In E. Spicer (ed.), *Plural society in the Southwest.* New York: Interbook/Weatherhead Foundation.

Lévi-Strauss, Claude. 1963. *Structural anthropology.* New York: Basic Books.

———. 1966. *The savage mind.* Chicago: University of Chicago Press.

Lewis, Oscar. 1951. *Life in a Mexican village: Tepoztlán restudied.* Urbana: University of Illinois Press.

Leyes y Códigos de México. [1971] 1982. *Ley Federal de Reforma Agraria.* México: Editorial Porrua.

Lister, Florenco, and Robert Lister. 1966. *Chihuahua: Storehouse of storms.* Albuquerque: University of New Mexico Press.

———. 1979. *Chihuahua: Almacén de tempestades.* Spanish translation by Rubén Osorio and Luis García Gutiérrez of their 1966 work in English. Chihuahua: Gobierno del Estado de Chihuahua.

Lloyd, Jane-Dale. 1983. La crisis económica de 1905 a 1907 en el noroeste de Chihuahua. *Humanidades Annuario 7.*

———. 1987. *El proceso de modernización capitalista del noroeste de Chihuahua, 1880–1910.* México: Universidad Iberoamericana.

———. 1988. *Rancheros and rebellion:* The case of northwestern Chihuahua, 1905–1909. In D. Nugent (ed.), *Rural revolt in Mexico and United States intervention.* San Diego: Center for U.S.-Mexican Studies.

———. 1991. Las actividades económicas de los rancheros de Galeana: Los usos y costumbres del trabajo asalariado. Paper presented to conference, "Popular Culture, State Formation and Revolutionary Mexico," Center for U.S.-Mexican Studies, University of California, San Diego, Mar. 1, 1991.

Long, Norman. 1984. Creating space for change: A perspective on the sociology of development. Inaugural lecture for Professorship of Empirical Sociology of Non-Western Countries, The Agricultural University, Wageningen, Netherlands, Nov. 15, 1984.

Loret de Mola, Carlos. 1986. *Que la nación me lo demande*. México: Grijalbo.

Lucas de Rouffinglac, Ann. 1985. *The contemporary peasantry in Mexico: A class analysis*. New York: Praeger.

Maitland, F. W. 1936. *Selected essays*. Cambridge: Cambridge University Press.

Malinowski, Bronislaw. 1922. *Argonauts of the western Pacific*. New York: E. P. Dutton. Paperback edition published in 1961.

Manual de Estadísticas Básicas del Estado de Chihuahua. 1983. Chihuahua: Secretaría de Programción y Presupuesto, Instituto Nacional de Estadística Geografía e Informática.

Marcus, George. 1986. Contemporary problems of ethnography in the modern world system. In J. Clifford and G. Marcus (eds.), *Writing Culture*. Berkeley: University of California Press.

Marcus, George, and Michael Fisher. 1985. *Anthropology as cultural critique*. Chicago: University of Chicago Press.

Margolies, Barbara Luise. 1975. *Princes of the earth*. Washington, DC: American Anthropological Association.

Marx, Karl. [1867] 1906. *Capital*. Vol. 1 Trans. Samuel Moore and Edward Aveling. Chicago: Charles Kerr (Modern Library reprint).

———. [1852] 1963. *The Eighteenth Brumaire of Louis Bonaparte*. New York: International Publishers.

———. [1857–58] 1973. *Grundrisse*. Trans. Martin Nicholaus. New York: Vintage.

Marx, Karl, and Friedrich Engels. [1871] 1971. *Writings on the Paris Commune*. Ed. Hal Draper. New York: Monthly Review Press.

———. 1975. *Selected correspondence*. 3d ed. Moscow: Progress Publishers.

Matson, Daniel S., and Albert H. Schroeder, eds. 1957. Cordero's description of the Apache—1796. *New Mexico Historical Review* 32 (3): 335:56.

Mendieta y Nuñez, Lucio. 1981. *El problema agrario de México y la Ley Federal de Reforma Agraria*. México: Ed. Porrua.

Meyer, Michael, and William Sherman. 1979. *The course of Mexican history*. New York: Oxford University Press.

Mintz, Sidney. 1973. A note on the definition of peasantries. *Journal of Peasant Studies* 1 (1): 91–106.

Mohanty, Chandra Talpade. 1991. Cartographies of struggle: Third World women and the politics of feminism. In Chandra Talpade Mohanty, Ann Russo, and Lourdes Torres (eds.), *Third World women and the politics of feminism*. Bloomington: Indiana University Press.

Monografías Municipales. 1982. Chihuahua: Dirección de Desarrollo Económico, Gobierno del Estado.

Moorhead, Max. 1975. *The presidio*. Norman: University of Oklahoma Press.

Nugent, Daniel. 1985. Anthropology, handmaiden of history?: An answer from the field. *Critique of Anthropology* 5 (2): 71–86.

————. 1987. Mexico's rural populations and *la crisis:* Economic crisis or legitimation crisis. *Critique of Anthropology* 7 (3): 93–112.

————. 1988. Rural revolt in Mexico, Mexican nationalism and the state, and forms of U.S. intervention. In D. Nugent (ed.), *Rural revolt in Mexico and U.S. intervention.* San Diego: Center for U.S.- Mexican Studies.

————. 1989a. "Are we not [civilized] men?": The formation and devolution of community in northern Mexico. *Journal of Historical Sociology* 2 (3): 206–39.

————. 1989b. Conflicting ideological views of the ejido in northern Mexico. Texas Papers on Mexico no. 88-03. Austin: Mexican Center of the Institute of Latin American Studies.

————. 1990. Paradojas en el desarrollo de la "cuestión agraria" en Chihuahua, 1885–1935. In Rubén Lau Rojo and Carlos González Herrera (eds.), *Actas del Primer Congreso de Historia Regional Comparada, 1989.* Juárez: Universidad Autónoma de Ciudad Juárez.

————. 1991. Revolutionary posturing, bourgeois land "reform": Reflections on the agrarian reform in northern Mexico. *Labour, Capital and Society.* 24 (1): 90–108.

————. 1992. Popular musical culture in rural Chihuahua: Accommodation or resistance? In John Calagione et al. (eds.), *Worker's expressions: Beyond accommodation and resistance on the margins of capitalism.* Albany: State University of New York Press.

Nugent, Daniel, and Ana María Alonso. 1994. Multiple selective traditions in the determination of agrarian struggle and popular culture: The ejido of Namiquipa, Chihuahua. In Gilbert Joseph and Daniel Nugent (eds.), *Everyday forms of state formation: revolution and the negotiation of rule in modern Mexico.* Durham, NC: Duke University Press. Forthcoming.

Nugent, Stephen. 1988. The "peripheral situation." *Annual Review of Anthropology* 17: 79–98.

Olea Arias, Heliodoro. 1961. *Apuntes historicos del 20 de noviembre de 1910 en Bachiniva.* Chihuahua: Impresora AIFFER.

Ollman, Bertell. 1971. *Alienation: Marx's conception of man in capitalist society.* Cambridge: Cambridge University Press.

Orlove, Benjamin. 1991. Mapping reeds and reading maps: The politics of representation in Lake Titicaca. *American Ethnologist* 18 (1): 3–38.

Ortiz Pinchetti, Francisco. 1986. Los Chihuahuenses quiere democracia y repudian al PRI. *Proceso* 496 (May 5): 16–21.

Ortner, Sherry. 1984. Theory in anthropology since the sixties. *Comparative Studies in Society and History* 26 (1): 126–66.

Osorio, Rubén. 1988. *Villismo:* Nationalism and popular mobilization in northern Mexico. In D. Nugent (ed.,) *Rural revolt in Mexico and U.S. intervention.* San Diego: Center for U.S.-Mexican Studies.

————. 1990. *Pancho Villa, ese desconocido.* Chihuahua: Gobierno del Estado.

————. n.d. Tomochic, la guerra del fin del mundo en la sierra. CRO.

Otero, Gerardo. 1986. Agrarian reform in Mexico: Capitalism and the state. Paper presented to the Research Seminar on Mexico and U.S.-Mexican Relations, Center for U.S.-Mexican Studies, University of California–San Diego, La Jolla, Oct. 1986.

Paige, Jeffrey. 1975. *Agrarian revolution: Social movements and export agriculture in the underdeveloped world.* New York: Free Press.

Palerm, Ángel. 1980. *Marxismo y anthropología.* México: Siglo Veintiuno.

Palmer, Bryan. 1990. *Descent into discourse: The reification of language and the writing of social history.* Philadelphia: Temple University Press.

Pérez Mendoza, Jaime. 1986. Campesinos de Anáhuac toman 62 silos de la Conasupo. *Proceso* 480 (Jan. 13): 27–29.

Ponce de León, José M. 1907. *Datos geográficos y estadísticos del estado de Chihuahua.* Chihuahua: Imprenta del Gobierno.

Post, Ken. 1978. *Arise, ye starvelings!* The Hague: Martinus Nijhoff.

———. 1986. Can one have an historical anthropology? Some reactions to Taussig and Chevalier. *Social Analysis* 19:78–84.

Prakash, Gyan. 1987. Terms of servitude: Representations of labor bondage in colonial India. Paper presented to the Mellon Symposium on Historical Anthropology, California Institute of Technology, Pasadena, May 1987.

Quevedo, Rodrigo M. 1935. Informe rendido por el gobernador constitucional. Supplement to *Periódico Oficial* 42 (Chihuahua).

Rebel, Hermann. 1989. Cultural hegemony and class experience: A critical reading of recent ethnological-historical approaches. Pt. 1. *American Ethnologist* 16 (1): 117–36.

Redclift, Michael. 1980. Agrarian populism in Mexico—the *via campesina. Journal of Peasant Studies* 7 (4): 492–502.

Redfield, Robert. 1930. *Tepoztlán.* Chicago: University of Chicago Press.

Reed, John. 1969. *Insurgent Mexico.* New York: International Publishers.

Reyes, Prisciliana. 1975. *Informe medico-sanitario de la comunidad de Namiquipa.* Chihuahua: Universidad Autónoma de Chihuahua, Escuela de Medicina.

Reyes, Sergio, et al. 1970. *Estructura agraria y desarrollo agrícola en México.* 3 vols. México: Centro de Investigaciones Agrarias.

Rocha Islas, Marta. 1979. *Del villismo y las defensas sociales en Chihuahua.* Lic. thesis, Universidad Nacional Autónoma de Mexico.

Rodríguez Gigena, Gonzalo, ed. 1983. *Economía mexicana, series temática: Sector Agropecuario.* México: Centro de Investigación y Docencia Económicas A.C.

Roseberry, William. 1978. Peasants as proletarians. *Critique of Anthropology* 3 (11): 3–18.

———. 1983. *Coffee and capitalism in the Venezuelan Andes.* Austin: University of Texas Press.

———. 1989. *Anthropologies and histories.* New Brunswick, NJ: Rutgers University Press.

———. 1991. Potatoes, sacks, and enclosures in early modern England. In Jay O'Brien and William Roseberry (eds.), *Golden ages, dark ages: Imagining the past in anthropology and history.* Berkeley: University of California Press.

Sahlins, Marshall. 1976. *Culture and practical reason.* Chicago: University of Chicago Press.

———. 1981. *Historical metaphors and mythical realities.* Ann Arbor: University of Michigan Press.

———. 1982. Individual experience and cultural order. In William Kruskal (ed.), *The social sciences: Their nature and uses.* Chicago: University of Chicago Press.

Salazar Quintana, Daniel. 1988. *Monografía del municipio de Namiquipa.* Chihuahua: Impresos y Offset Gaytan.

Sanderson, Steven. 1986. *The transformation of Mexican agriculture.* Princeton: Princeton University Press.

Sanderson, Susan R. Walsh. 1984. *Land reform in Mexico, 1916–1980.* New York: Academic Press.

Sayer, Derek. 1987. *The violence of abstraction.* Oxford: Basil Blackwell.

———. 1990. British reaction to the Amritsar massacre, 1919–20. *Past and Present* 131: 130–64.

Scholte, Bob. [1972] 1974. Toward a reflexive and critical anthropology. In Dell Hymes (ed.), *Reinventing anthropology.* New York: Vintage.

———. 1986. The Charmed Circle of Geertz's Hermeneutics. *Critique of Anthropology* 6 (1): 5 : 15.

———. 1987. The literary turn in contemporary anthropology. *Critique of Anthropology* 7 (1): 33–47.

Schryer, Frans J. 1980. *The rancheros of Pisaflores.* Toronto: University of Toronto Press.

Schulze, Karl. 1990. La idea y la política agrarias de Francisco Villa: La situacíon social agraria en Chihuahua a fines del Porfiriato y durante la Revolución. In Rubén Lau Rojo and Carlos Gonzalez Herrera (eds.), *Actas del Primer Congreso de Historia Regional Comparada.* Juárez: Universidad Autónoma de Ciudad Juárez.

Secretaría de Programación y Presupuesto. 1981. Carta topográfica. Oscar Soto Maynez, H13C42, Chihuahua. México: Coordinación General de los Servicios Nacionales de Estadística, Geografía e Informática.

Semo, Enrique. 1979. Reflexiones sobre la revolución mexicana. In Héctor Aguilar Camin et al., *Interpretaciones de la revolución mexicana.* México: Editorial Nueva Imagen.

———, ed. 1983. *México: Un pueblo en la historia.* 3 vols. México: Universidad Autónoma de Puebla and Editorial Nueva Imagen.

Sepúlveda, Ximena. 1975. *La Revolución en Bachiniva.* Serie de Estudios no. 7. México: Departamento de Etnología y Antropología Social, Instituto Nacional de Antopología e Historia.

Service, Elman R. [1958] 1971. *Profiles in ethnology.* Rev. ed. New York: Harper and Row.

Shanin, Teodor. 1987a. Introduction: Peasantry as a concept. In T. Shanin (ed.), *Peasants and peasant societies.* Oxford: Basil Blackwell.

———, ed. [1971] 1987b. *Peasants and peasant societies.* Oxford: Basil Blackwell. 2d ed., amplified; originally published by Penguin.

Shannon, Elaine. 1988. *Desperados: Latin Drug Lords, U.S. Lawmen, and the War America Can't Win.* New York: Viking.

Sheridan, Thomas. 1988. *Where the dove calls: The political ecology of a peasant corporate community in northwestern Mexico.* Tucson: University of Arizona Press.

Sheridan, Thomas, and Thomas Naylor. 1979. *Rarámuri*. Flagstaff: Northland Press.

Sider, Gerald. 1980. The ties that bind: Culture and agriculture, property and propriety in the Newfoundland village fishery. *Social History* 5.

Silverman, Sydel. 1979. The peasant concept in anthropology. *Journal of Peasant Studies* 7 (1): 49–69.

Simpson, Eyler. 1937. *The ejido: Mexico's way out*. Chapel Hill: University of North Carolina Press.

Smith, Carol. 1984. Local history in global context. *Comparative Studies in Society and History* 26 (2): 193–228.

Smith, Raymond T. 1984. Introduction. In R. T. Smith (ed.), *Kinship Ideology and Practice in Latin America*. Chapel Hill: University of North Carolina Press.

Solis, Gregorio. 1936. *Acontecimientos chihuahuenses*. Chihuahua: Ed. "La Prensa" Bonifacio S. Martínez y Hnos.

Spicer, Edward. 1962. *Cycles of conquest*. Tucson: University of Arizona Press.

Stavenhagen, Rodolfo. 1969. *Las clases sociales en las sociedades agrarias*. México: Siglo Veintiuno.

———. 1970. Social aspects of agrarian structure in Mexico. In Rodolfo Stavenhagen (ed.), *Agrarian problems and peasant movements in Latin America*. New York: Doubleday.

———. 1978. Capitalism and the peasantry in Mexico. *Latin American Perspectives* 5 (3): 27–37.

Stern, Steve J., ed. 1987. *Resistance, rebellion and consciousness in the Andean peasant world, eighteenth to twentieth centuries*. Madison: University of Wisconsin Press.

Tannenbaum, Frank. 1930. *The Mexican agrarian revolution*. Washington, DC: Brookings Institute.

Taylor, John. 1979. *From development to underdevelopment*. London: Macmillan.

Terrazas, Joaquin. 1905. *Memorias del Sr. Coronel D. Joaquin Terrazas*. Juárez: "El Agricultor Mexicano" Escobar Hnos.

Terrazas, Silvestre. 1985. *El verdadero Pancho Villa*. México: Ediciones Era.

Terrazas Sánchez, Filiberto. 1973. *La Guerra Apache en México (viénto de octubre)*. México: B. Costa-Amic.

Tompkins, Frank. 1934. *Chasing Villa*. Harrisburg, PA: Military Service Publishing Company.

Torres, Elías. 1975. *Vida y hechos de Francisco Villa*. México: Ed. Epoca.

Tyler, Stephen. 1986. Post-modern ethnography: From document of the occult to occult document. In Clifford and G. Marcus (eds.), *Writing Culture*. Berkeley: University of California Press.

———. 1987. Still rayting. *Critique of Anthropology* 7 (1): 49–51.

Vargas Valdez, Jesús. 1988. Algunas notas para el estudio de la historia de Chihuahua. *Cuadernos del Norte* 1 (1): 15–20.

———. 1989. La fragua de los tiempos: El agrarismo en Chihuahua. Series published in *El Heraldo de Chihuahua* in eight parts, May–July 1989.

Warman, Arturo. 1978. The revolutionary potential of the Mexican peasant. In Stanley Diamond (ed.), *Toward a Marxist Anthropology*. The Hague: Mouton.

————. [1976] 1980. *We come to object: The peasants of Morelos and the national state*. Trans. Stephen Ault. Baltimore: Johns Hopkins University Press.

————. 1988a. Los estudios campesinos: Veinte años después. *Comercio Exterior* 38 (7): 653–58.

————. 1988b. The political project of zapatismo. In Friedrich Katz (ed.), *Riot, rebellion, and Revolution*. Princeton: Princeton University Press.

Wasserman, Mark. 1975. Oligarchy and foreign enterprise in Porfirian Chihuahua, Mexico, 1876–1911. Ph.D. diss., University of Chicago.

————. 1980. The social origins of the 1910 revolution in Chihuahua. *Latin American Research Review* 15 (1): 15–38.

————. 1984. *Capitalists, caciques and revolution*. Chapel Hill: University of North Carolina Press.

Weber, Max. [1918] 1958. Politics as a vocation. In H. Gerth and C. W. Mills (eds.), *From Max Weber*. New York: Oxford University Press.

West, Robert C. 1949. The mining community in northern New Spain: The Parral mining district. *Ibero-Americana* 30.

Whetten, Nathan. 1948. *Rural Mexico*. Chicago: University of Chicago Press.

Whiteford, Scott, and Laura Montgomery. 1985. The Political economy of rural transformation: A Mexican case. In Billie R. De Walt and Pertti J. Pelto (eds.), *Micro and macro levels of analysis in anthropology*. Boulder, CO: Westview Press.

Williams, Raymond. 1977. *Marxism and literature*. Oxford: Oxford University Press.

Wolf, Eric. 1966. *Peasants*. Englewood Cliffs, NJ: Prentice-Hall.

————. 1969a. On peasant rebellions. In T. Shanin (ed.), *Peasants and peasant societies*. Oxford: Basil Blackwell.

————. 1969. *Peasant wars of the twentieth century*. New York: Harper & Row.

————. 1982. *Europe and the people without history*. Berkeley: University of California Press.

————. 1987. The peasant war in Germany: Friedrich Engels as social historian. *Science & Society* 51 (1): 82–92.

Wolpe, Harold. 1980. Introduction. In H. Wolpe (ed.), *The articulation of modes of production*. London: Routledge and Kegan Paul.

Womack, John. 1969. *Zapata and the Mexican Revolution*. New York: Vintage Books.

————. 1986. The Mexican Revolution. In Leslie Bethell (ed.), *The Cambridge history of Latin America*. Vol. 5. Cambridge: Cambridge University Press.

Zamosc, Leon. 1986. *The agrarian question and the peasant movement in Colombia*. New York: Cambridge University Press.

INDEX

213